IMAGES
of America

BLUE ISLAND'S RACEWAY PARK

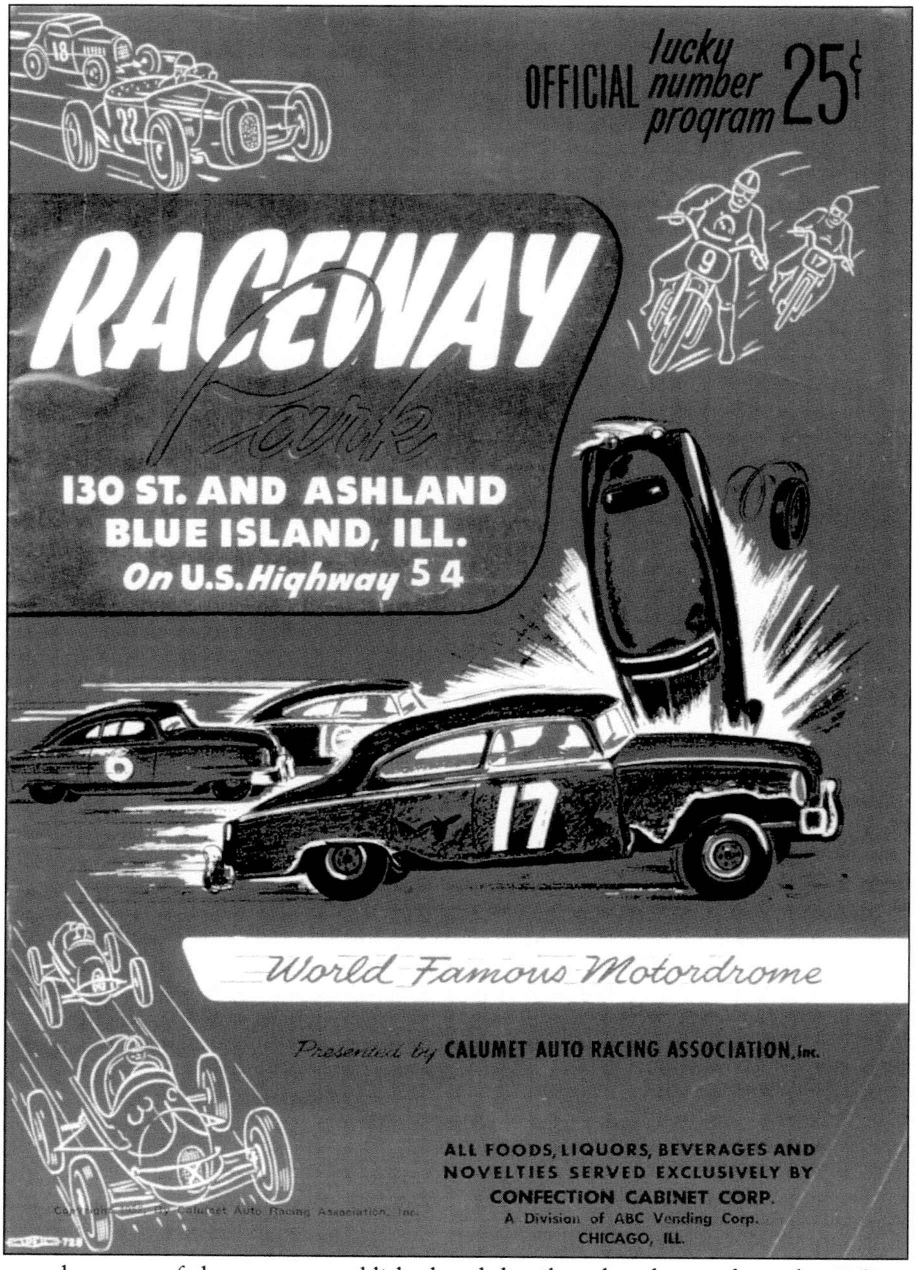

This was the cover of the program published and distributed each year from the 1950s to the early 1970s at Raceway Park. Although the program would slightly differ each year, whether by the color of the cover or by the cars on the cover, each contained advertisements from local businesses, rosters of the competitors in each division, and a lucky program number. (Courtesy of Stan Kalwasinski.)

On the cover: The 300 Lap Classic became a Raceway Park staple, and the 1956 edition, seen here in this Bud Norman photograph, was won by Bob Perrine. Perrine, the innermost car, fought off Bryant Tucker (25) and Robert "Legs" Whitcomb (V2) for his only "300 lapper" victory. (Courtesy of Stan Kalwasinski.)

IMAGES
of America

Blue Island's Raceway Park

Stan Kalwasinski and Samuel Beck

ARCADIA
PUBLISHING

ISBN 978-0-7385-7743-2

Published by Arcadia Publishing
Charleston, South Carolina

Printed in the United States of America

Library of Congress Control Number: 2009941374

For all general information contact Arcadia Publishing at:
Telephone 843-853-2070
Fax 843-853-0044
E-mail sales@arcadiapublishing.com
For customer service and orders:
Toll-Free 1-888-313-2665

Visit us on the Internet at www.arcadiapublishing.com

This book is dedicated to the families of track owner Pete Jenin, announcer Wayne Adams, and all of the officials, drivers, crew members, and fans who made Raceway Park one of the premier entertainment facilities in the Chicago area for 62 years. The track may now be gone, but the memories stemming from it will not be forgotten.

Contents

ACKNOWLEDGMENTS

We have many people to thank for contributing to this project, as it is not the easiest task trying to fit the amount of history seen at Raceway Park in its 62 years of existence into a book. However, we had a job to get done, and we are very proud of this book.

First off, we must thank longtime announcer Wayne Adams. Not only did Wayne volunteer to author the introduction to the book, but over his many years of announcing, he kept each and every program from events he worked. Oftentimes, we would call Wayne at his home in Dolton asking about the name of a driver from the 1940s, and the following day, he would have the answer to our question. He and his wife, "Boots," deserve enormous thanks for accommodating us when we would stop by to interview him.

Next, we must acknowledge the efforts of our photograph contributors: Bob Sheldon, Wayne Adams, Bob Talaski, Stan Kalwasinski, Paul Beck, and Bob Pilsudski. Without the participation and cooperation of these gentlemen, this book would never have been completed to our satisfaction. They documented the 62-year history of Raceway Park through the lens of a camera, and they graciously offered us their time and photographs for the book.

We also have to thank our editors, Jeff Reutsche and John Pearson, for keeping in contact with us as well as answering any questions that we had. It was a joy working with these two gentlemen.

Finally, we have to thank the numerous drivers, officials, crew members, car owners, and race fans who provided stories and background information on the drivers and race cars. There are too many people to name, and we do not want to leave anybody out. We also want to thank the family of track owner/promoter Pete Jenin for keeping the racetrack open for as long as it was, providing innumerable Chicagoans entertainment for many decades. Many of us meet up on a regular basis to share photographs, videos, and stories, and these "parties" were really the motivation to write this book. We wanted to preserve the history of Raceway Park through this book, and we think that we have certainly achieved that.

INTRODUCTION

"Well, good evening ladies and gentlemen! Once again, Wayne Adams bidding you welcome to Raceway Park on behalf of owner and promoter, Pete Jenin."

That is pretty much the way I started announcing each and every program I ever did at Raceway Park over those 42 years I was there. There might have been a little change here and there, but for the most part, that was my opening.

I remember going to the first event at Raceway Park in 1938 as a fan. I do not recall how many races they ran that year, but it was not very many as they did not start racing there until September. The one thing I distinctly remember about the first time I saw the track is that it was square. It had two short straightaways and four corners. I was going out there and watching them build it.

It was dirt and it had an excellent surface. The racing was great because all of the top midget drivers from the area competed there. Man, did they have a lot of cars. Harry McQuinn, one of the top midget drivers in the country, won that first midget feature race. Ed Rippe and Harry Malone headed up the group that built the track and promoted those first races. There was some talk that the track was actually built for greyhound dog racing, but that never really materialized.

Art Folz and Wally Zale, as I recall, did the promotion at Raceway Park in 1941. I was still just a fan and taking pictures at the races. Zale, who was probably the winningest midget driver in the country before World War II, and I were pretty good friends, and he asked me if I could score races.

I did not really know much about scoring races, but before you know it, I was the scorer at Raceway Park. Still, in my mind, I wanted to announce auto races. That would have to wait as World War II brought a halt to racing sometime in July 1942.

I was in the army for three and a half years, and, when I got out, I started going to the races again. Raceway Park was one of the first tracks to hold midget races after the war in 1945.

The United Auto Racing Association (UARA) was formed in the winter of 1946–1947 for B class cars, which were cars that were not powered by the expensive Offenhauser ("Offy") engines. They were mostly powered by Ford V8s. UARA had planned a full schedule of racing at Hanson Park on Chicago's northwest side. I knew all of the UARA people as I had begun again to cover local racing for *Illustrated Speedway News*, which was a weekly racing newspaper published in Brooklyn, New York.

Most of the UARA officials knew I wanted to announce races. After their first race of the season in 1947, UARA president Lou Scally called me and asked if I would like to be their announcer. I said I sure would and I felt I had done a good job my first time. After the races, Nick and Pete Jenin, owners of Raceway Park, along with one of their top drivers—Bud Koehler—came down and talked to me and offered me the announcer's job at Raceway Park. A few weeks later, Art Folz, who was promoting the races at Soldier Field, called and asked if I would like to announce there too. Here I was, a young guy from Missouri, announcing three shows a week at the area's top tracks.

In 1948, I was announcing at both Raceway Park and Soldier Field in addition to doing races for UARA, many of them at Gill Stadium in Chicago. Folz came to me one day and said I had to make up my mind—either announce at Raceway or Soldier Field, not both. I figured the Jenins owned Raceway Park and Folz was just leasing Soldier Field, so I went with Raceway and that decision pretty much "set in stone" my association with Raceway Park.

The midgets were the top draw at Raceway for years. In 1948, the track held its first stock car races with front-running midget driver Danny Kladis, driving a Jeep, winning the track's first 300 Lap Classic. The next year (1949), Raceway held weekly stock car racing events, and that pretty much started the long history of stock car racing at the track. I remember those early stock car races as I announced at both Raceway and Gill Stadium that first year. The fans loved the races. There was a lot of action. They screamed and hollered and cheered every time those stock cars crashed and flipped. They were exciting shows.

Before you knew it, the midgets were replaced at Raceway with stock car races as the schedule sometimes called for racing four nights a week. Tens of thousands of fans would come out to watch the races each week. The Jenins built the backstretch grandstands because they needed more room. Stock car drivers were making more money racing during the week than they could working a regular job. The Jenins had remodeled the track when they took ownership and paved it shortly after the 1951 season began with 80 race meets held that summer.

The racing was intense. During the early years, the drivers literally knocked each other out of the way. The fans loved it and definitely had their favorites. Bud Koehler, Bob Pronger, and Bill Van Allen had to be three of the greatest short-track stock car drivers anywhere. If you never saw those three guys in one race, competing against one another, you never saw a stock car race.

The competition was unbelievable. People saw a show, an entertaining show. The fact that thousands came each week, four nights a week, proves the type of show it was back then. It was definitely a spectator's program.

The Jenins bought the track prior to the 1947 season. The place was in pretty bad shape and, as I recall, the property had been condemned. Pete Jenin did a lot of the renovation work himself, and his brother, Nick, handled the front office. Nick sold his interest in the track to Jimmy Derrico in 1952 with Derrico and Jenin being partners until Pete Jenin became the sole promoter in 1970. Others were involved in the promotion there from time to time, but it was pretty much Pete's racetrack over the years.

One of my biggest thrills as an announcer was when my son Wayne Jr. won the novice division championship in 1966. I did not know he and his buddies put a car together. He was racing under a fake name—Smada Enyaw, which is Wayne Adams spelled backwards. One night, somebody called from the pits and told me that that was my son out there racing. Not to be outdone by their older brother, my daughter, Jill, and youngest son, Craig, also raced at the track.

Raceway Park lasted 62 years, and I was there for 42 of them as the announcer. If I had to do it over, I would not change a thing.

I hope you enjoy Stan Kalwasinski and Samuel Beck's efforts here, chronicling the history of Raceway Park—"the World's Busiest Track." And as I used to say each night after the races, "on behalf of all of our drivers, mechanics, and members of the Championship Stock Car Club, this is your announcer Wayne Adams asking you to please drive carefully all the way home," and for one final time here, "we'll see you later."

—Wayne Adams

One

The 1930s and 1940s

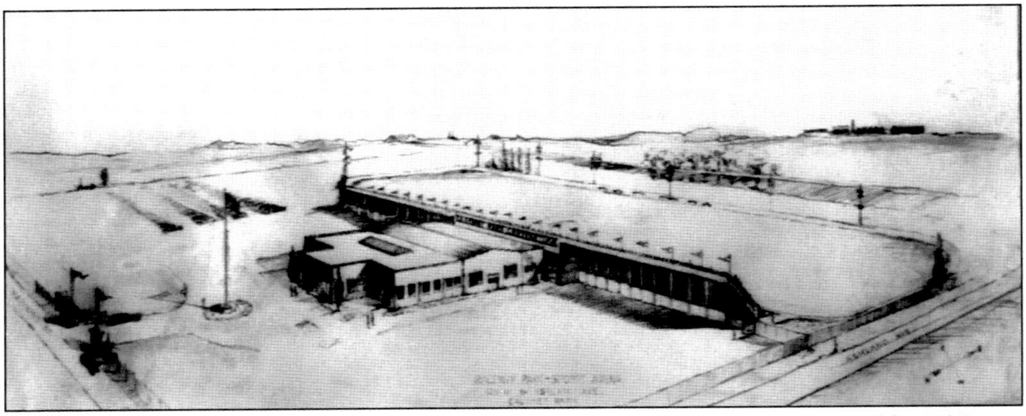

Raceway Park opened its doors for the first time on September 24, 1938. Operated by Ed Rippe and Harry Malone, the track was originally constructed for dog racing, a sport that was never legalized in Illinois. Instead, the quarter-mile track began hosting midget races on its dirt surface, drawing large crowds and car counts. Pictured is a June 1938 artist's conception of Raceway Park–Sports Arena, 129th Place and Ashland Avenue, Calumet Park. (Courtesy of Bob Sheldon.)

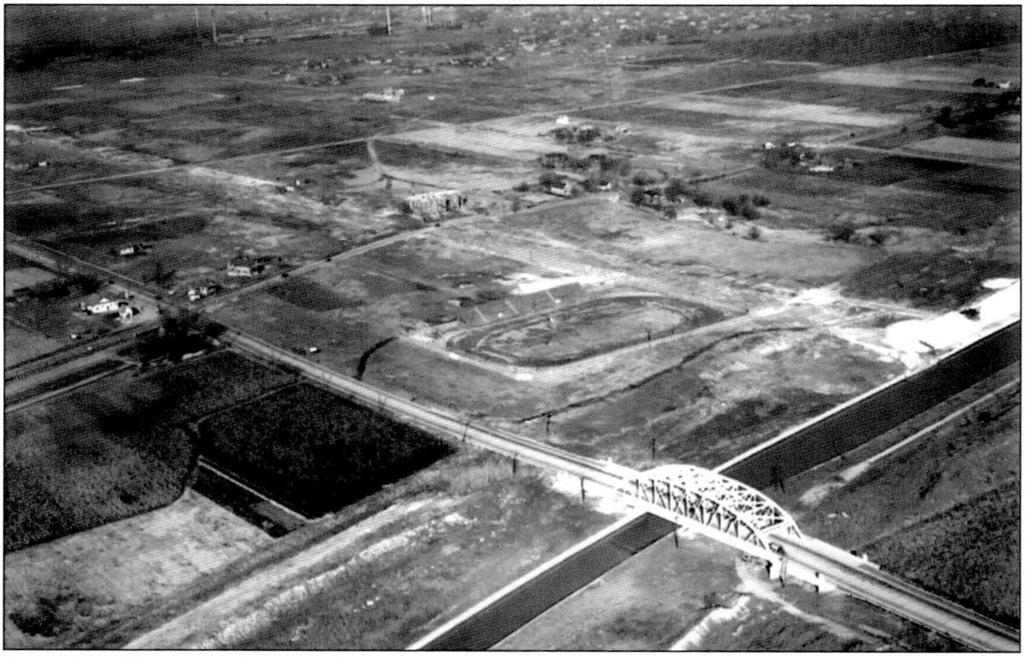

A pre–World War II photograph shows Raceway Park way out in the country during its initial years. Ashland Avenue, the bridge going over the Calumet-Sag Channel, and the corner of Vermont Street and Ashland can be picked out in this photograph. Chicago's city limits were less than a mile north and east of the track. (Courtesy of Bob Talaski.)

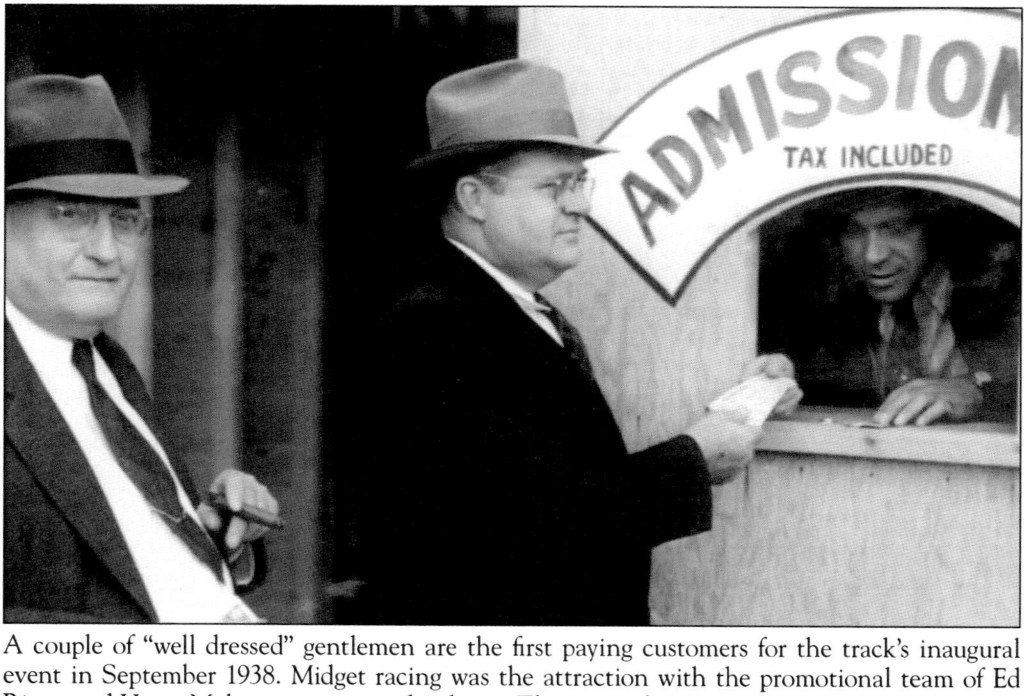

A couple of "well dressed" gentlemen are the first paying customers for the track's inaugural event in September 1938. Midget racing was the attraction with the promotional team of Ed Rippe and Harry Malone putting on the shows. The original opening date of September 17 was rained out with the racing action finally getting under way a week later on September 24, 1938. (Courtesy of Bob Sheldon.)

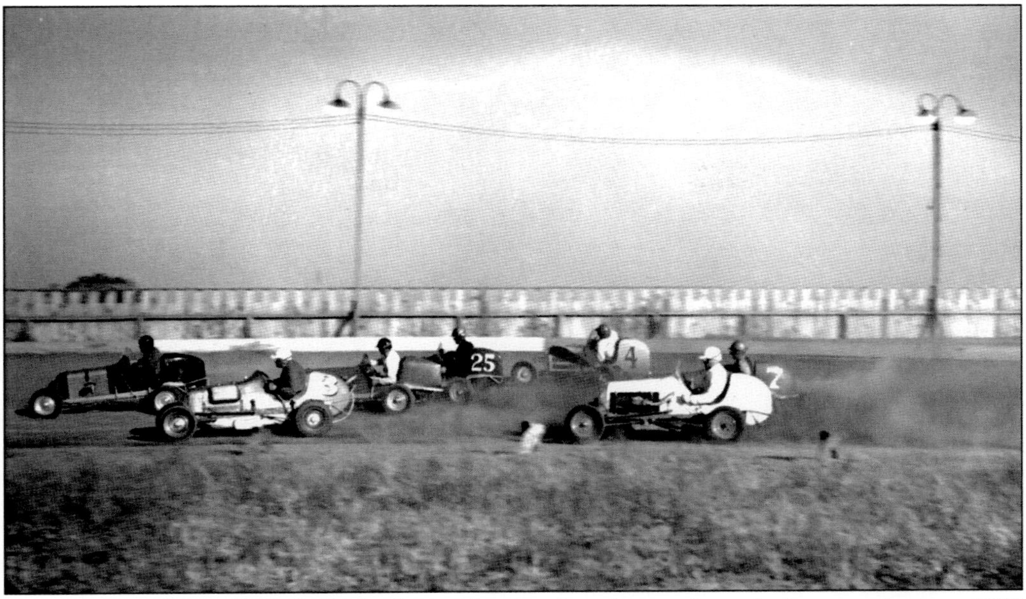

Big and powerful Wally Zale (3) leads a pack of midget drivers through the turn during a 1939 competition at Raceway Park. Zale won 47 main events at tracks throughout the Midwest in 1939 and posted a record 67 wins the following year. He was reported to have won a total of 178 midget feature wins prior to his death in April 1942. Zale and fellow racer Frank Perrone were killed in an automobile/train accident on Route 6 (159th Street), just west of Cicero Avenue, in Oak Forest. (Courtesy of Wayne Adams.)

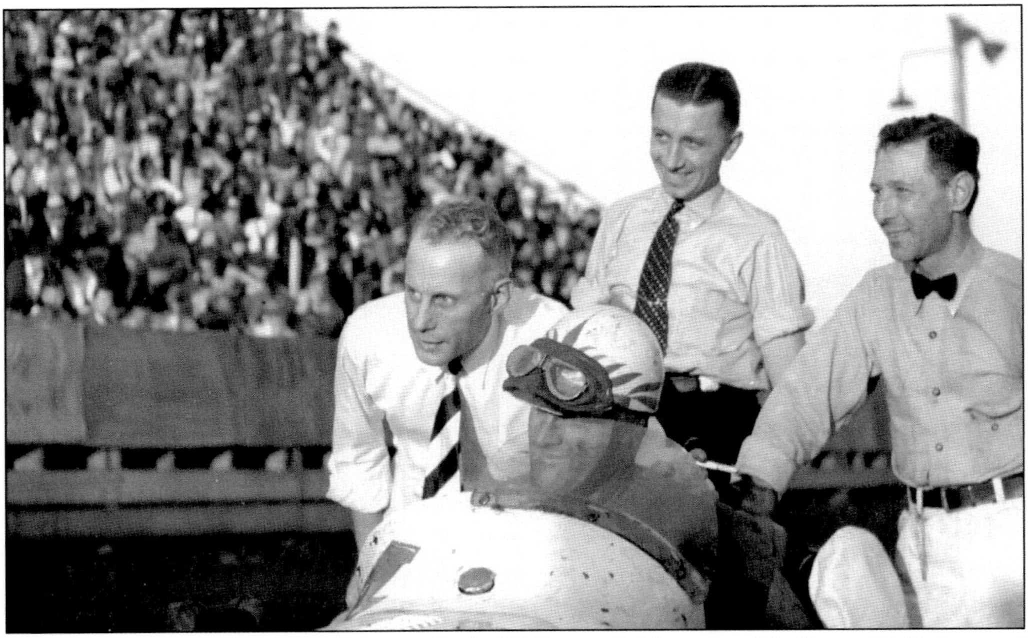

Heading the group that built Raceway Park, Ed Rippe (left) poses with Harry McQuinn and two other gentlemen on October 16, 1938. McQuinn, who hailed from Indianapolis, won the inaugural midget feature race at the speedway—the 40-lap Calumet Sweepstakes—on September 24, 1938. McQuinn competed several times in the Indianapolis 500 and was later an official at the famed speedway. (Courtesy of Bob Sheldon.)

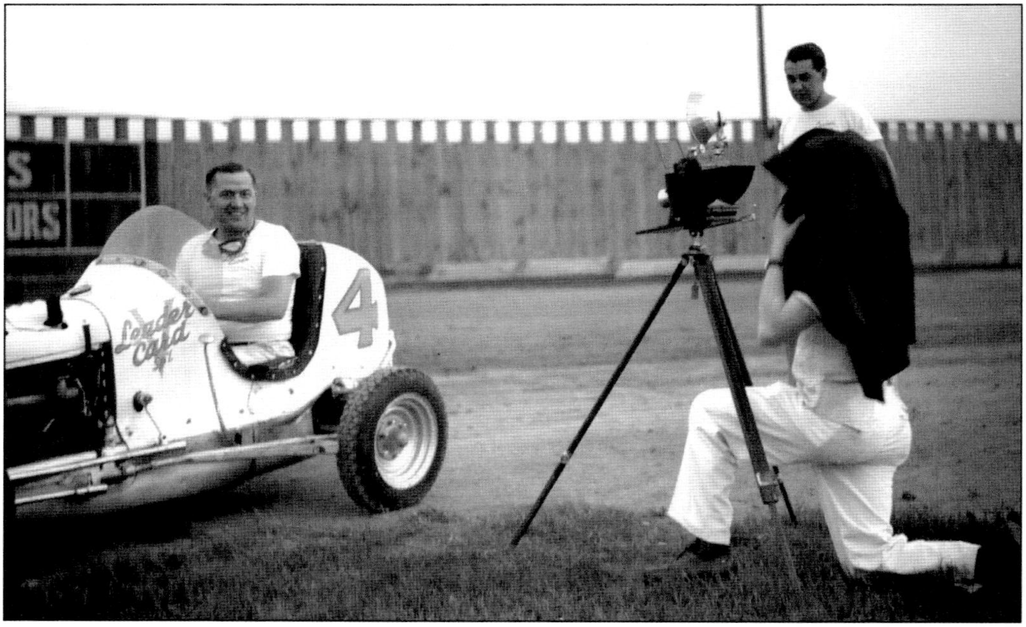

Myron Fohr sits in his Leader Card Spl. (4) midget just inside the track's backstretch as photographer Ed Kirchner prepares to get a posed picture of the Milwaukee speedster in 1939. Young photographer Wayne Adams came along and snapped this picture. This shot shows the old wooden fence that surrounded the track at one time and partially shows the scoreboard (behind Fohr) that was used for semipro baseball games that were held in the infield. (Courtesy of Wayne Adams.)

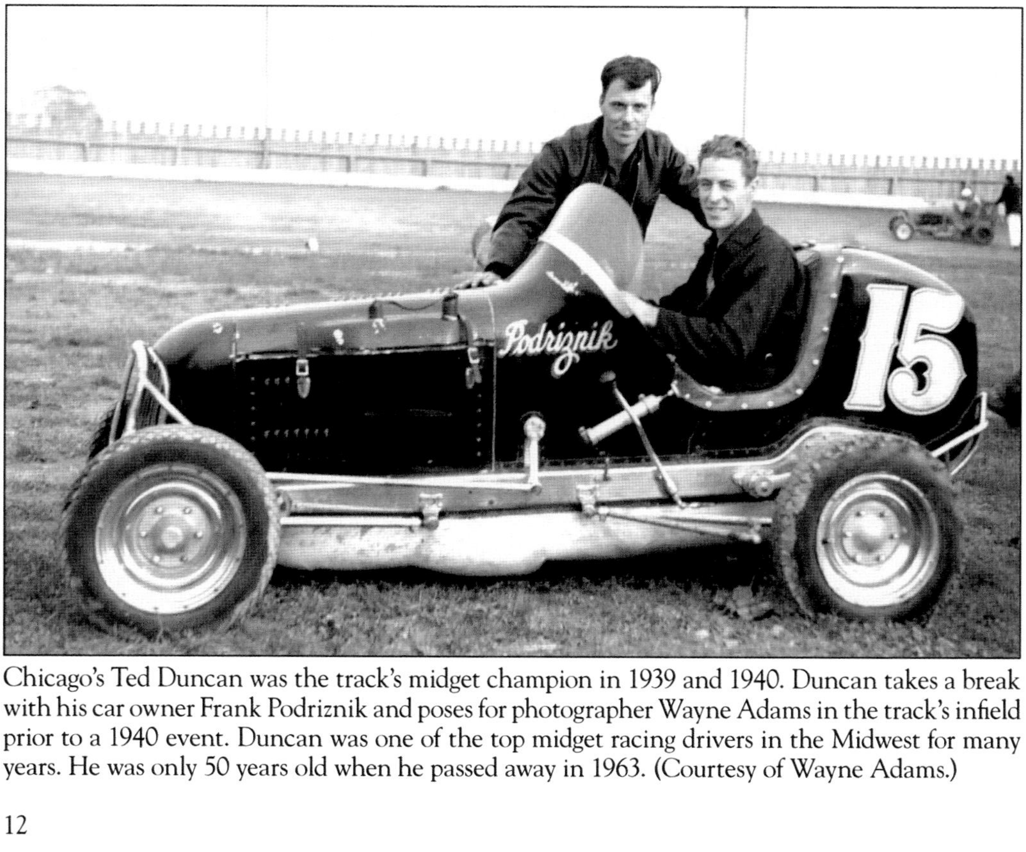

Chicago's Ted Duncan was the track's midget champion in 1939 and 1940. Duncan takes a break with his car owner Frank Podriznik and poses for photographer Wayne Adams in the track's infield prior to a 1940 event. Duncan was one of the top midget racing drivers in the Midwest for many years. He was only 50 years old when he passed away in 1963. (Courtesy of Wayne Adams.)

The cover of a 1942 official program shows Raceway Park located at 129th Place and Halsted Street with racing every Saturday night under the management of the Chicago Auto Racing Association. Someone made a mistake, as the track was really located approximately at 129th and Ashland Avenue, also known as old U.S. Highway 54. Years later, 130th Street and Ashland Avenue was used in newspaper advertisements and other publications as the track's location. (Courtesy of Bob Sheldon.)

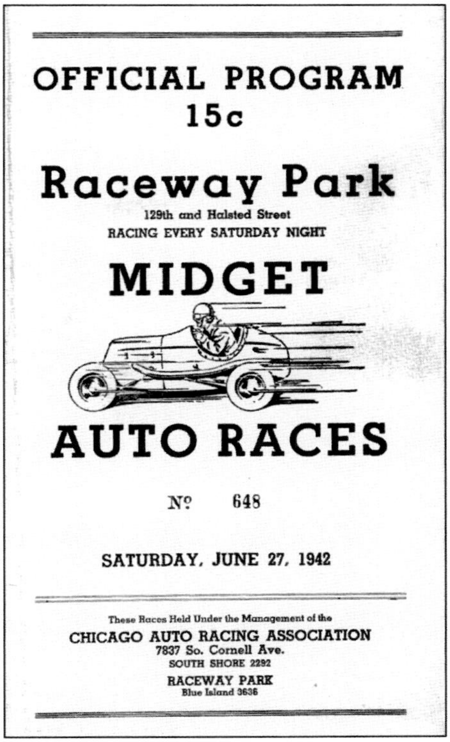

OFFICIAL PROGRAM
15c

Raceway Park
129th and Halsted Street
RACING EVERY SATURDAY NIGHT

MIDGET

AUTO RACES

№ 648

SATURDAY, JUNE 27, 1942

These Races Held Under the Management of the
CHICAGO AUTO RACING ASSOCIATION
7837 So. Cornell Ave.
SOUTH SHORE 2292
RACEWAY PARK
Blue Island 3636

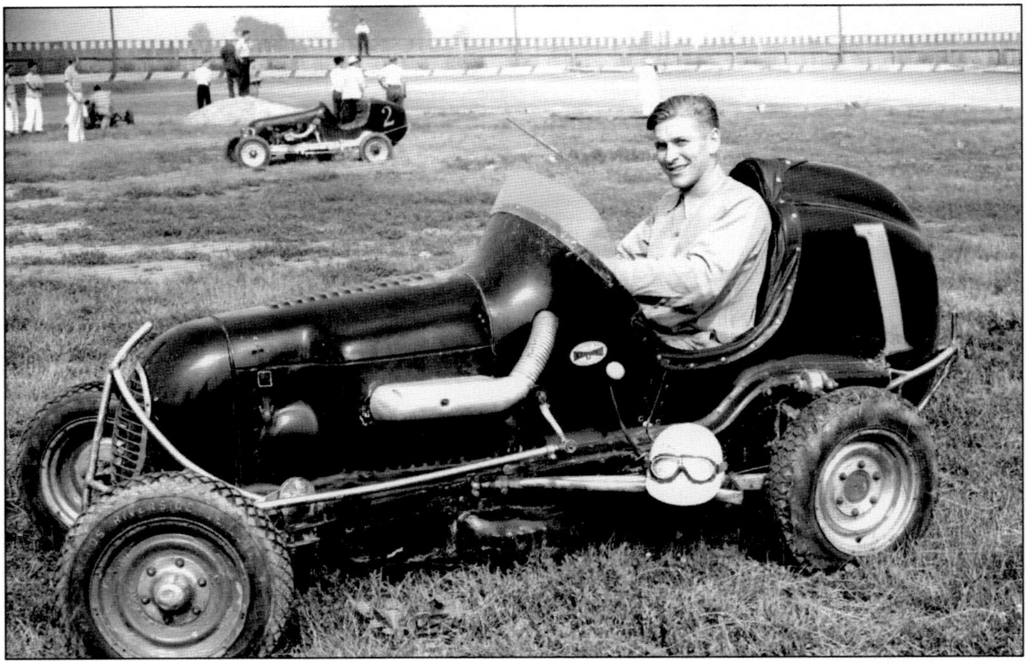

Melvin Eugene "Tony" Bettenhausen of Tinley Park poses in his Rudy Nichels midget (1) at Raceway Park in 1942. Behind the wheel of the former Wally Zale–driven car, Bettenhausen established himself as a midget-racing winner throughout the Midwest. Bettenhausen, who was killed in a practice crash at the Indianapolis Motor Speedway in 1961, was Raceway's midget champion in 1941, 1942, and 1947. (Courtesy of Bob Sheldon.)

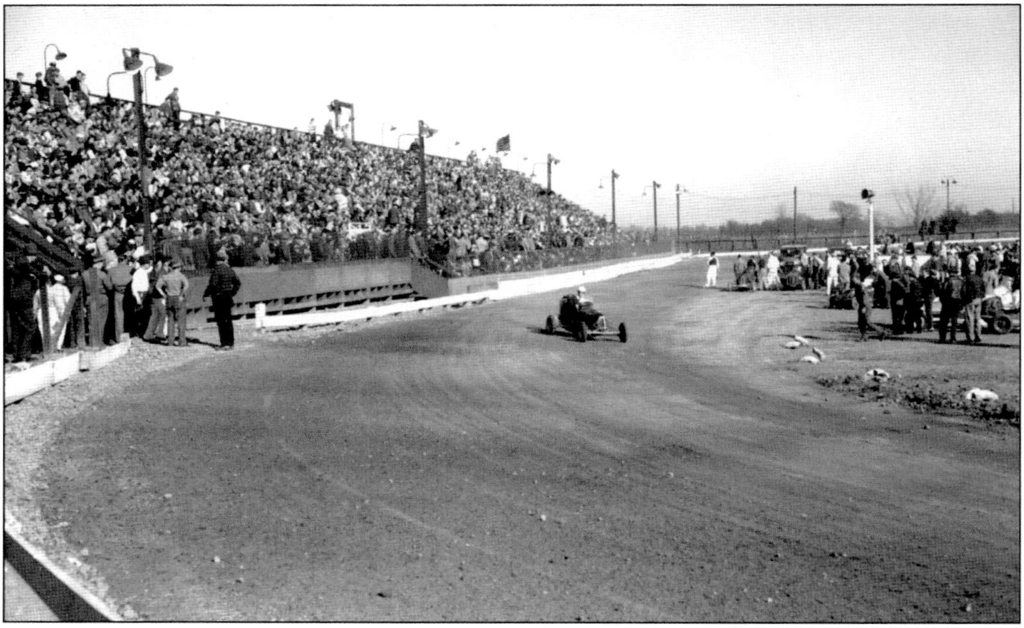

With World War II coming to a close, Raceway Park was perhaps the first track in the United States to hold a midget-racing program. Racing returned to the Chicago area oval on August 25, 1945, with Tinley Park's Tony Bettenhausen claiming the feature win. Bettenhausen is seen here wheeling the Nichels black No. 1 into Raceway's turn one before a packed house in October 1945. (Courtesy of Bob Sheldon.)

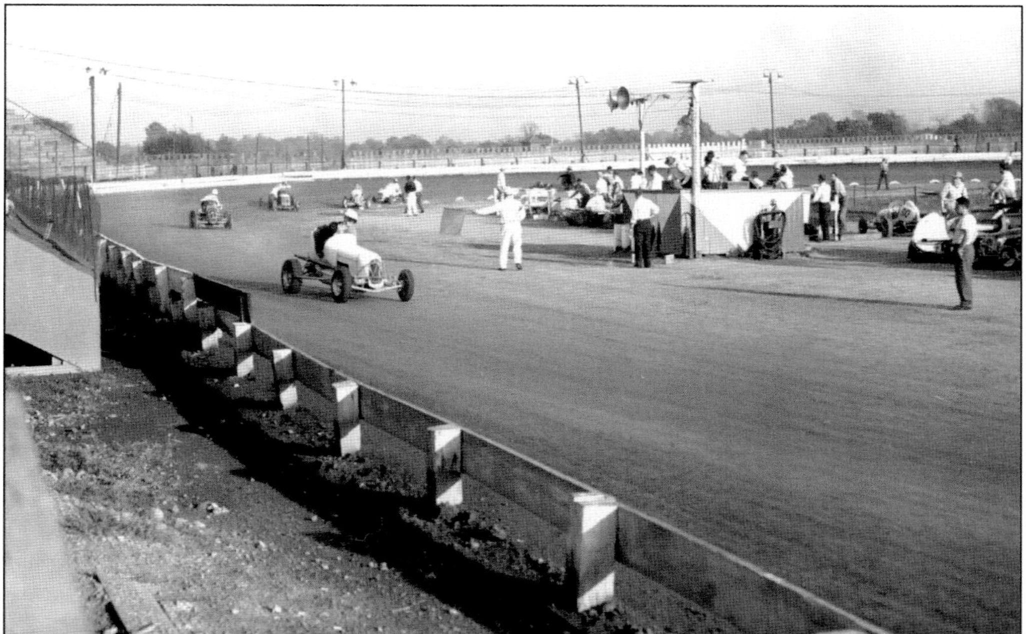

The green flag is displayed as midget drivers race down the track's main straightaway in 1947. As seen in this photograph, the cars were pitted in the track's infield as the track's pit area was yet to be built outside of turns three and four. The officials' stand was also in the infield at the time this picture was taken. (Courtesy of Bob Sheldon.)

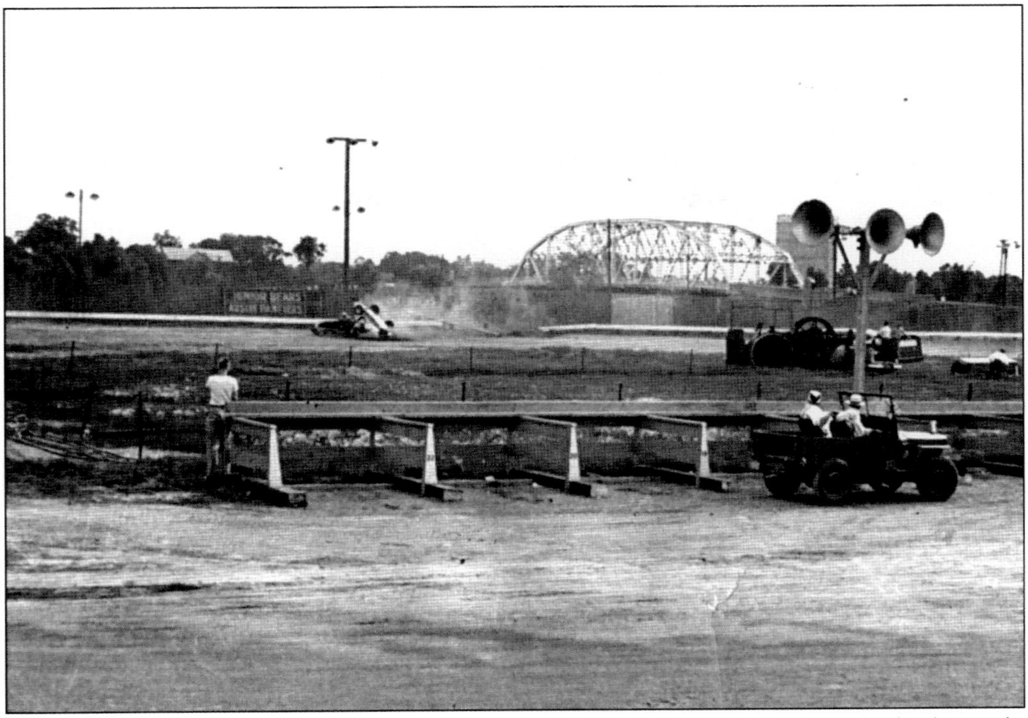

In this 1947 scene, midget driver Shorty Sorenson flips while in the middle of the backstretch. The backstretch grandstands were not built until the early 1950s. (Courtesy of Bob Sheldon.)

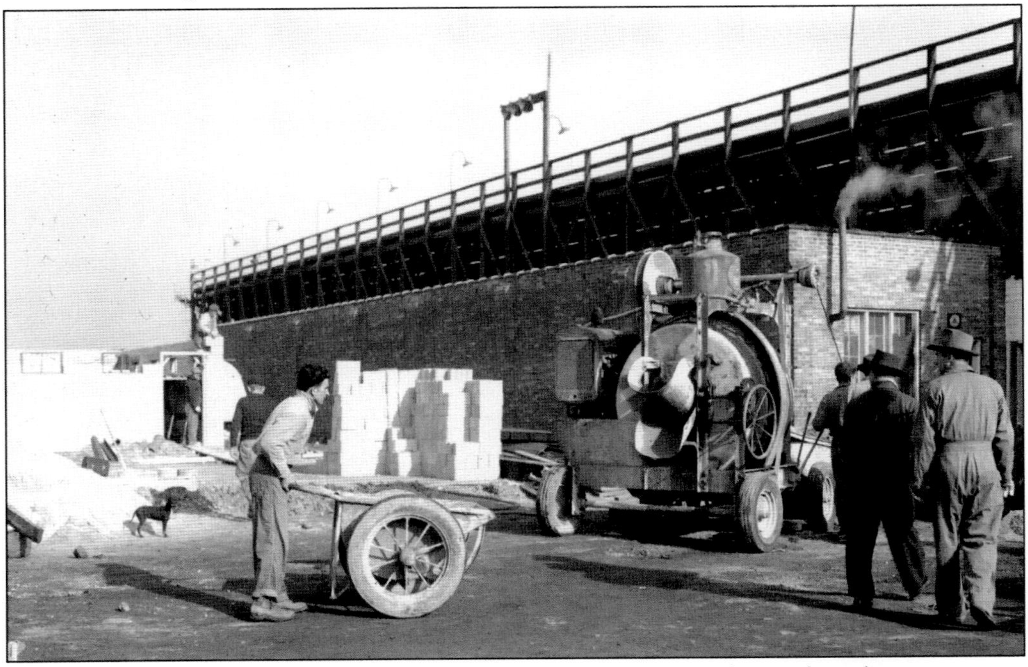

Workmen, cement blocks, and mortar are seen in this picture as the track undergoes a major facelift before the 1948 racing season began. The Jenin brothers, Nick and Pete, took over the speedway's ownership and promoted their first midget-racing program at the track on June 4, 1947. (Courtesy of Bob Sheldon.)

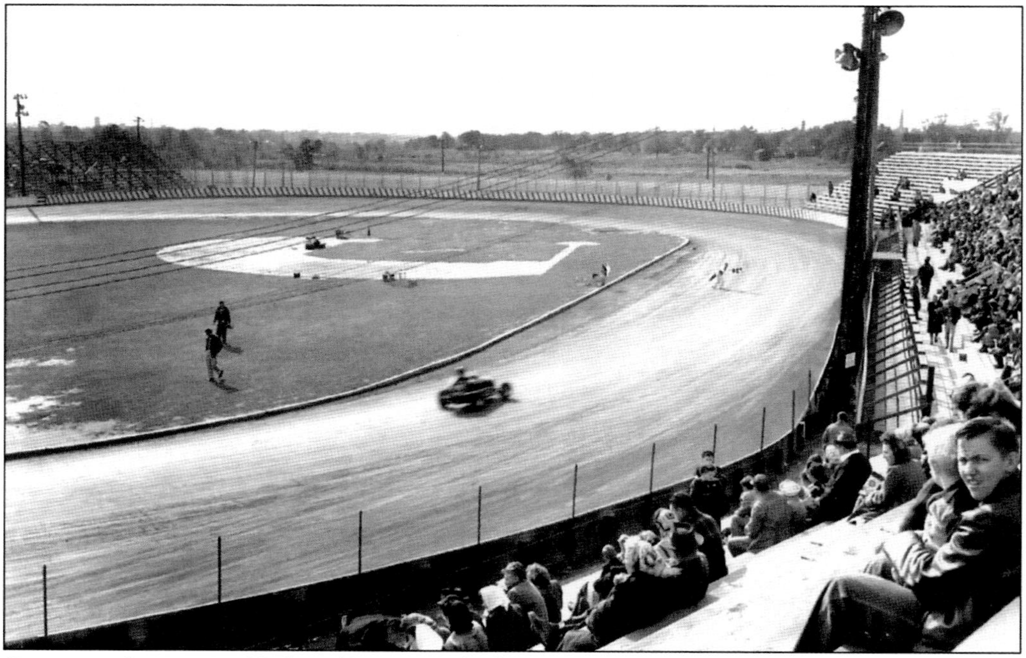

Owners and promoters Nick and Pete Jenin had pretty much completed the track's modernization program when this picture was taken in 1948. Notice the baseball diamond in the infield. (Courtesy of Bob Sheldon.)

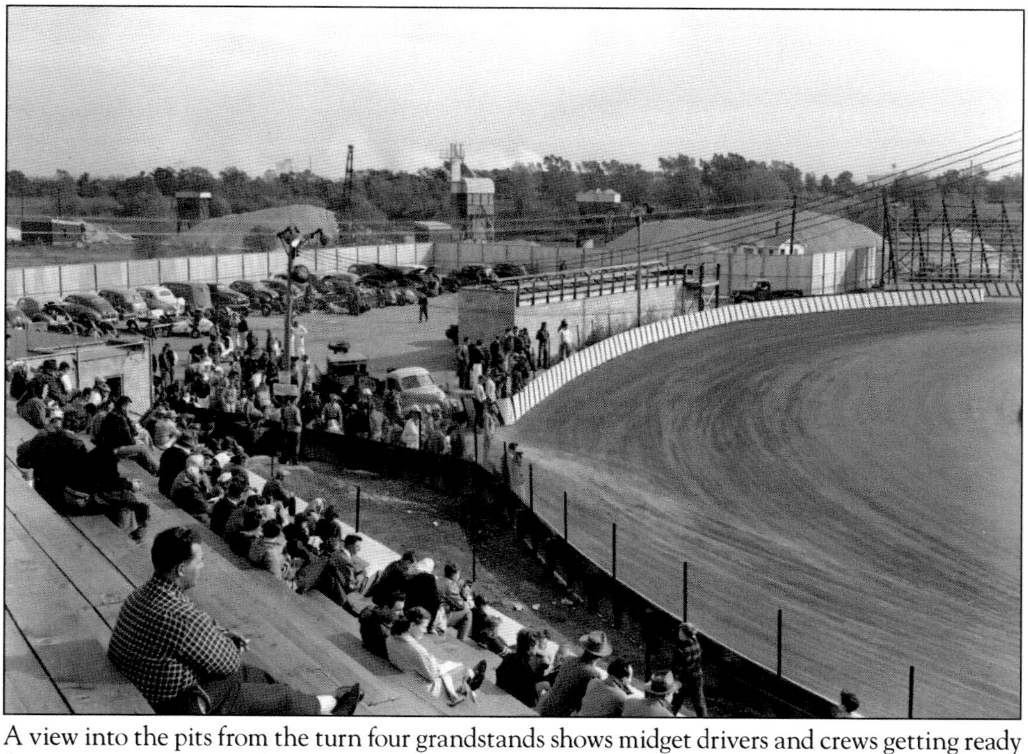

A view into the pits from the turn four grandstands shows midget drivers and crews getting ready for competition in October 1948. (Courtesy of Bob Sheldon.)

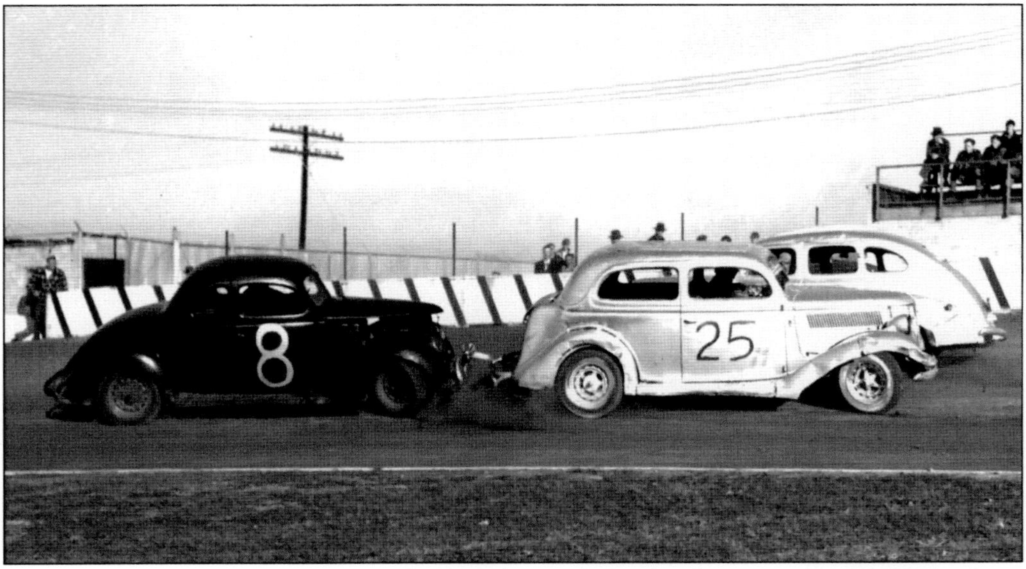

The year 1948 saw stock car racing held at the track for the first time. Danny Kladis drove a four-wheel-drive Jeep to victory in the track's first event—a 300-lap battle on October 31, 1948. The 300 Lap Classic would become an annual event at the Raceway oval for many years. A week later, Raceway closed its season with a 100-lap feature, which was won by Bill Van Allen. During the season finale, Tony Saylor (8) and Harvey Sheeler (25) are seen spinning around as an unidentified competitor motors around the outside of the spinning duo. (Courtesy of Bob Sheldon.)

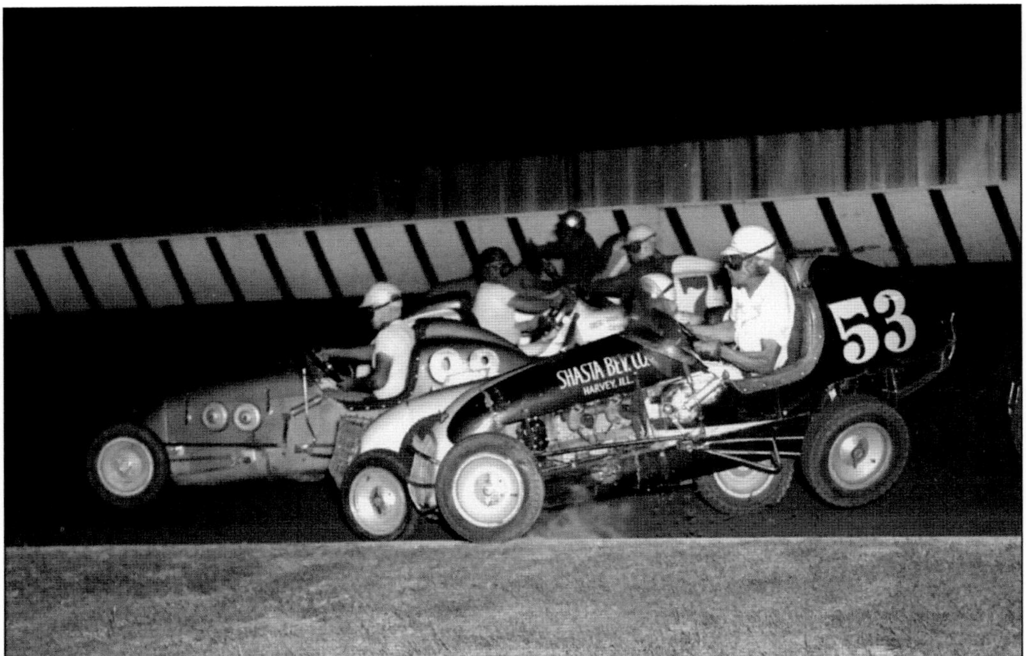

Byron Fisher (53) has a few wheels off the ground in some 1948 midget-racing action at the track. If one looks closely, they are six cars wide in this shot taken by photographer Bob Sheldon. (Courtesy of Bob Sheldon.)

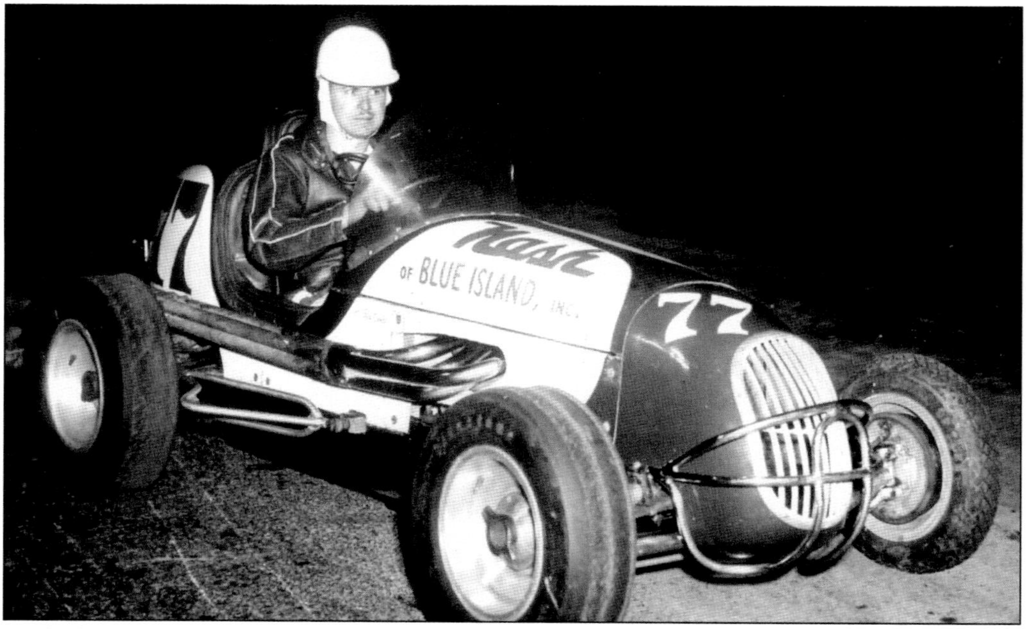

With the track minutes away from his Blue Island home, Robert "Bud" Koehler was a well-established midget-racing driver in the Midwest before stock cars made their first appearance at Raceway Park in 1948. Koehler (77) was the midget track champion at the speedway in 1949, 1951, and 1952. For the record, Koehler won 10 midget feature races and 490 late model main events during his career at the track. (Courtesy of Bob Sheldon.)

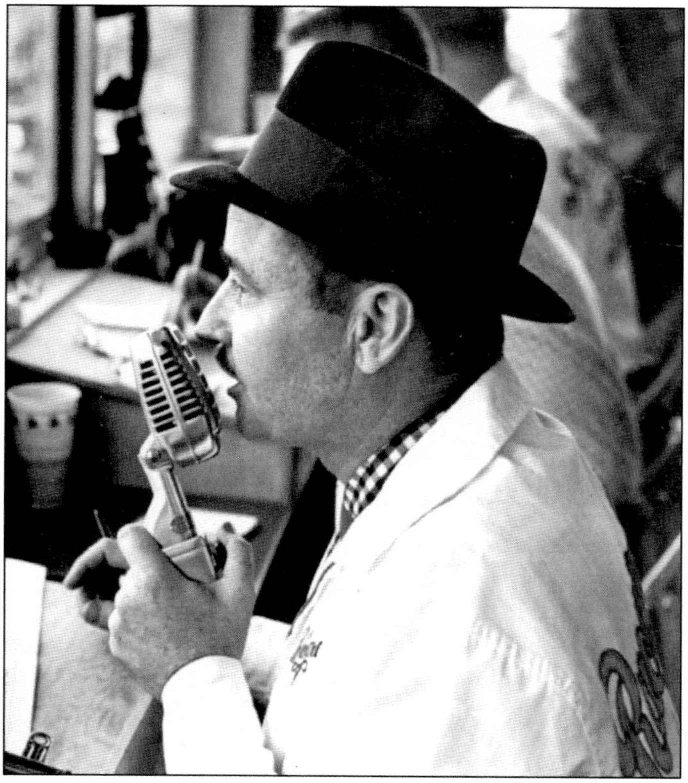

Wayne Adams was the track's announcer from 1946 until he retired after the 1989 season ended. Adams announced more than 2,000 racing events at the speedway and chronicled the track's history with his detailed notes and statistics. Adams began his association with Raceway Park as simply a fan, but later began taking pictures at the track and scored the races before taking over the microphone duties. (Courtesy of Stan Kalwasinski.)

Two

The 1950s

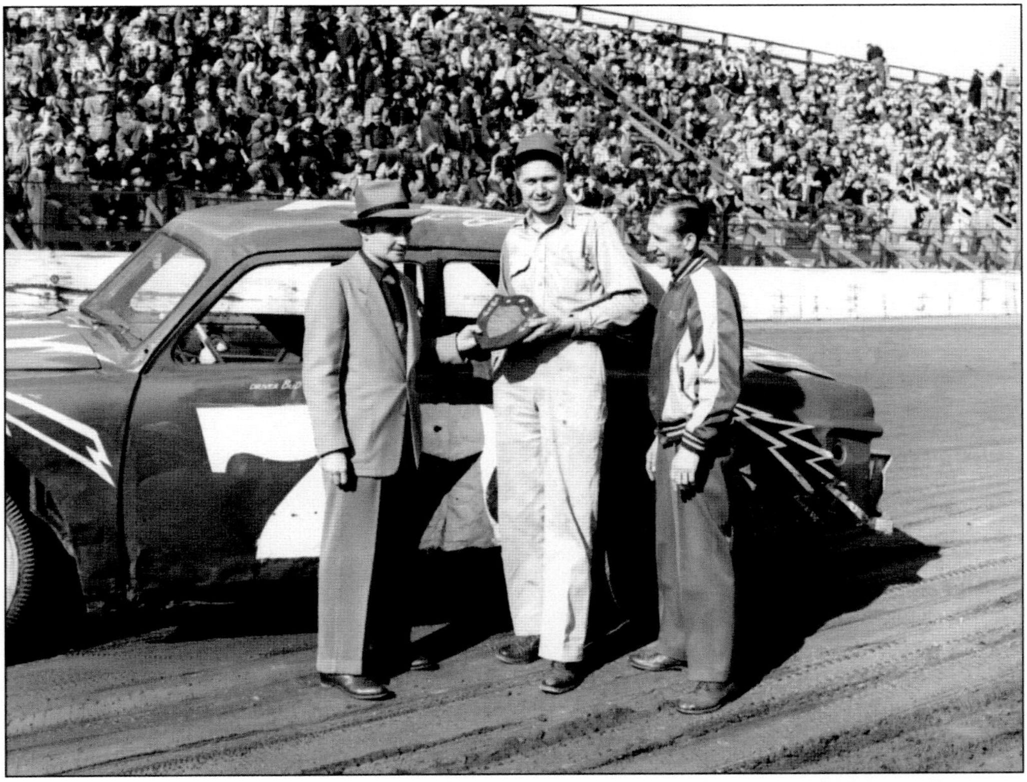

In the 1950s, stock cars took over from midgets as the most popular racing division at Raceway Park, and the track was paved during the 1951 racing season. To accommodate large crowds, the Jenins added grandstands along the backstretch. Drivers such as Stanley "Stash" Kullman, Ray Young, Ted Janecyk, and Harry Simonsen, big-name competitors that ran at Raceway for at least three decades a piece, began their careers at the track in the 1950s. Here Bud Koehler (77), of Blue Island, accepts an award from dapper announcer Wayne Adams (left) as owner/promoter Pete Jenin (right) looks on. (Courtesy of Bob Sheldon.)

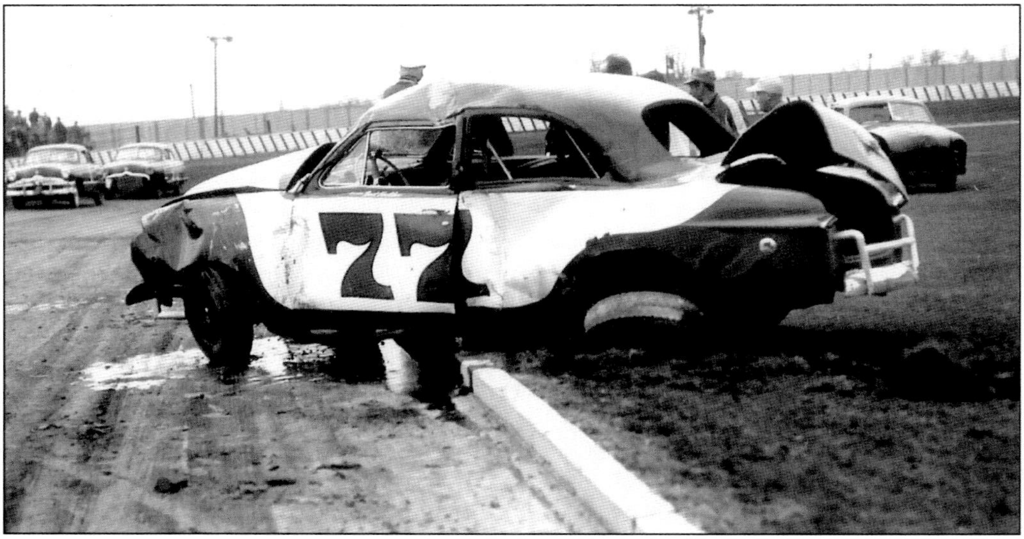

Bud Koehler's 1949 Ford looks a little worn after Koehler tangled with Bob Williams and flipped during the track's season-opening program in 1950. After this crash, Koehler and Williams would race each other in some real heated battles for pretty much the rest of their careers. (Courtesy of Bob Sheldon.)

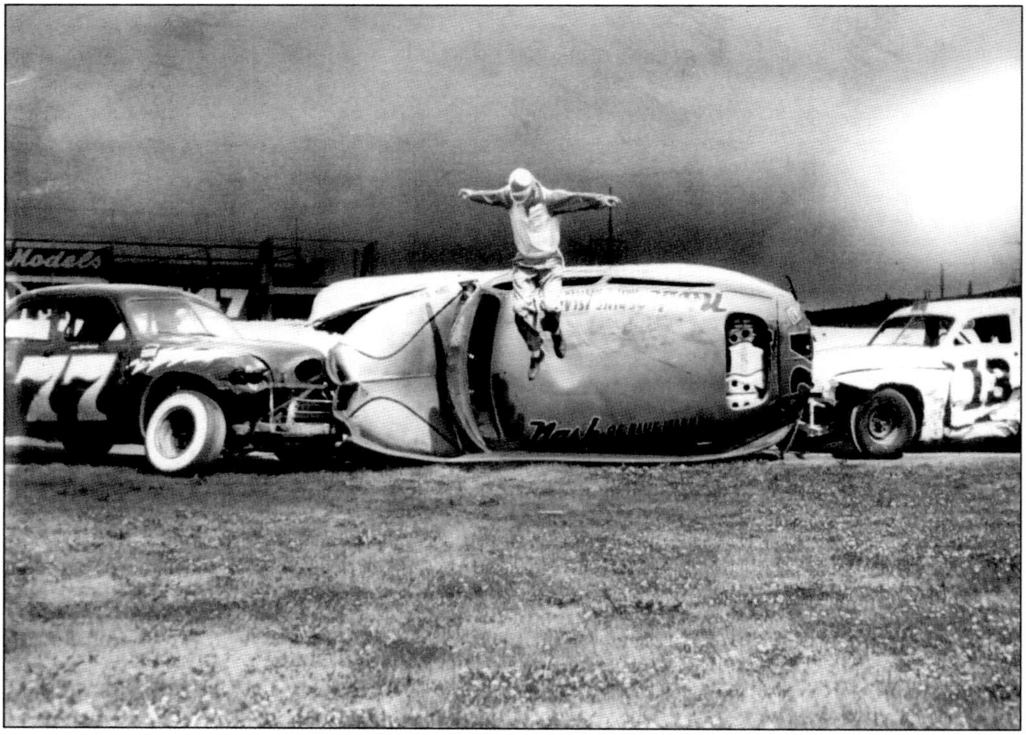

Raceway Park was years ahead of NASA. In this 1951 scene, Eddie Anderson (24) floats seemingly from space as he leaps from his rolled-over 1950 Nash. Also involved in this incident were Bud Koehler (77) and Henry Smith (13). Anderson, along with Chuck Scharf, founded the Championship Auto Race Drivers' Association, the sanctioning body of Raceway Park. (Courtesy of Bob Sheldon.)

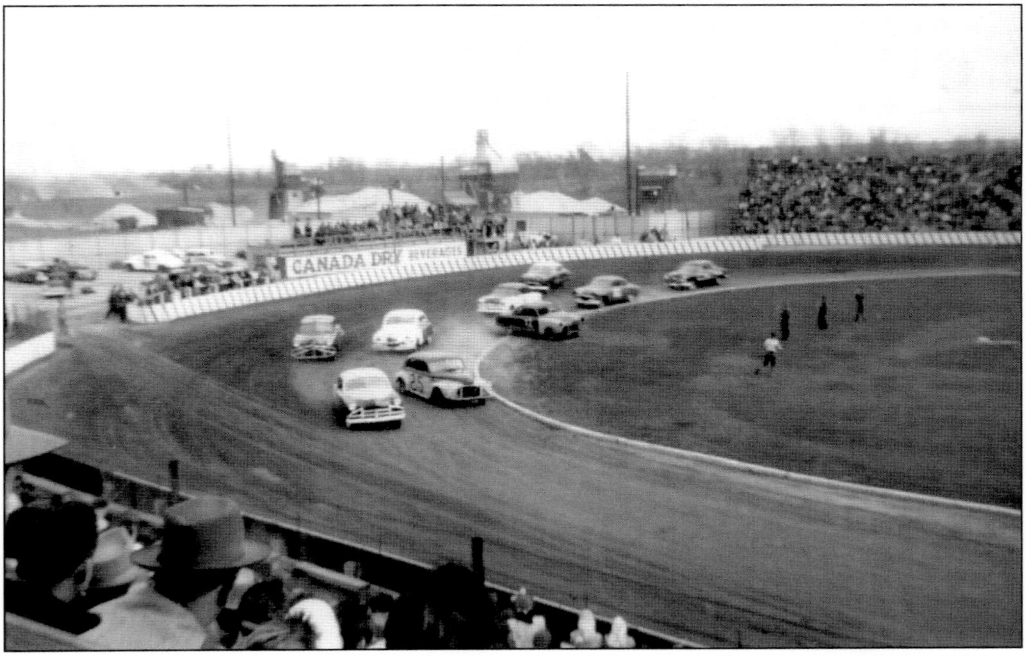

Race fan Vince Mayer captured this photograph while sitting in the grandstands attending a Sunday-afternoon event in the early 1950s. The track was not yet paved, so drivers work the dirt surface with Bryant Tucker (25) trying to move his Buick into the lead during a heat race. (Courtesy of Stan Kalwasinski.)

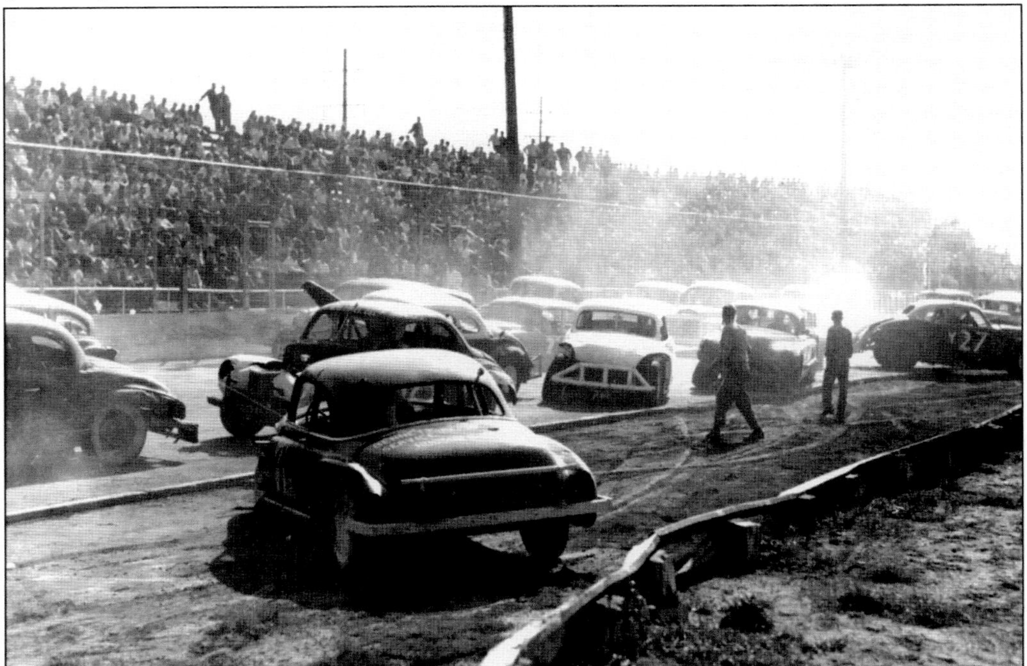

In this 1950 scene, the backstretch is jammed with cars and spectators as the action gets pretty wild. Plenty of dust was kicked up, but Raceway Park's track surface was paved the following year. (Courtesy of Bob Sheldon.)

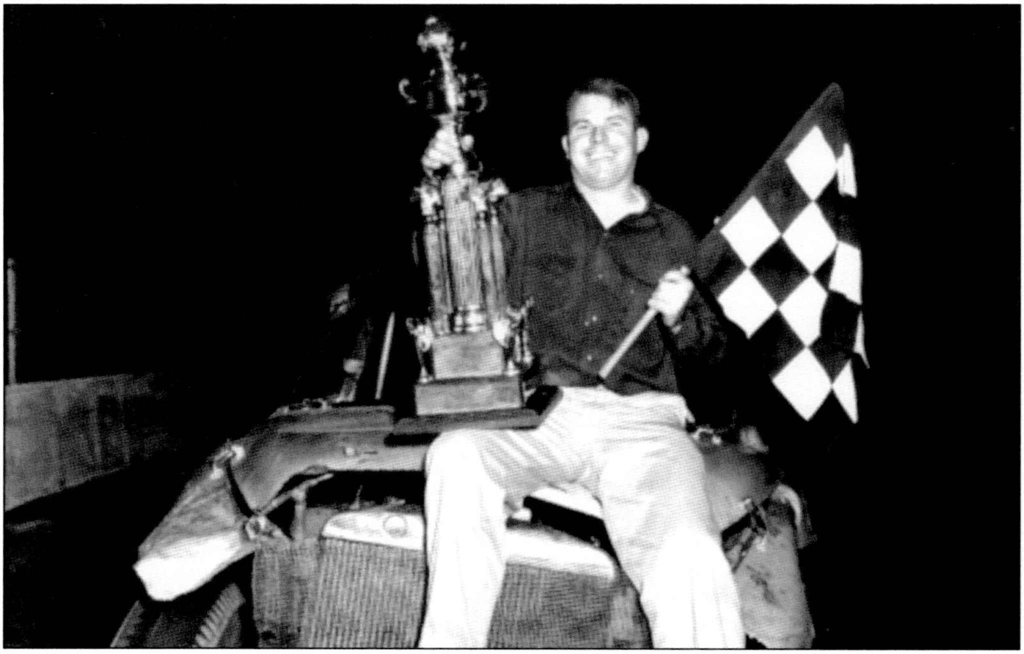

Hal Ruyle, who grew up in southern Illinois across the Mississippi River from St. Louis, Missouri, was the track's stock car champion in 1950. Nicknamed the "Farmer Boy" from St. Louis, Ruyle sits on the hood of his Hank Salat–owned Packard after winning the track's third annual 300 Lap Classic. (Courtesy of Bob Sheldon.)

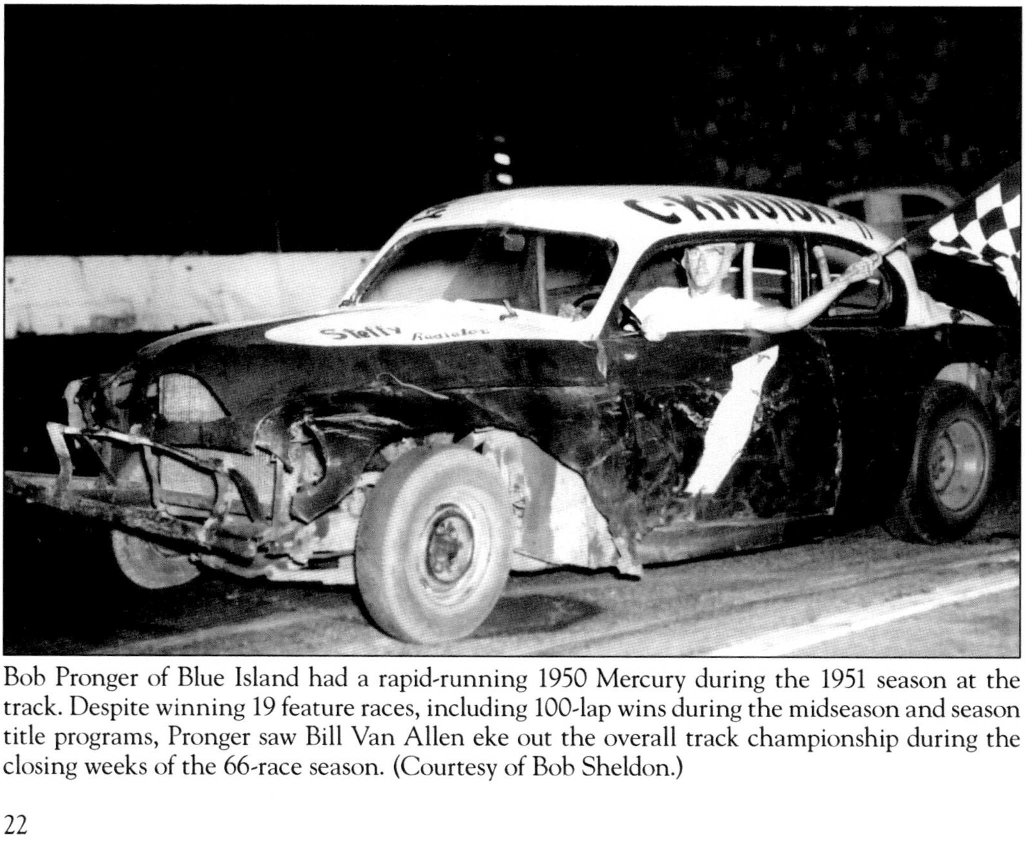

Bob Pronger of Blue Island had a rapid-running 1950 Mercury during the 1951 season at the track. Despite winning 19 feature races, including 100-lap wins during the midseason and season title programs, Pronger saw Bill Van Allen eke out the overall track championship during the closing weeks of the 66-race season. (Courtesy of Bob Sheldon.)

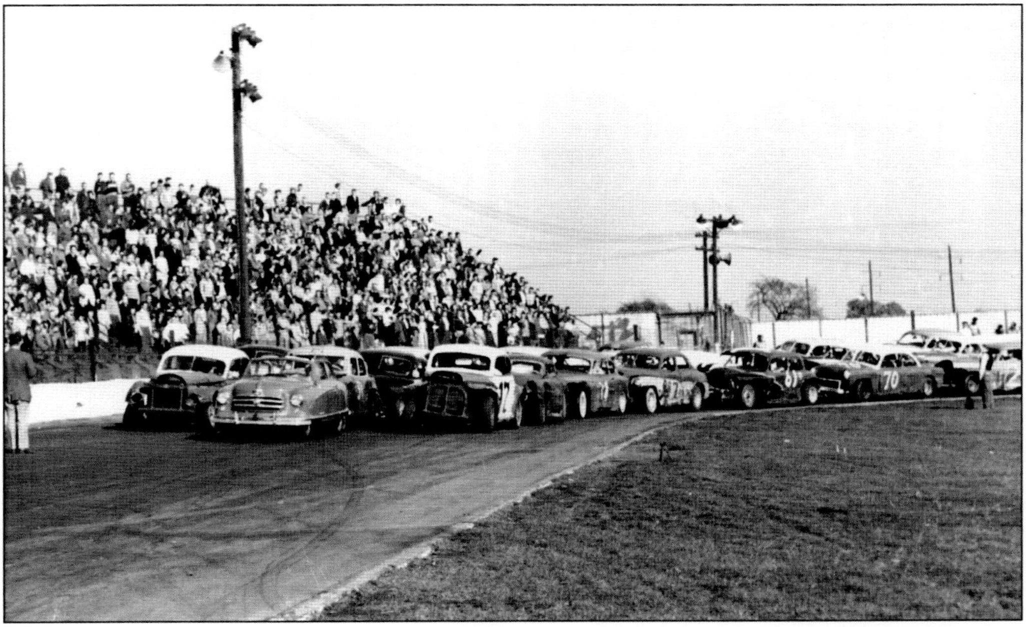

A brand new Nash convertible leads the field to the start of the 1951 300 Lap Classic. Bill Van Allen (6), of Justice, would take home the victory. The pace car was awarded later that afternoon to a lucky fan who entered in a raffle to win the car. The year 1951 was the first year that the track was paved, and Raceway Park held over 80 racing programs that year, earning the moniker "World's Busiest Track." (Courtesy of Bob Sheldon.)

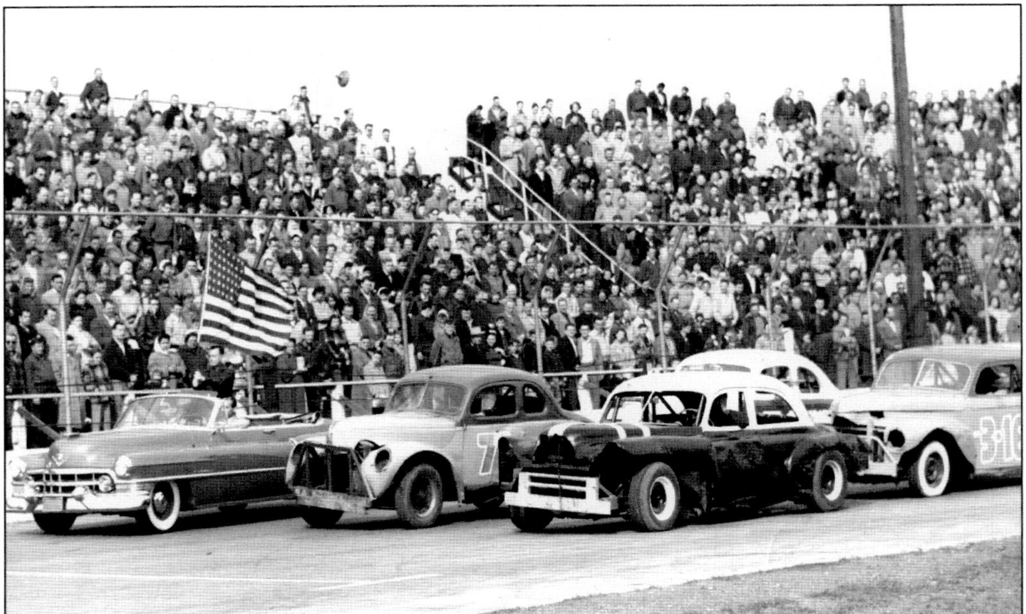

The Cadillac pace car cruises by as the packed near-capacity crowd stands while tribute is paid to the United States through the playing of the national anthem. Lined up and ready to race in 1952's opening day are Gene Orris (71), Cliff Tatro (unmarked car), and Skip Brueggeman (3-16). (Courtesy of Bob Sheldon.)

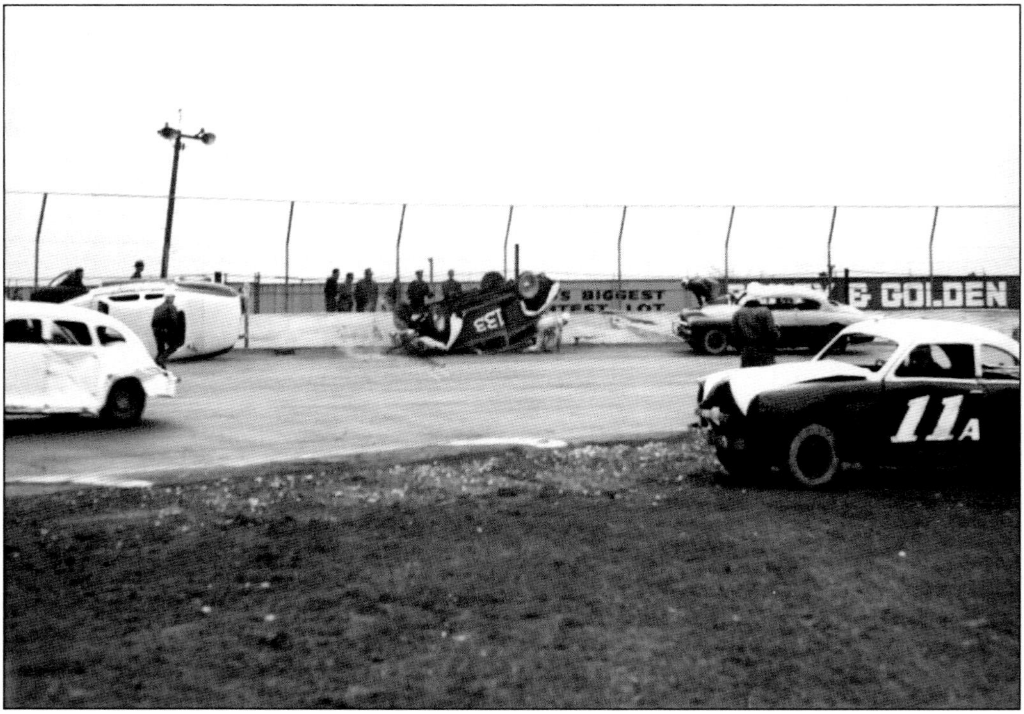

Traffic is halted at the west end of the track as one car rests on its side and another (133) is on its roof between turns one and two. (Courtesy of Bob Sheldon.)

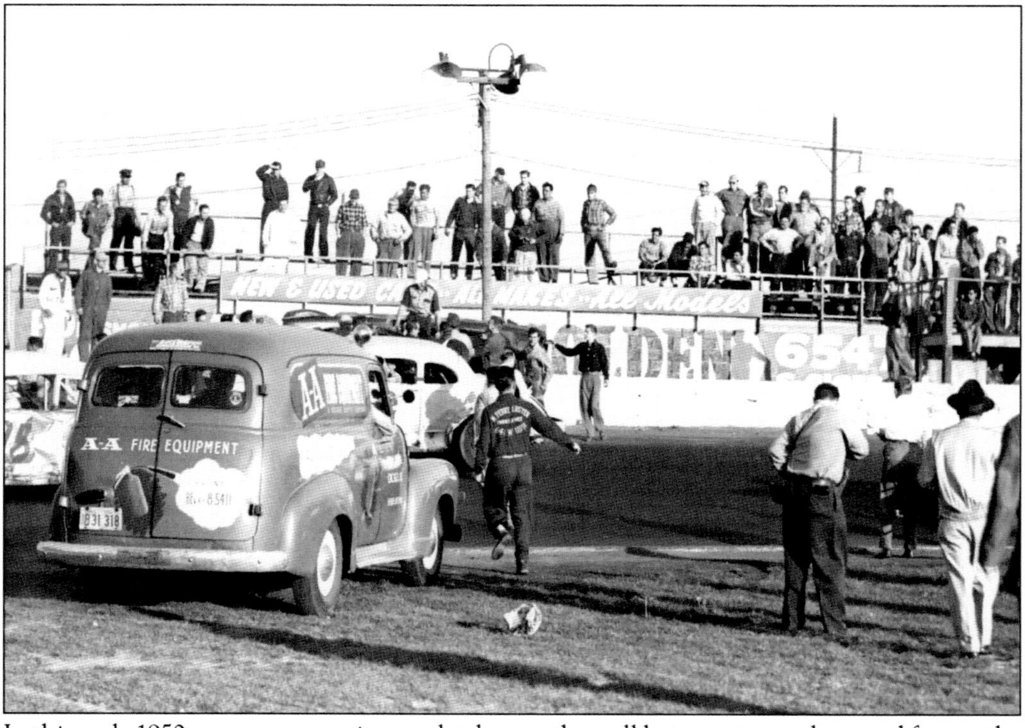

In this early-1950s scene, one car is completely over the wall between turns three and four as the driver climbs out. Plenty of help is on the way! (Courtesy of Bob Sheldon.)

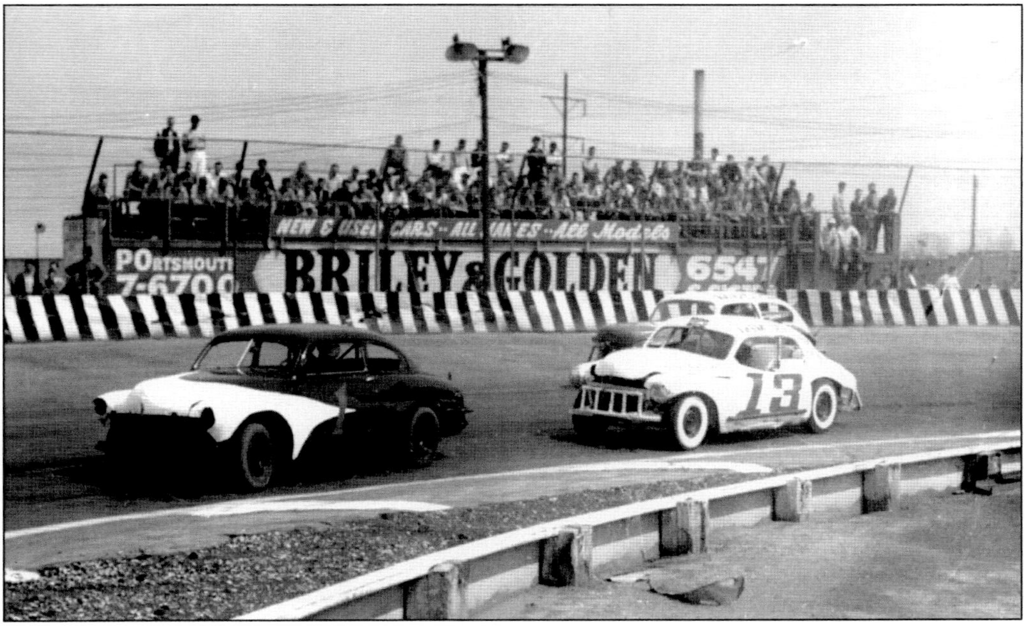

Bob Pronger (1) leads Henry Smith (13) around turn four in this 1952 racing scene. Pronger, Don Oldenberg, Bill Cornwall, and several other Raceway regulars would travel south to Daytona Beach, Florida, for several years during the 1950s to race on the sands of Daytona Beach in the NASCAR races held each February. In 1953, Pronger did not even complete a lap, having rolled his racecar while entering turns one and two. (Courtesy of Bob Sheldon.)

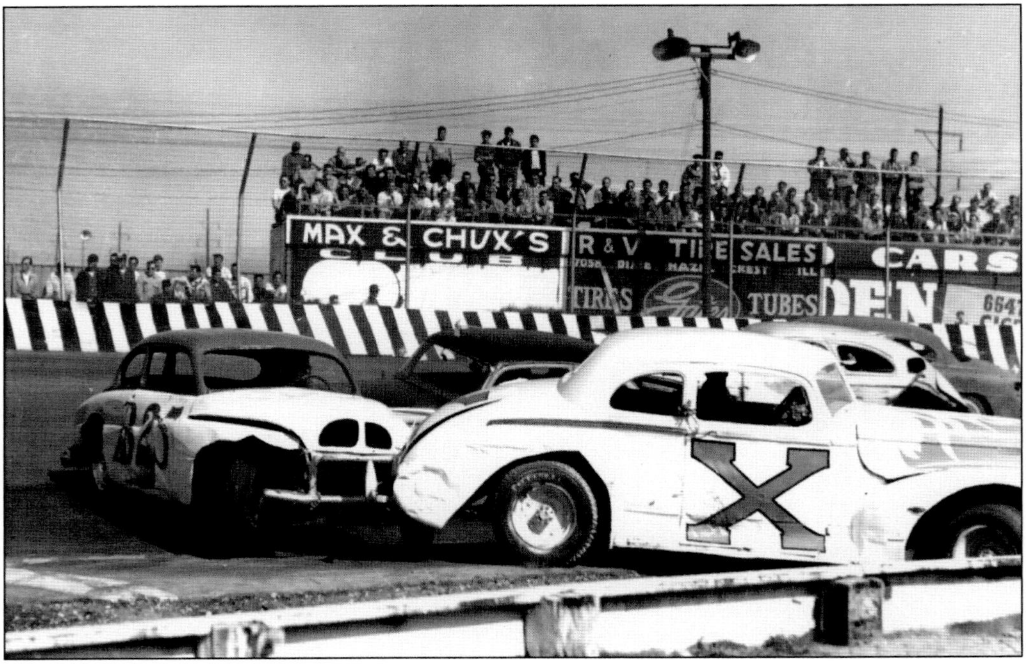

Bun Emery (B25) and Johnny Slowiak (X) get turned around in turn four as traffic swings by on the outside in this 1953 scene. The elevated grandstands in the background were on the roof of the pit bathrooms and allowed drivers and crew members to watch the action without having to enter the general grandstands. (Courtesy of Bob Sheldon.)

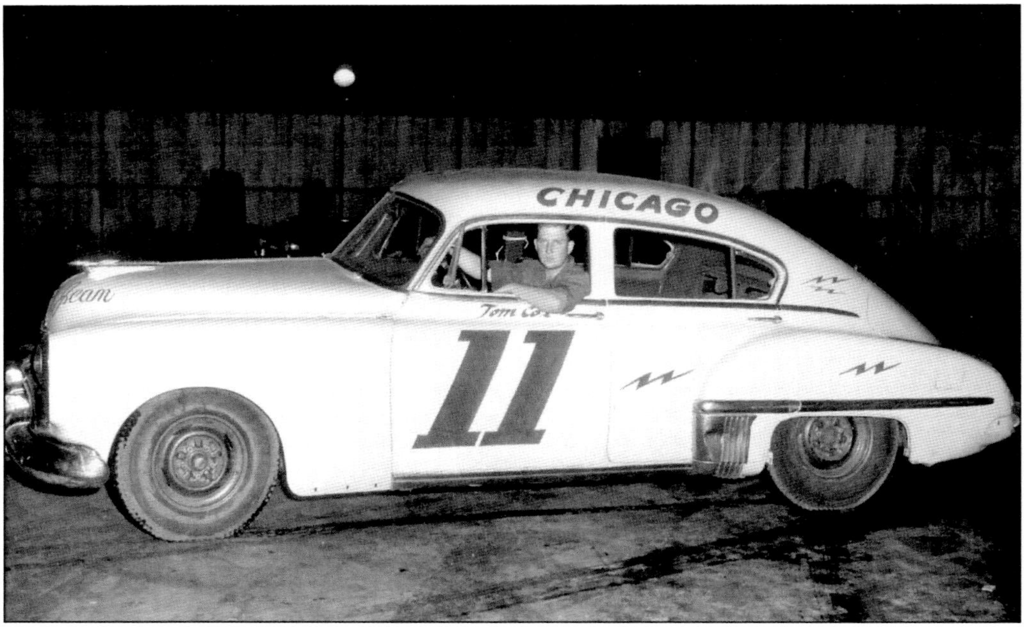

Tom Cox (11) was one of the early stock car frontrunners at the speedway. Hailing from Chicago and later calling Villa Park home, Cox was the track's stock car champion in 1955, winning 22 feature races during the season. Cox, who was among the drivers in competition during the first year of stock car racing in 1948, is shown here in a four-door Oldsmobile ready to do battle in the early 1950s. (Courtesy of Stan Kalwasinski.)

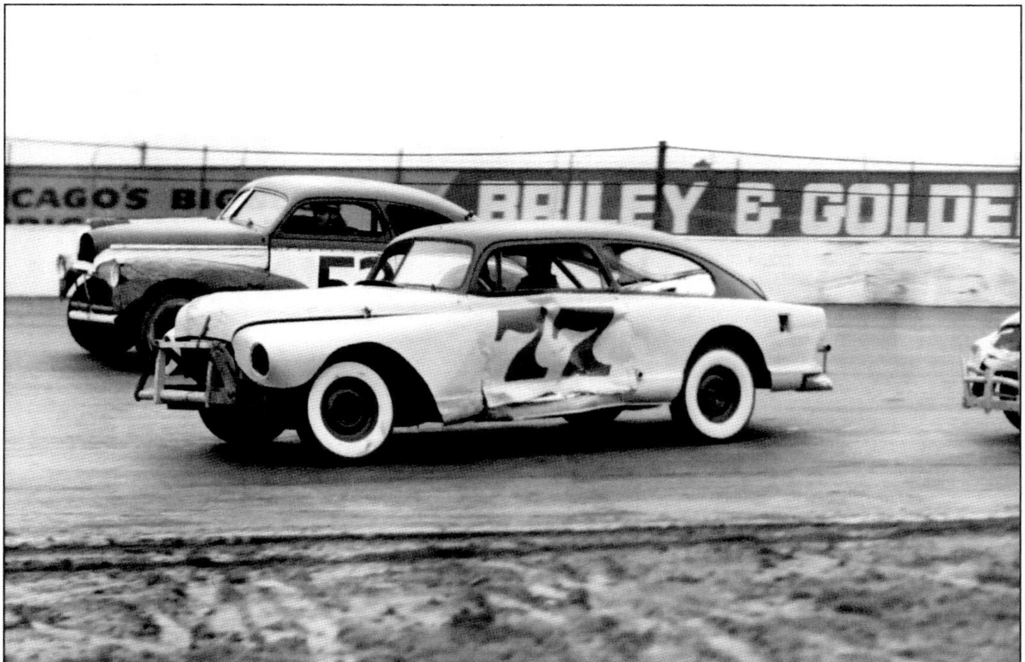

Bud Koehler (77) slides inside of Bill Cornwall (53) in this 1952 scene. Both Koehler and Cornwall were track champions who started driving at Raceway in the 1940s. (Courtesy of Bob Sheldon.)

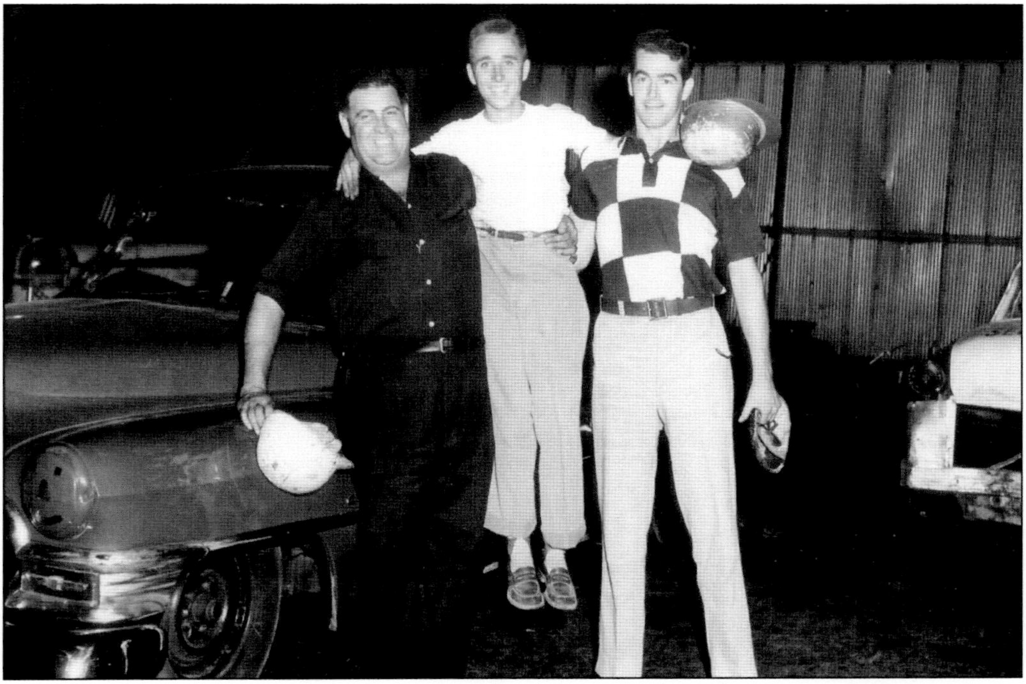

Pete Clark (left), Jack Lighthart (center), and Bob Pronger show that Raceway Park stock car drivers came in all different sizes as evident in this early-1950s photograph. Pronger, who hailed from Blue Island, enjoyed the most success at Raceway Park of the trio, winning late model championships there in 1961 and 1969. Pronger, who set NASCAR qualifying records at Daytona Beach, Florida, in 1953, was reported to be involved with Chicagoland car stealing operations and disappeared in 1971. (Courtesy of Bob Sheldon.)

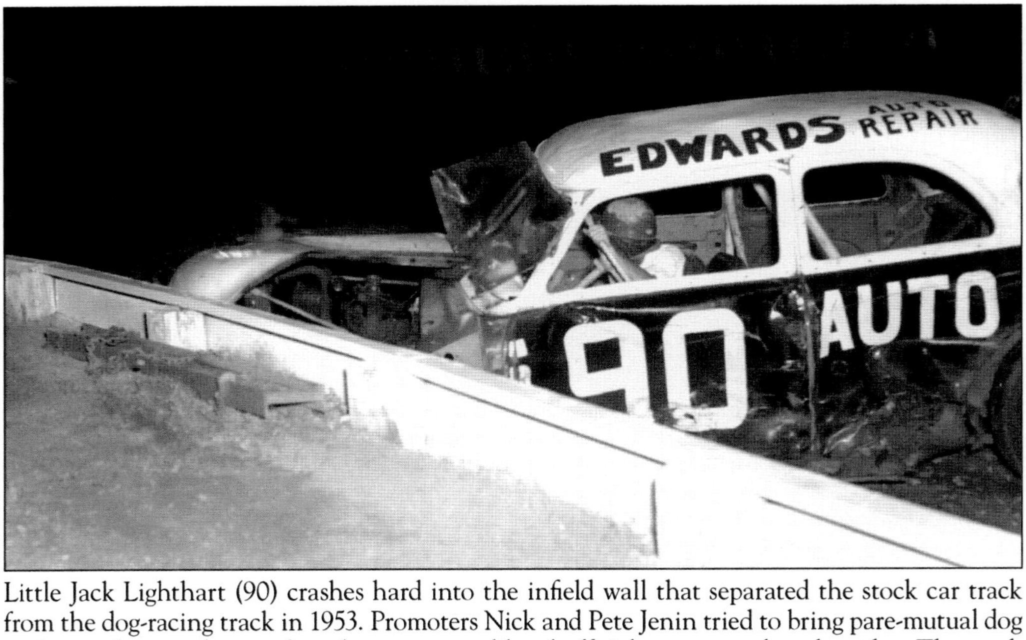

Little Jack Lighthart (90) crashes hard into the infield wall that separated the stock car track from the dog-racing track in 1953. Promoters Nick and Pete Jenin tried to bring pare-mutual dog racing to the speedway only to have state and local officials put an end to that idea. The track did host exhibition dog-racing events in 1953. (Courtesy of Bob Sheldon.)

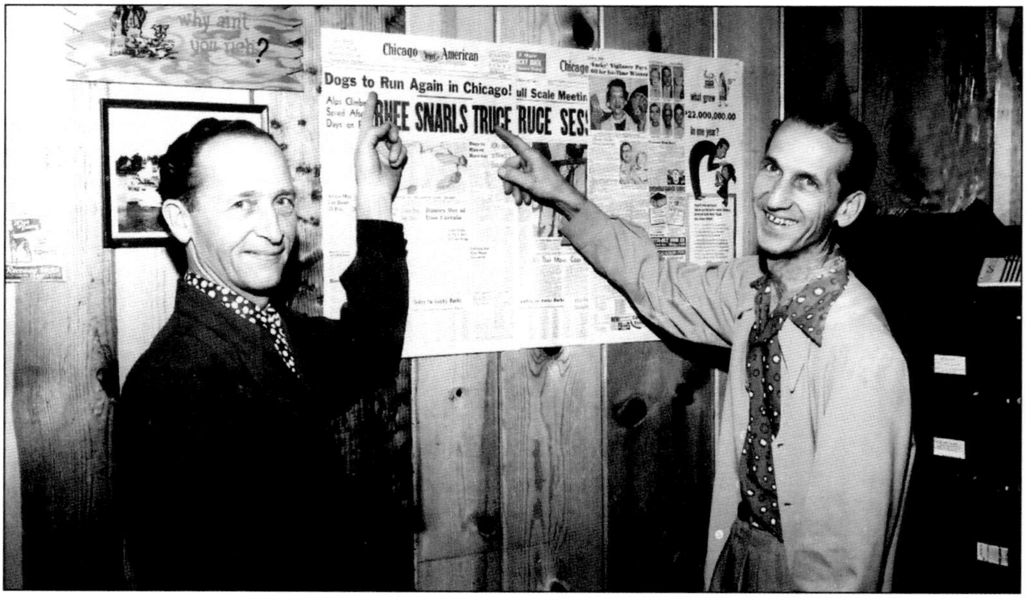

"Dogs to Run Again in Chicago!" the *Chicago American* newspaper headline declared in 1953. In their office, Nick Jenin (left) and his brother Pete point to the newspaper banner as they prepared to host dog-racing programs at their speedway. A special dog track was built in the infield of the auto-racing track with the idea of betting on the pooches. State and local officials never let Nick and Pete actually hold betting events at the track, although the Jenins presented several exhibition dog races. (Courtesy of Bob Sheldon.)

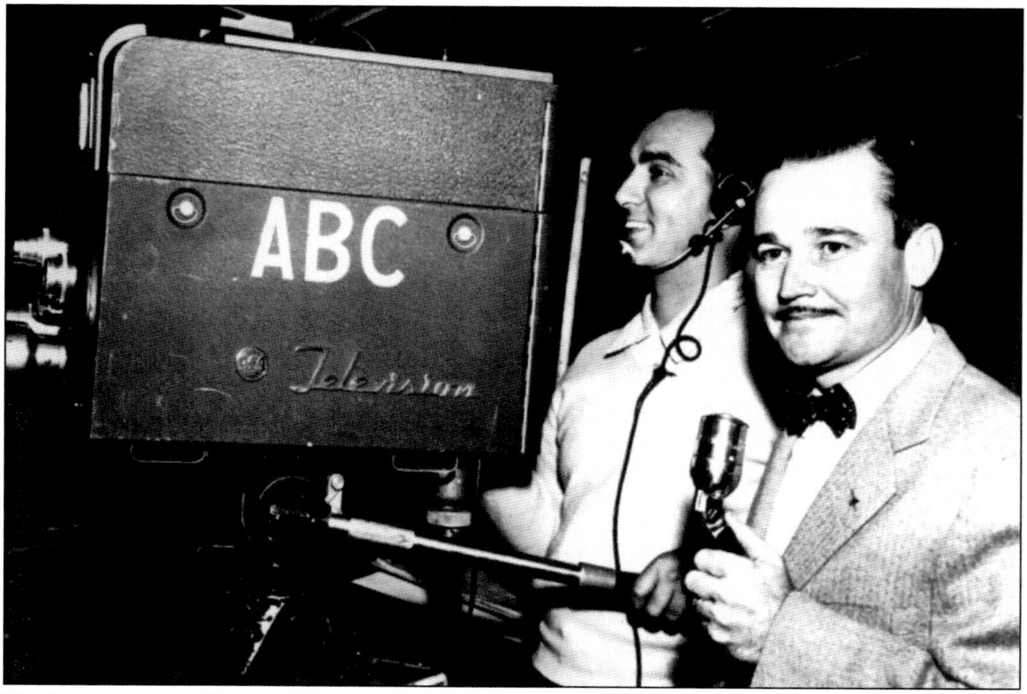

Track announcer Wayne Adams poses next to the ABC television camera before a night of television work during the track's 1954 season. WBKB-TV, channel 7, televised the stock car races live from 9:30 p.m. to 10:30 p.m. on 17 Sunday nights. (Courtesy of Stan Kalwasinski.)

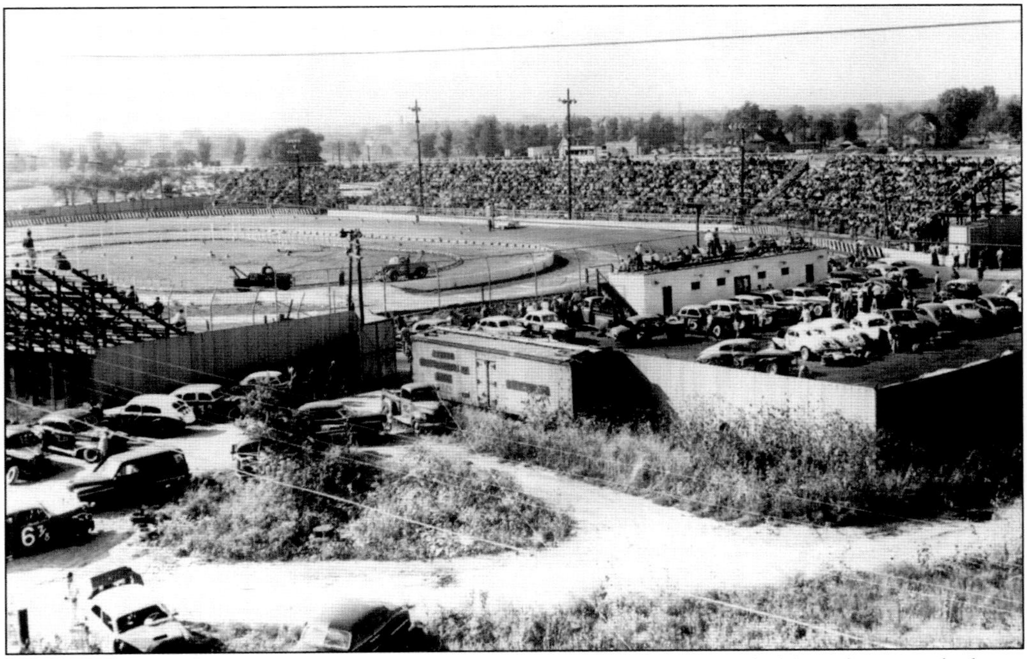

Fans wait for stock car racing to begin at the track in 1953. This Bob Sheldon photograph shows the speedway's pit area as well as part of the newly added backstretch grandstands. The pits were later expanded to accommodate a larger amount of cars. The dog-racing track around the infield is visible in this photograph. (Courtesy of Bob Sheldon.)

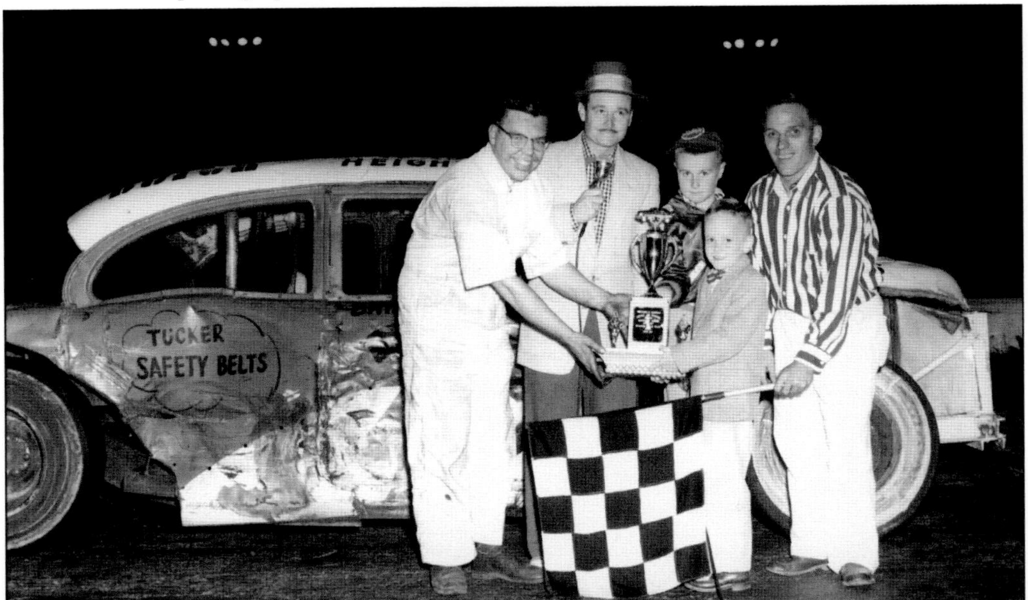

Pictured left to right are driver Bryant Tucker (25), announcer Wayne Adams, Roger Koehler (son of late model driver Bud), Joe Fisher (son of a Dressel's Bakeries executive, the sponsor of the race), and starter Smokey Smith celebrating Tucker's 100-lap season title race victory in 1956. Tucker was known for his seat belt manufacturing company, and he often ran at Soldier Field and even participated in some early NASCAR events. (Courtesy of Stan Kalwasinski.)

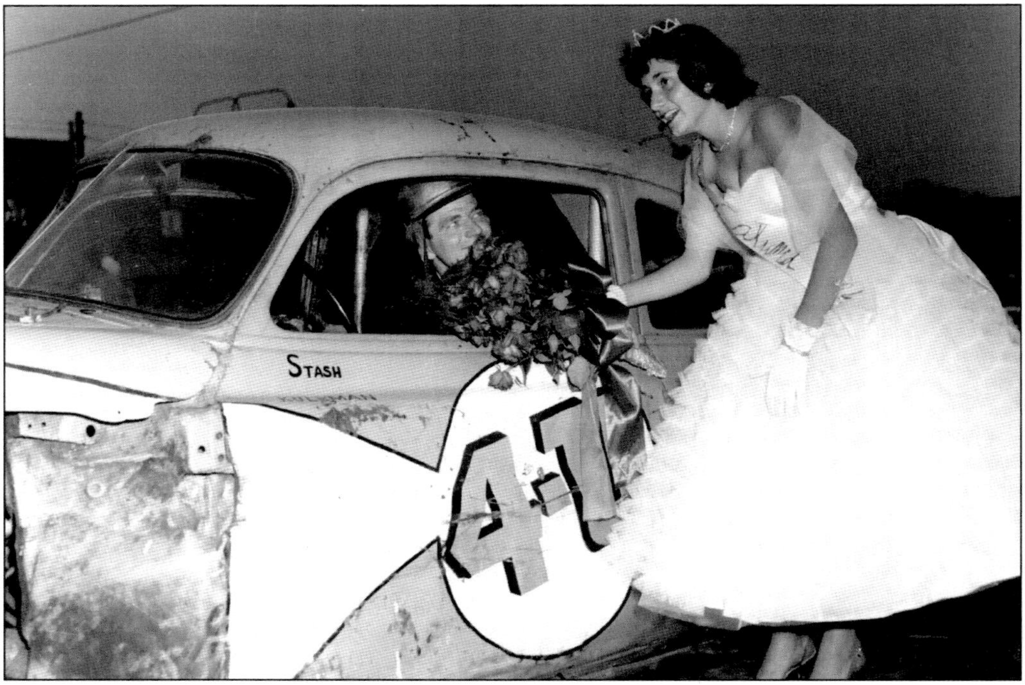

Although this is the car of Stanley "Stash" Kullman (4U), it is actually Ted Janecyk behind the wheel, as he talks to a beauty pageant participant. We hope that she did not get her dress dirty after a long day at the track. (Courtesy of Stan Kalwasinski.)

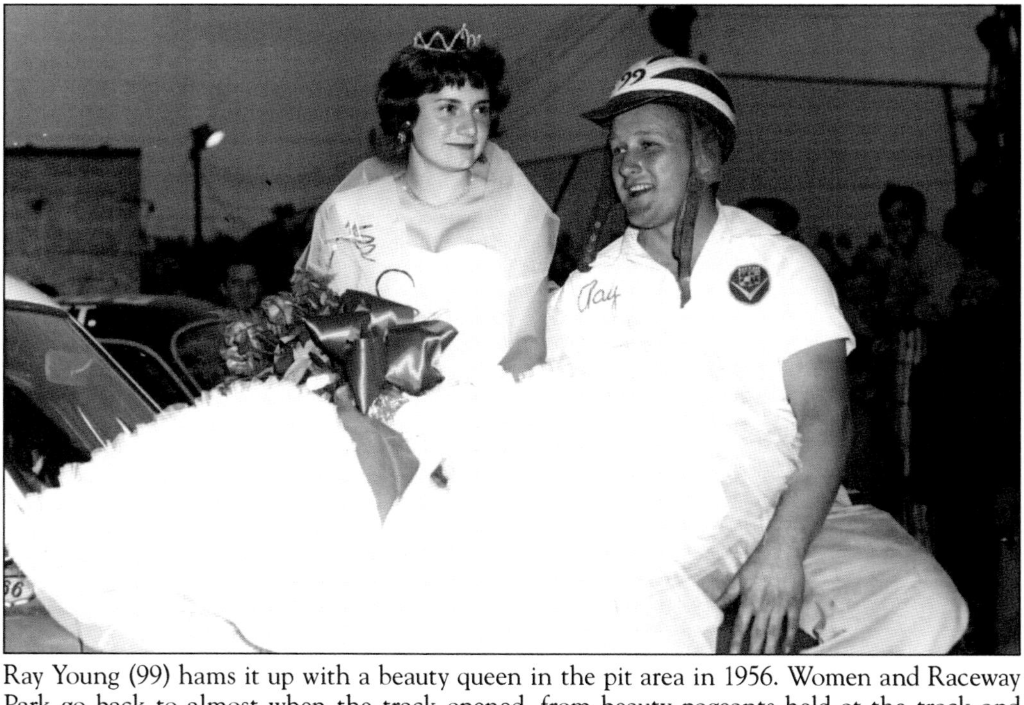

Ray Young (99) hams it up with a beauty queen in the pit area in 1956. Women and Raceway Park go back to almost when the track opened, from beauty pageants held at the track and women drivers such as Reggie Taylor to Bill Wildt and his showgirls of the 1990s. (Courtesy of Stan Kalwasinski.)

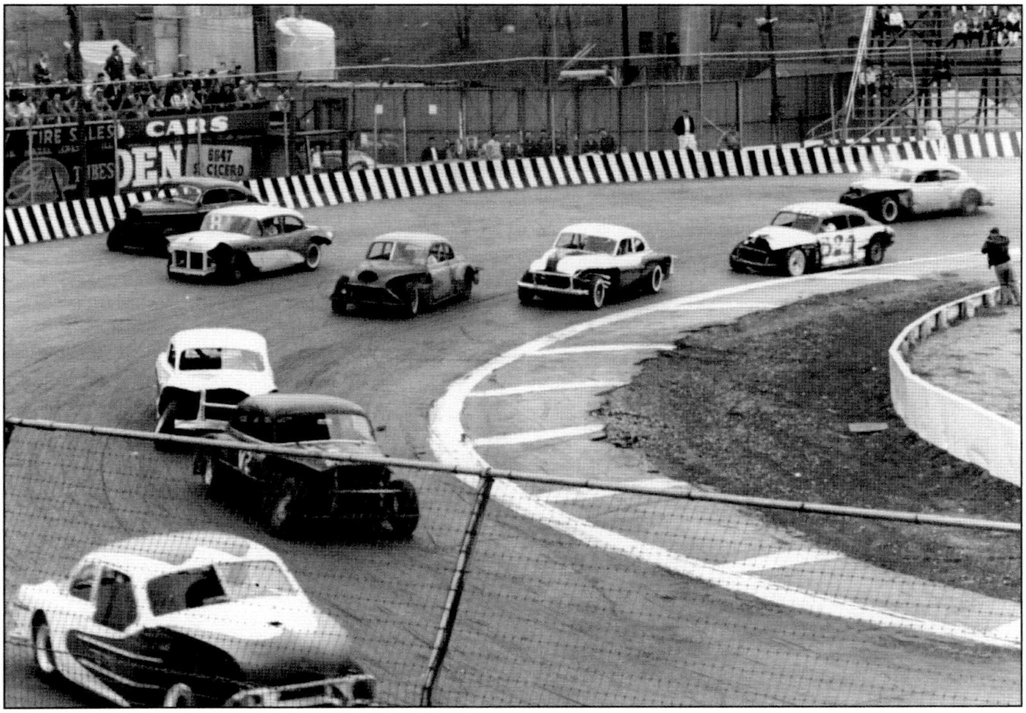

In this 1956 late model scene, Harry Simonsen (TS1) and Legs Whitcomb (V2) lead a gang of cars coming out of turn four. (Courtesy of Stan Kalwasinski.)

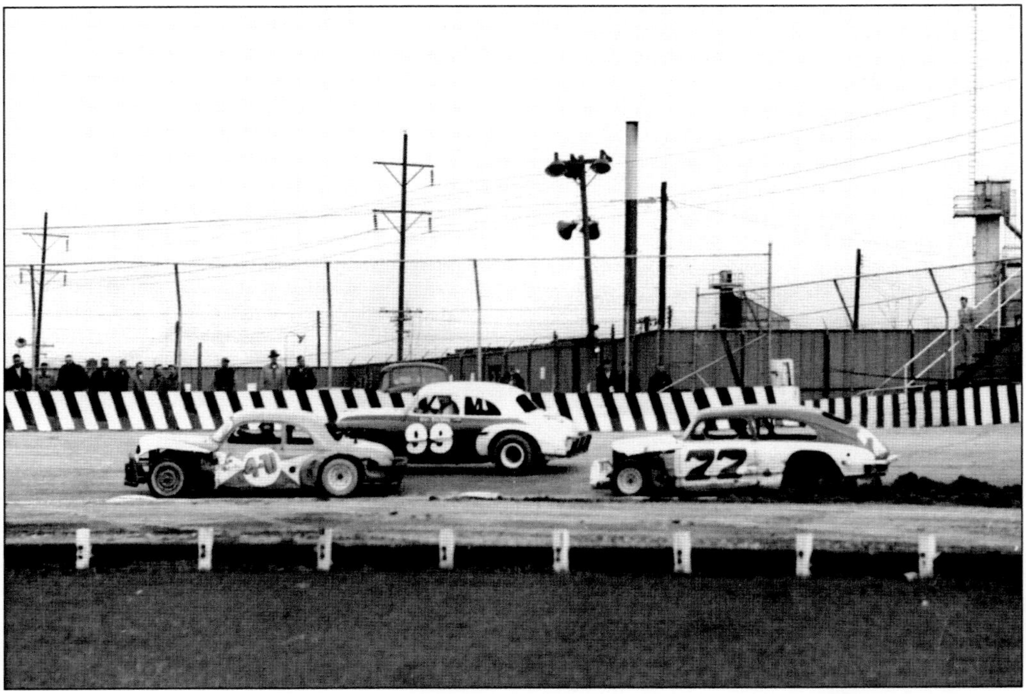

Stash Kullman (4U) leads Ray Young (99) and Bud Koehler (77) around turn three in mid-1950s late model action. These three drivers would compete against each other at Raceway Park for nearly three decades. (Courtesy of Bob Sheldon.)

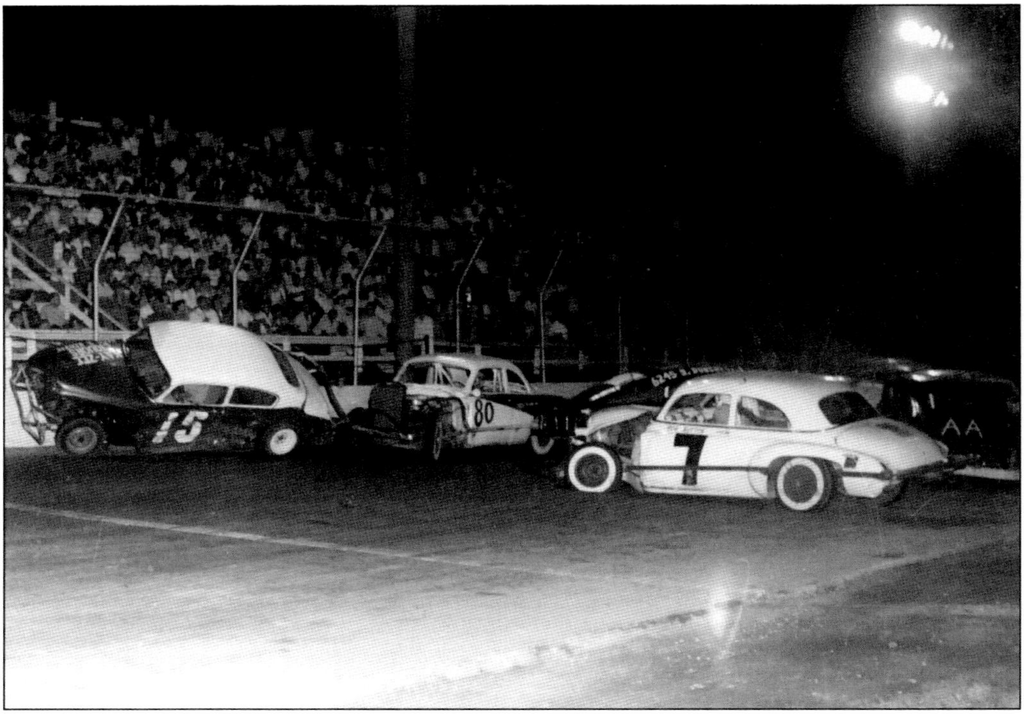

In this 1956 racing scene, Bob Button (7) faces the grandstands as other late models crash around him. (Courtesy of Stan Kalwasinski.)

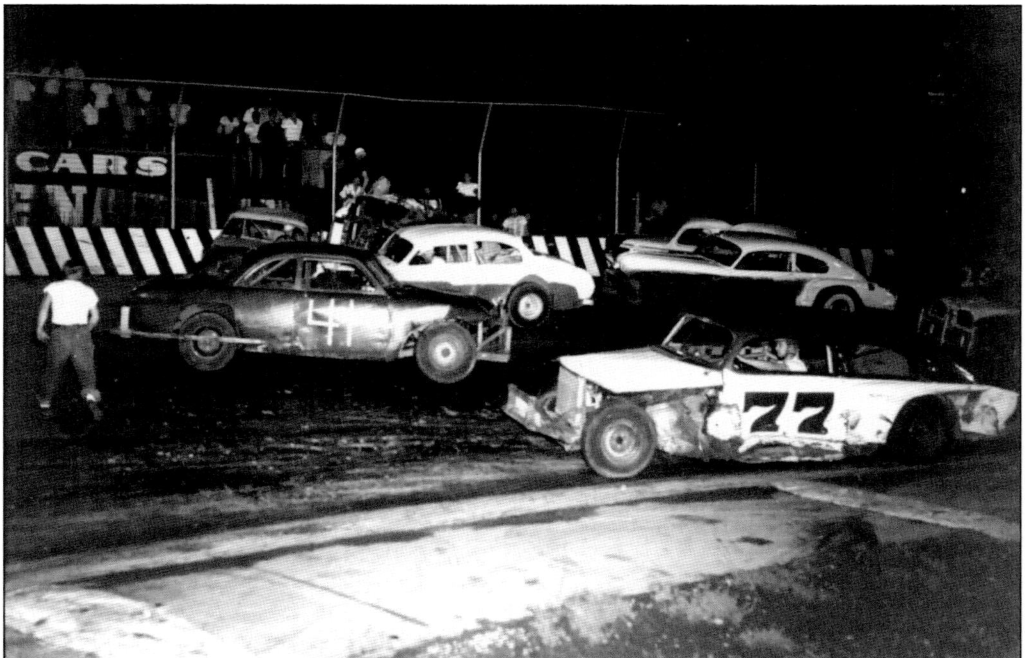

Bud Koehler (77) looks on as cars tangle all around him in turn three during the 1956 racing season. An unidentified driver is climbing out of his rolled automobile while drivers and crew members in the pit area look on. (Courtesy of Stan Kalwasinski.)

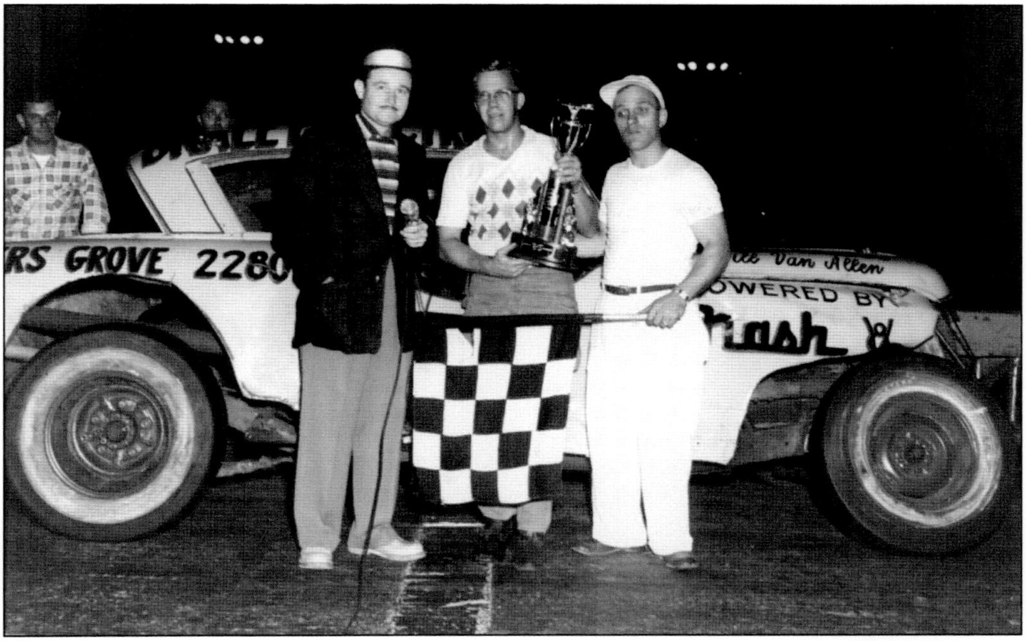

Little Bill Van Allen celebrates another big victory in 1956 with track announcer Wayne Adams and starter Roger "Smokey" Smith. Van Allen would leave Raceway midway through the 1964 racing season, preferring to race at other speedways such as Santa Fe. Van Allen passed away in the early 1970s after a bout with cancer. (Courtesy of Stan Kalwasinski.)

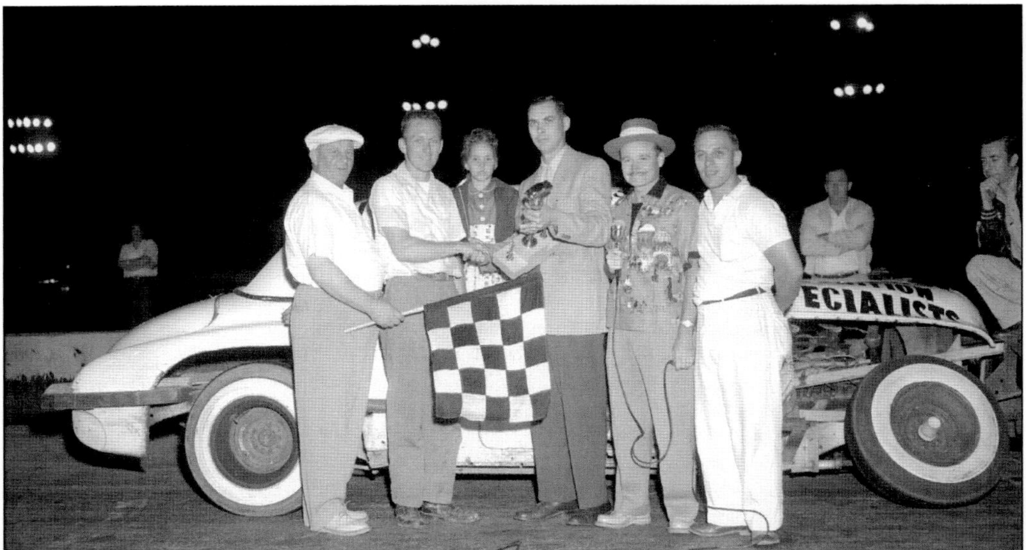

Bob Button (second from left) of Midlothian garnered top stock car honors in 1956 by winning eight feature races during the year. Button, who operated a Shell gas station and taxi company in his hometown, had the distinction of winning six 50-lap races in a row at the World's Busiest Track. Button started his string by winning Twin 50s on Labor Day 1955. He is shown here after a Fourth of July 1956 win with starter Tom Plouzek (left), local car dealer Marvin Miller, announcer Wayne Adams (second from right), and assistant starter Roger "Smokey" Smith (far right). (Courtesy of Stan Kalwasinski.)

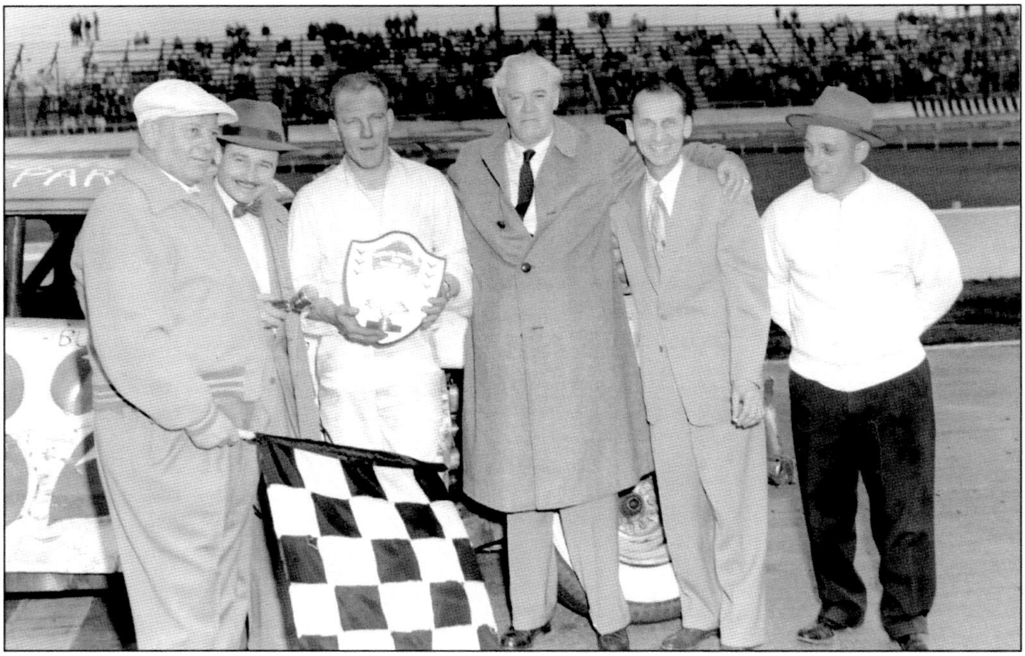

Bun Emery (B25), third from left, celebrates a victory in 1956 by receiving the Illustrated Speedway News award with, from left to right, starter Tom Plouzek, announcer Wayne Adams, *Illustrated Speedway News* publisher Walter Bull, track promoter Pete Jenin, and assistant starter Roger "Smokey" Smith. (Courtesy of Stan Kalwasinski.)

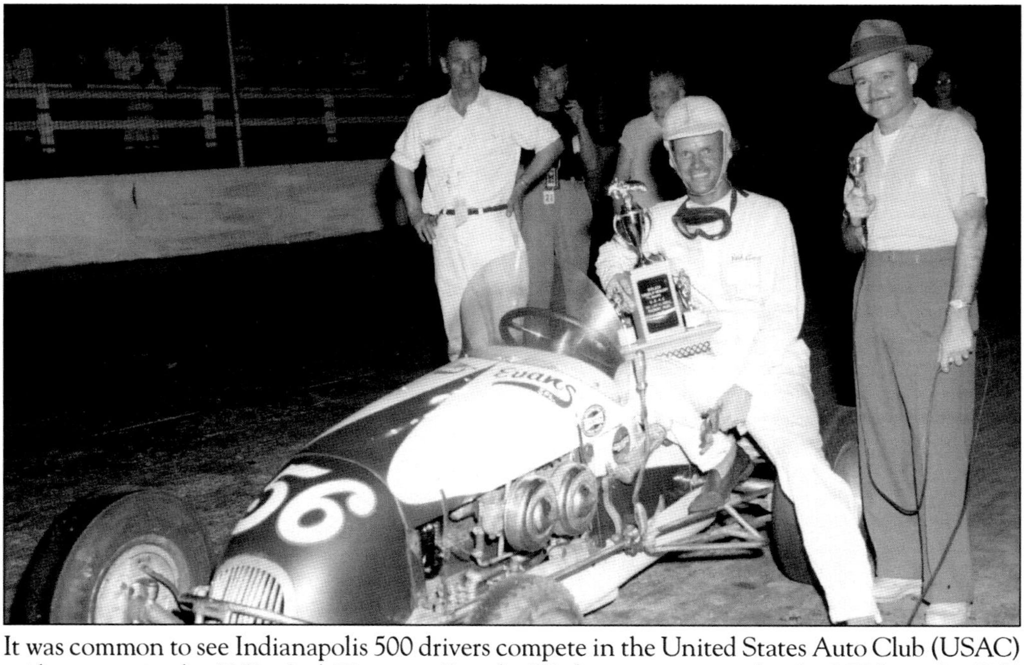

It was common to see Indianapolis 500 drivers compete in the United States Auto Club (USAC) midget races in the 1950s. Jack Turner, a Seattle, Washington, native, finished 25th in the 1956 Indy 500 and, a few weeks later, won a USAC midget race at Raceway Park. Turner (56) is shown here with his trophy as Wayne Adams is ready to perform a postrace interview. (Courtesy of Stan Kalwasinski.)

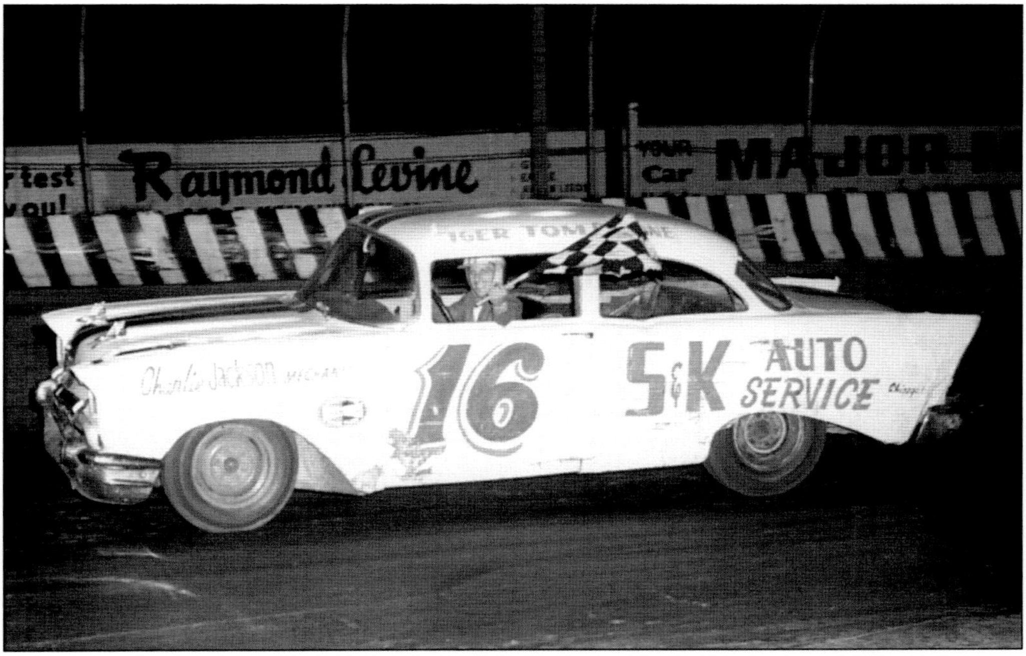

"Tiger" Tom Pistone (16) guides his 1957 Chevrolet around the track in a victory lap after winning Raceway's midseason title race of 1957. Pistone would go on to success in NASCAR, and his nephew Pete Pistone would become a successful racing commentator in the Chicagoland area. (Courtesy of Stan Kalwasinski.)

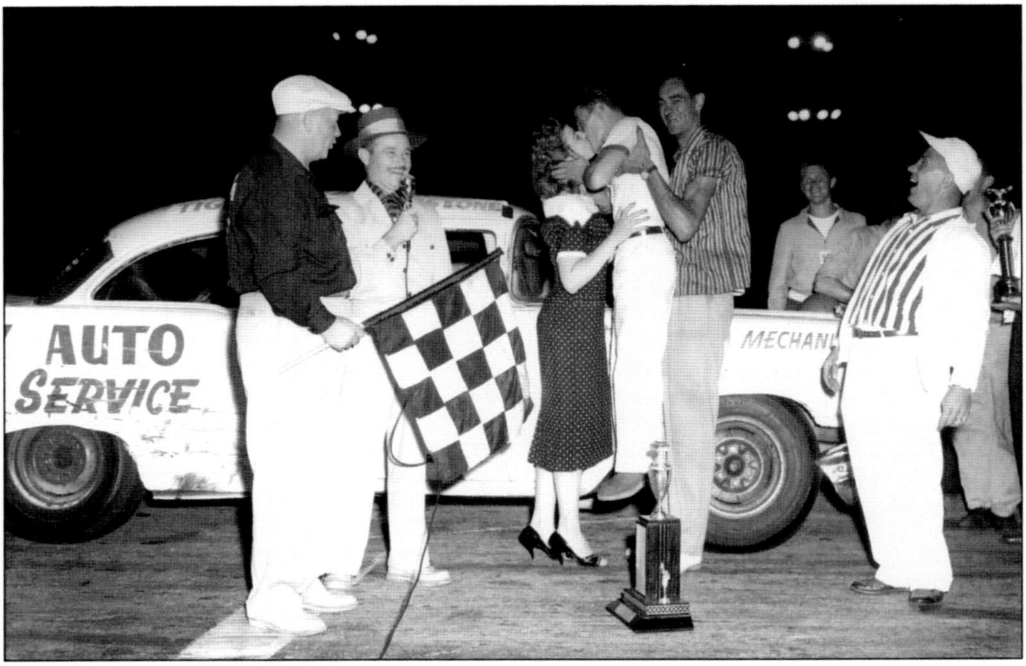

Pistone's mechanic, Charlie Jackson, gives "Tiger" Tom a lift after his victory in the 1957 midseason title race. Pistone's five-foot-two-inch frame was hoisted into a kissing position with Darlene Werner as starters Tom Plouzek (far left), Smokey Smith (far right), and track announcer Wayne Adams (second from left) look on. (Courtesy of Stan Kalwasinski.)

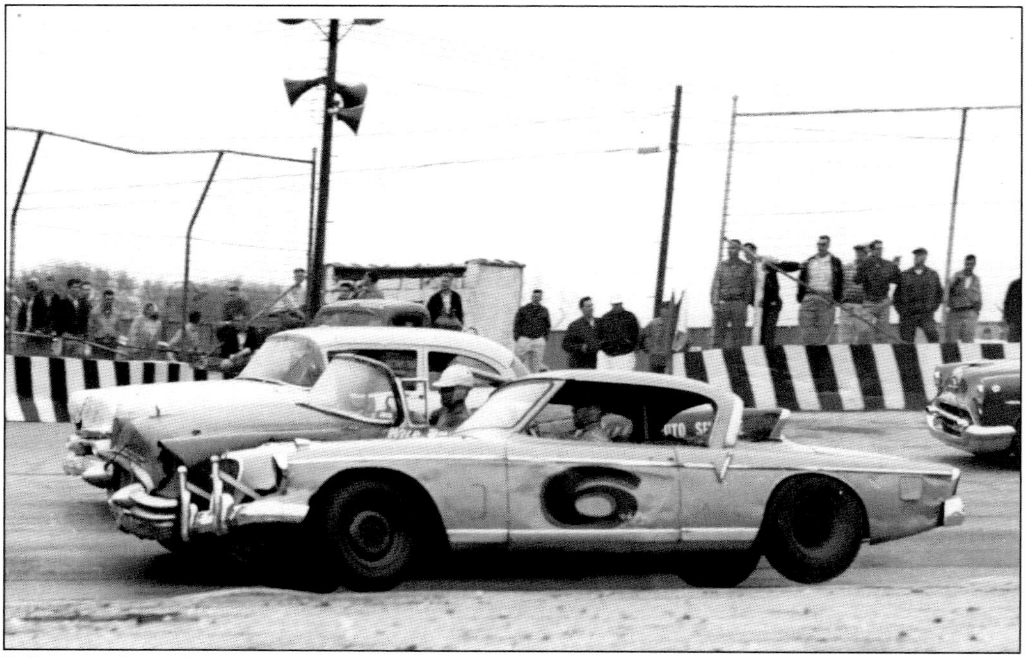

Bill Van Allen (6) guides his Studebaker across the bumps inside of the racing groove as he passes traffic in turn four in this 1958 racing scene. They are three-wide exiting turn four, and the middle car is in fact a convertible. In the late 1960s, Harry Simonsen drove the last convertible to compete at Raceway Park. (Courtesy of Bob Sheldon.)

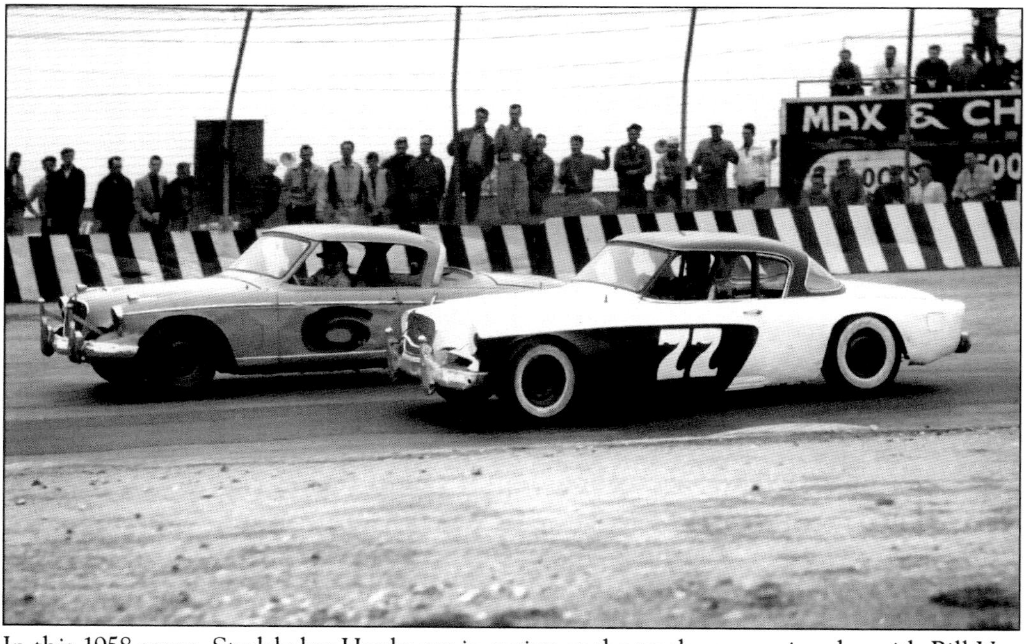

In this 1958 scene, Studebaker Hawks are in action at the track on opening day with Bill Van Allen (6) and Bud Koehler (77) doing the driving. Over the years, these two speedsters had some real battles on the speedway, always providing an exciting show for the fans. Koehler won the season-opening 30-lapper on April 20, 1958, defeating Van Allen. (Courtesy of Bob Sheldon.)

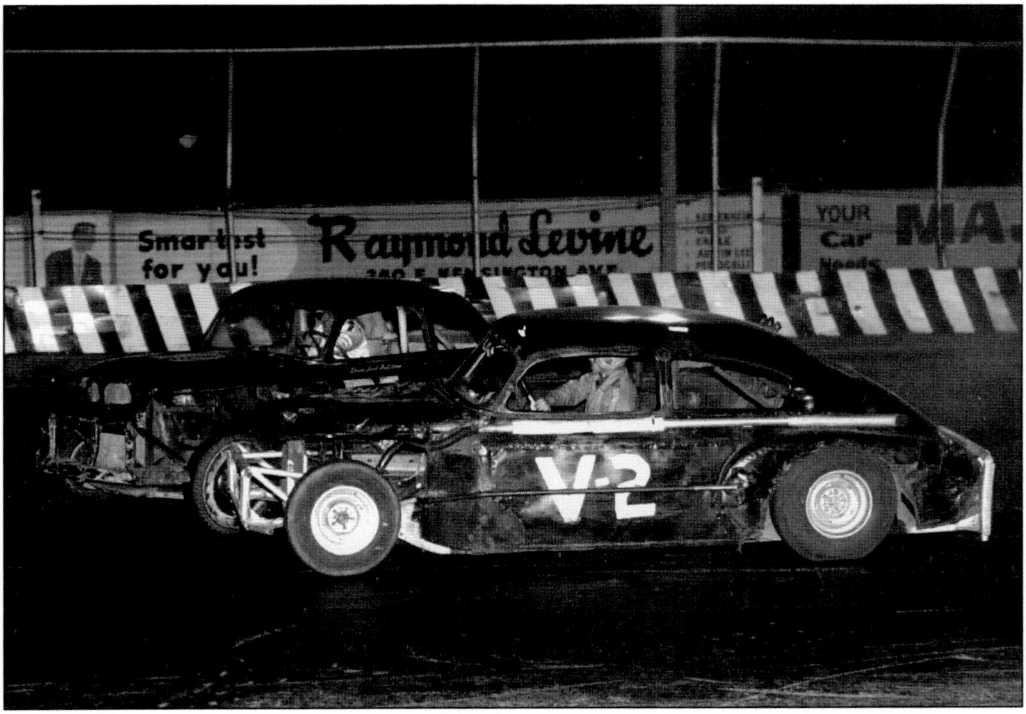

Legs Whitcomb (V2) and Jack Helstern bump and bang their way through turn two during a 1956 late model race. (Courtesy of Stan Kalwasinski.)

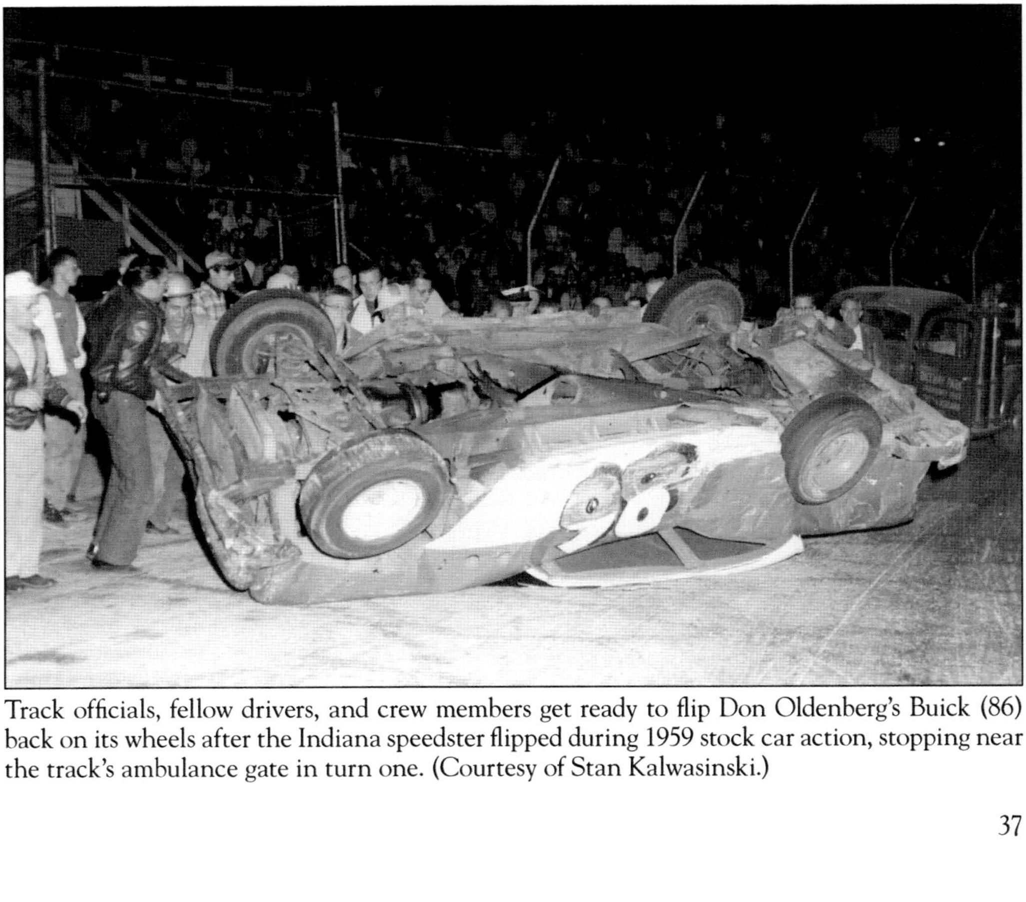

Track officials, fellow drivers, and crew members get ready to flip Don Oldenberg's Buick (86) back on its wheels after the Indiana speedster flipped during 1959 stock car action, stopping near the track's ambulance gate in turn one. (Courtesy of Stan Kalwasinski.)

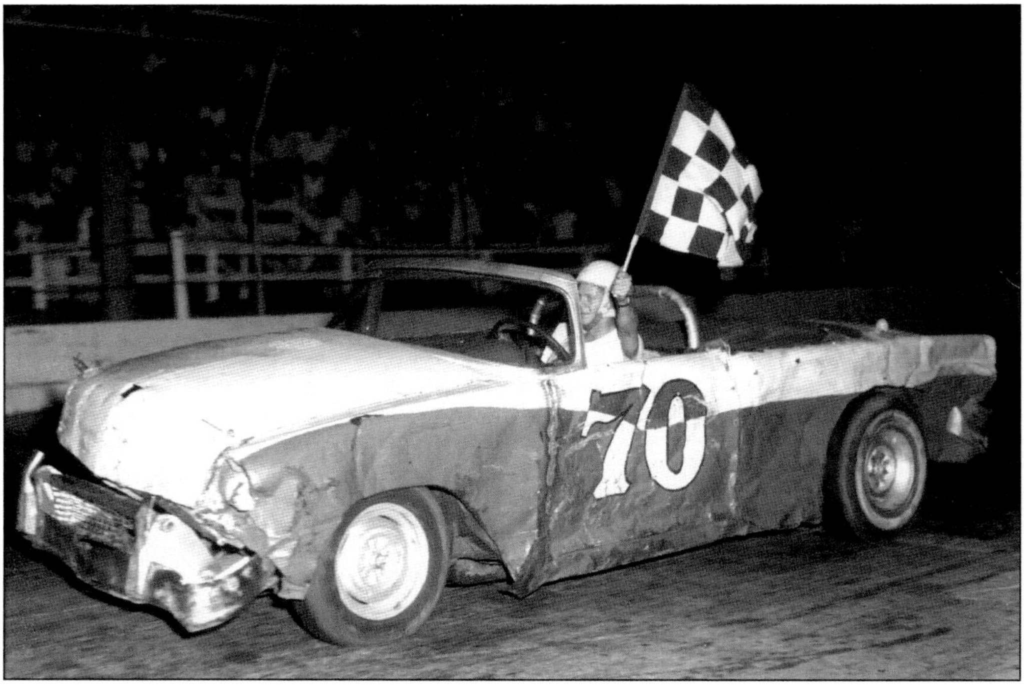

In this 1958 scene, Bob Williams takes a victory lap in his 1955 Ford convertible (70). The following year, Williams would win the late model championship after archrival Bud Koehler was forced to serve a two-week suspension for rough driving. (Courtesy of Stan Kalwasinski.)

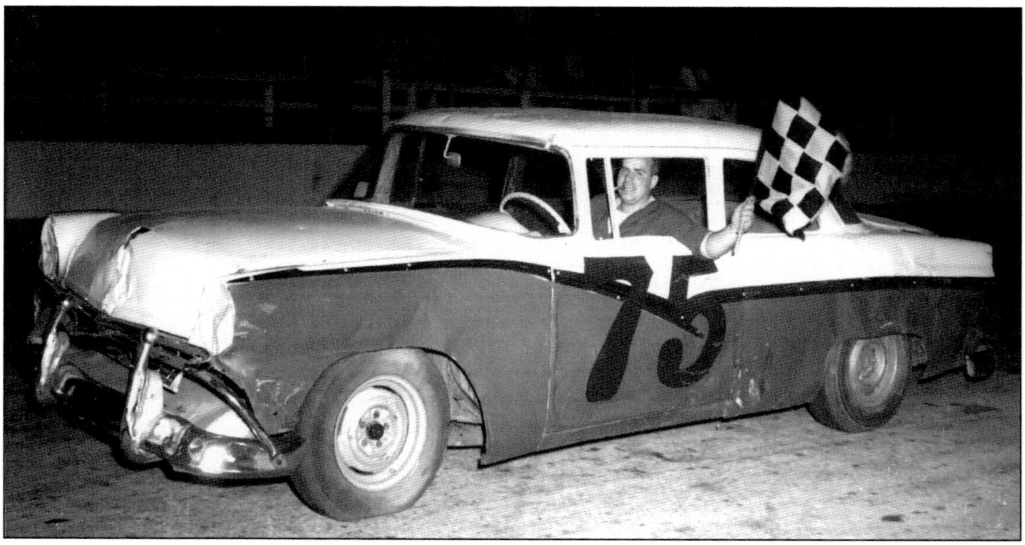

With his ever-present cigar clenched between his teeth, Louie Panico of Evergreen Park carries the checkered flag after scoring a 1959 victory in his Ford. Panico, who operated a flower shop and was known as the "Racing Florist" at the track, was a longtime participant in the popular team races held between 1955 and 1963. The Louie Panico team would face off against the Johnny Schipper team each night in a Roller Derby–type battle with one of each team's three cars trying to complete a designated number of laps to score a victory. Each team would do everything in its power to stop and demolish the other team's lead car, making for some exciting action. (Courtesy of Stan Kalwasinski.)

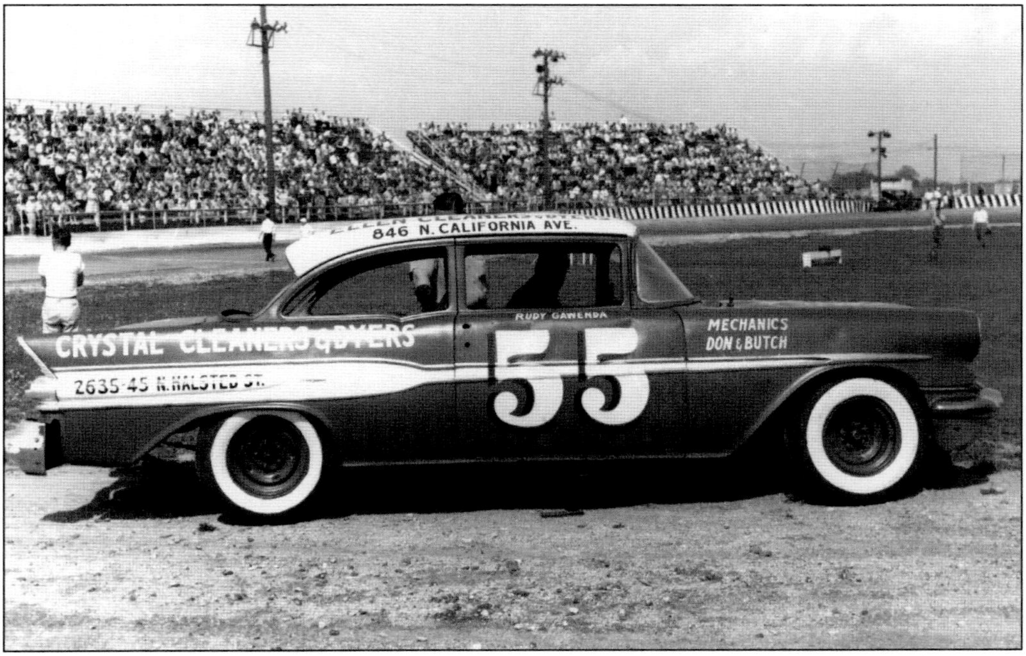

Rudy Gawenda (55) parks his Pontiac on the turn two infield prior to lining up for a race on opening day in 1959. The grandstands are nearly full, and by this time, the fence of the dog-racing track was removed. The inner track would later be paved and used as a go-karting track. (Courtesy of Stan Kalwasinski.)

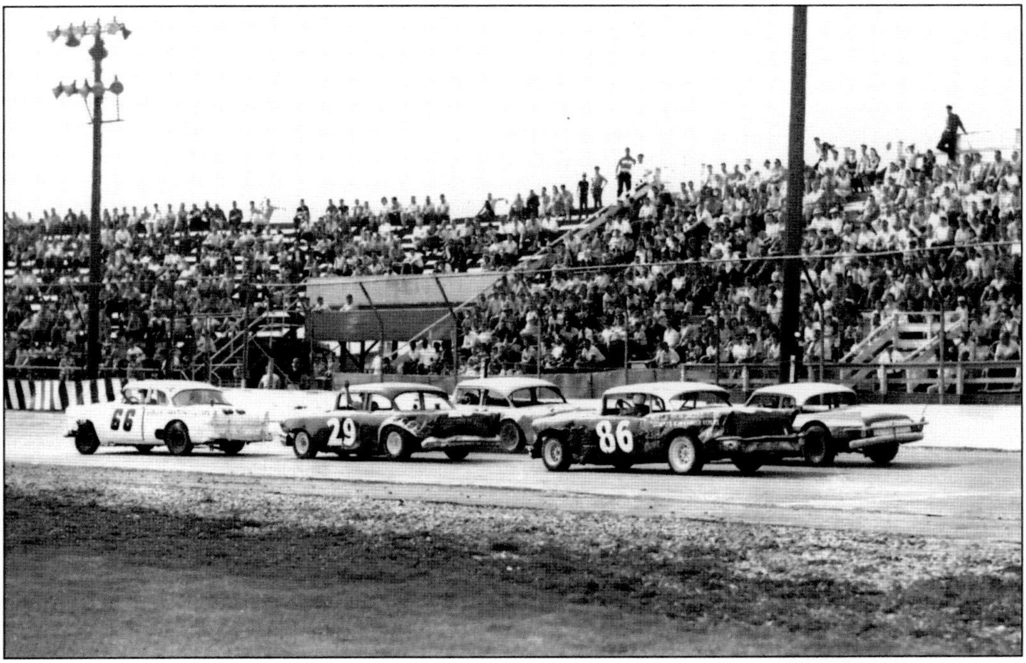

"It's Trophy Dash time!" as Wayne Adams would announce. Opening Day 1959 finds Bob Vickery (66) leading Tom Cox (29), Jerry Welch (000), Don Oldenberg (86), and Ray Young (99). The crowd is enjoying the nice weather as an Andy Frain usher keeps spectators away from the fence. (Courtesy of Stan Kalwasinski.)

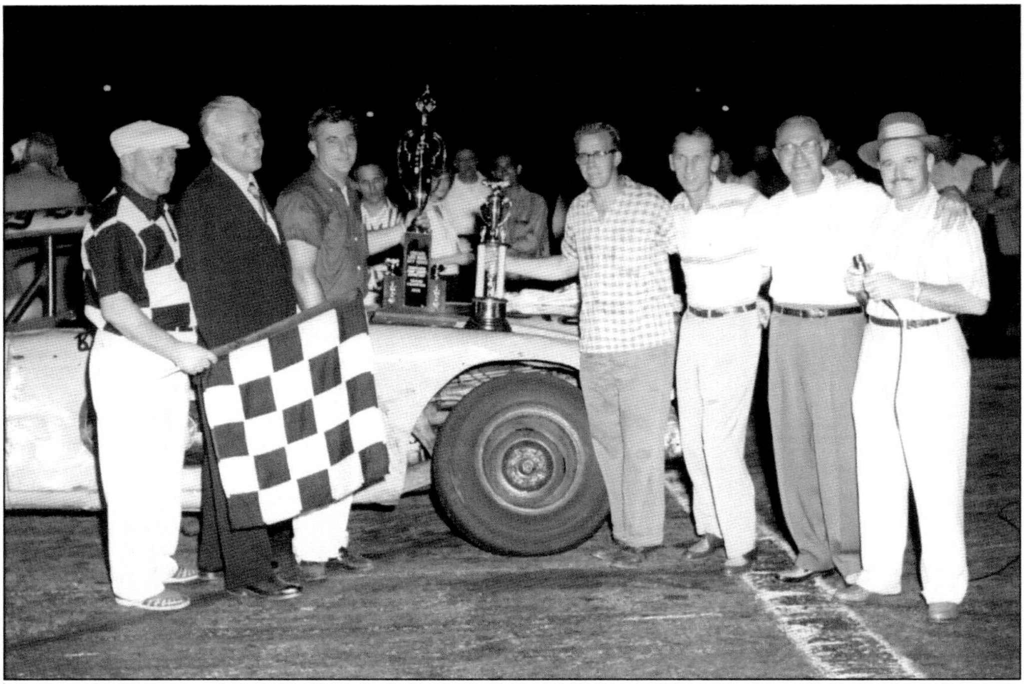

Raceway Park, along with O'Hare Stadium in Schiller Park and Chicago's Soldier Field, participated in a special City Series stock car series in 1958. Each track held a special Friday-night program that was highlighted by a 100-lap feature. Future NASCAR star Fred Lorenzen won both 100-lappers at Soldier Field and O'Hare. Bill Van Allen (6) won the 100-lapper at Raceway, and he is seen here (fourth from right) posing with, from left to right, starter Tom Plouzek, O'Hare Stadium promoter Bill Cherney, City Series champion Bill Lutz, Raceway Park promoters Pete Jenin and Jimmy Derrico, and announcer Wayne Adams. (Courtesy of Stan Kalwasinski.)

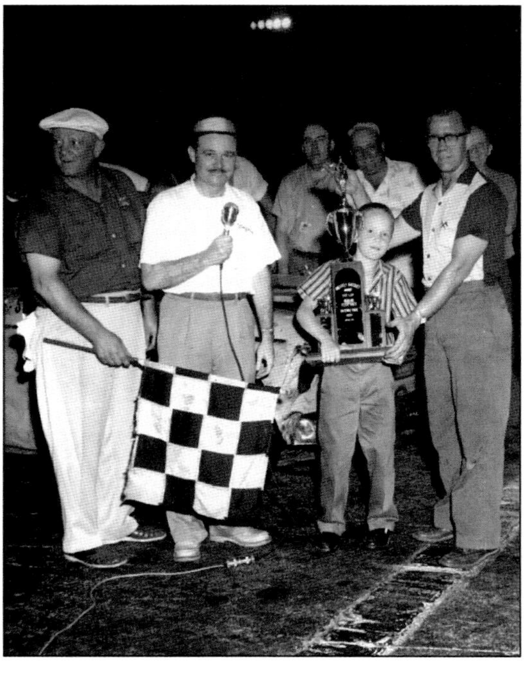

Bill Van Allen (6) drove his Studebaker Lark to victory in 1959's season title race. Presenting the Dressel's Bakeries trophy to Van Allen and a young fan are Tom Plouzek and Wayne Adams. (Courtesy of Stan Kalwasinski.)

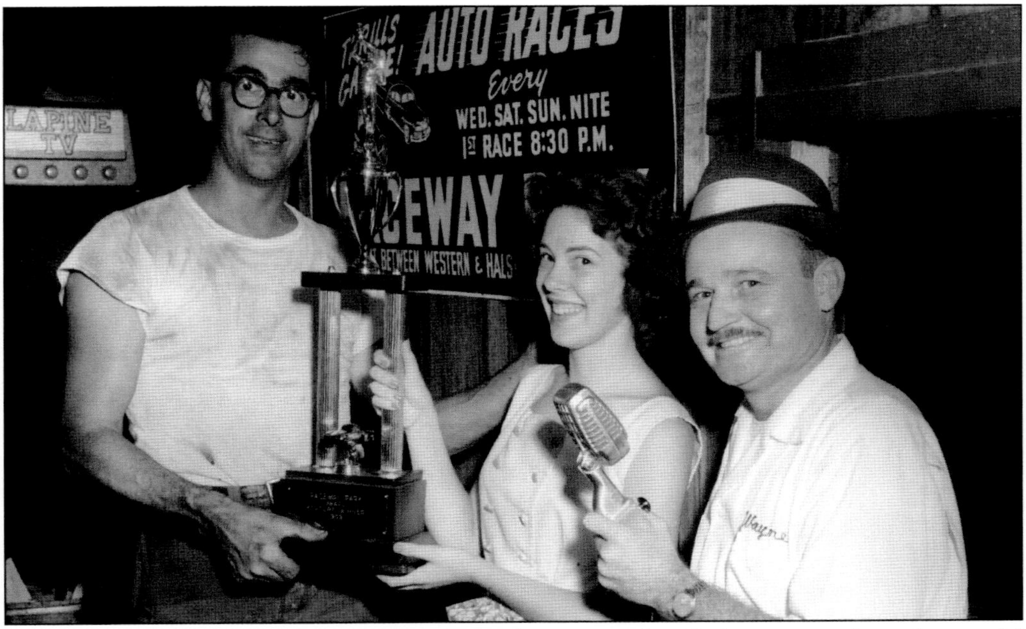

The legendary Bob Pronger receives his trophy from an unidentified presenter after a late model feature victory in 1959, as track announcer Wayne Adams joins in on the presentation. The sign in the background of the judges' stand proclaims "Thrills Galore—Auto Races—Every Wed., Sat., Sun., Nite." Pronger was among the many that provided those thrills, winning 148 feature races during his career. (Courtesy of Stan Kalwasinski.)

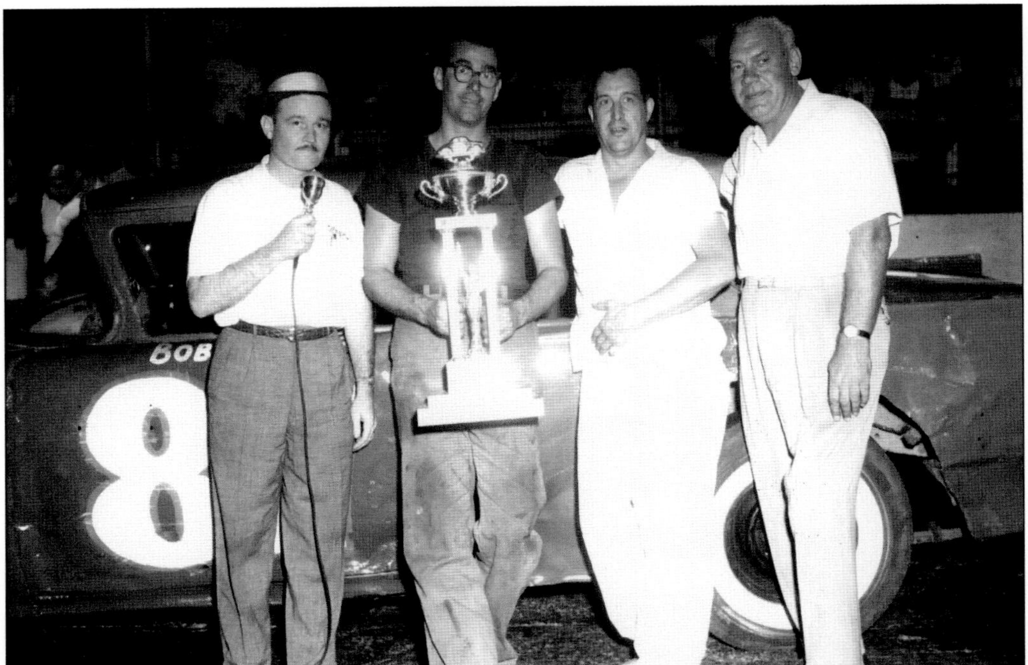

Bob Pronger (87), second from left, celebrates another victory in 1959. Pronger would end up second on Raceway Park's all-time feature race winners list. Only Bud Koehler, with 490 late model and 10 midget feature wins, had more wins than Pronger. (Courtesy of Stan Kalwasinski.)

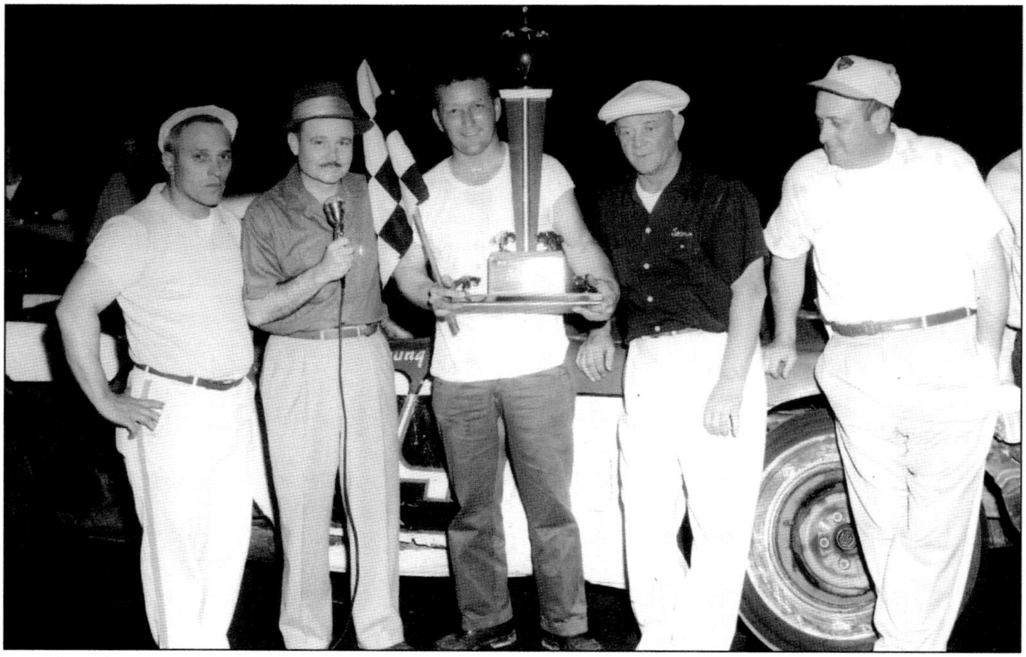

Popular driver Ray Young (99) scores the midseason championship victory in 1959. Young moved to Chicago from Tennessee as a teenager, and he would enjoy driving race cars around the Midwest for over 30 years. Young was a true driver, as his day job was driving a semi truck across the country. (Courtesy of Stan Kalwasinski.)

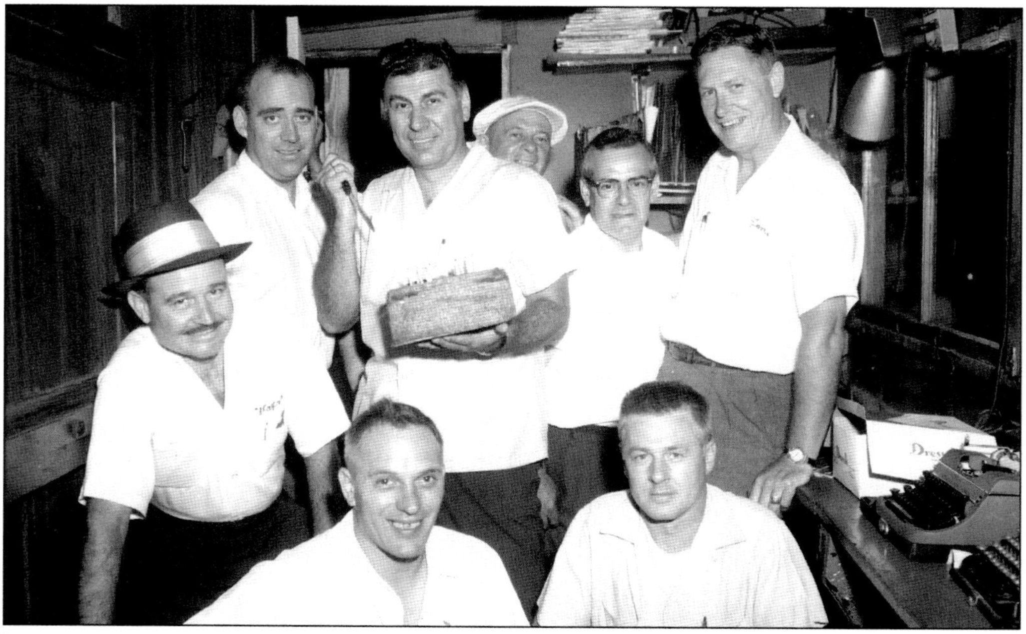

Longtime Raceway Park official Joe Uzelac gets ready to cut into a Dressel's whipped cream cake during a birthday celebration in the judges' stand in the late 1950s. Among Uzelac's well-wishers are (clockwise from left) track announcer Wayne Adams, publicity director Paul Sigler, starter Tom Plouzek, sound technician Tony Sisco, official timer Jim Shigley, scorer Jimmy Fox, and assistant starter Smokey Smith. (Courtesy of Stan Kalwasinski.)

Three

THE 1960S

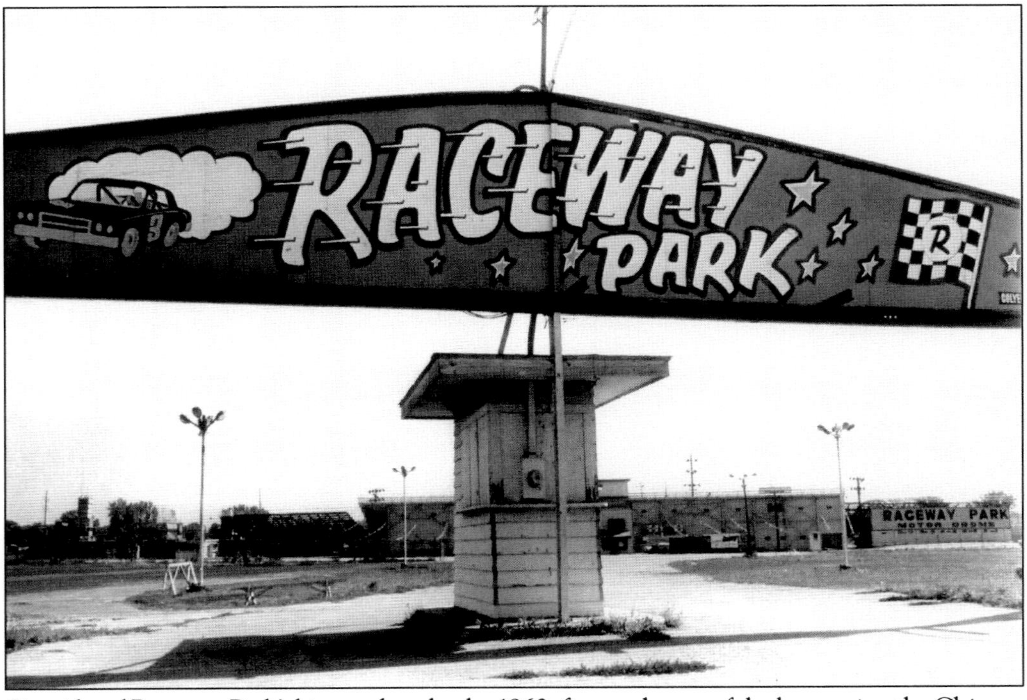

Considered Raceway Park's biggest decade, the 1960s featured some of the best racing the Chicago area has ever witnessed. Racing occurred four nights a week (Wednesday, Friday, Saturday, and Sunday), and the track was leased to N. Perry Luster in 1968 and 1969. Fans coming into the main entrance at the track in 1964 drove under this sign as they entered the parking lot. Painted by local sign painter and racecar driver Dan Colyer, the sign honors Bill Cornwall's 1963 late model championship ride (3). (Courtesy of Paul Beck.)

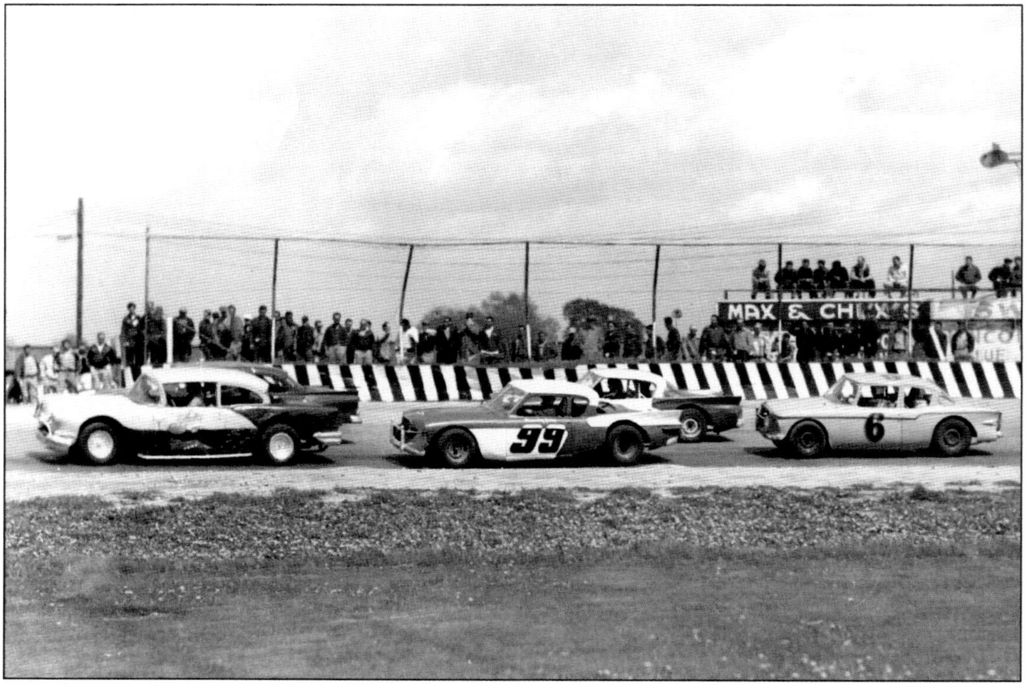

The five fastest qualifiers start the opening day trophy dash in 1960. The field includes Johnny Kapovich (37), Don Oldenberg (86), Ray Young (99), Bud Koehler (77), and Bill Van Allen (6). (Courtesy of Bob Sheldon.)

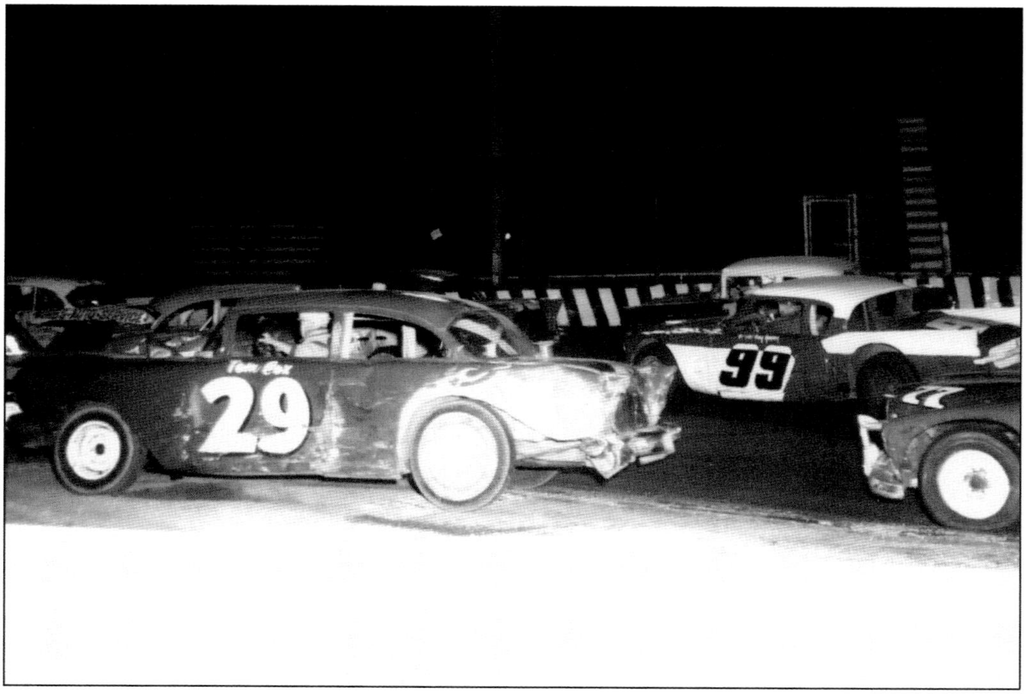

Exiting turn two and accelerating down the backstretch could often be challenging. In this 1960 late model scene, eight cars try to squeeze their way out of the turn. (Courtesy of Stan Kalwasinski.)

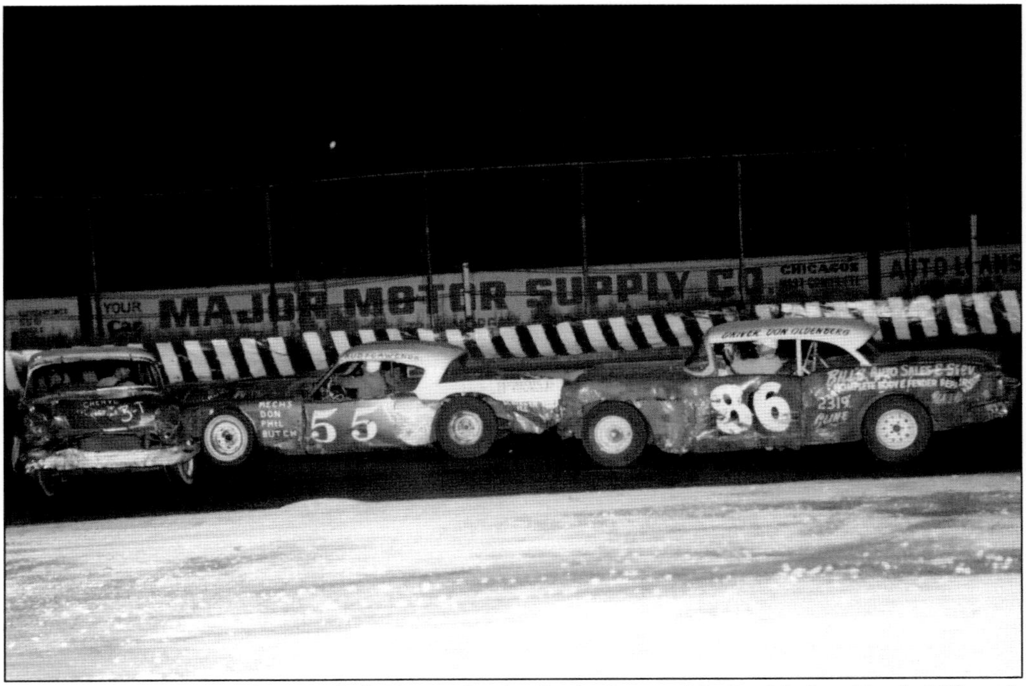

In this 1960 scene, Ted Janecyk (3T) gets hit by Rudy Gawenda's Studebaker Hawk (55) with Don Oldenberg's Buick (86) ready to join the mayhem. All three drivers were among the top 20 in the final points standings. (Courtesy of Stan Kalwasinski.)

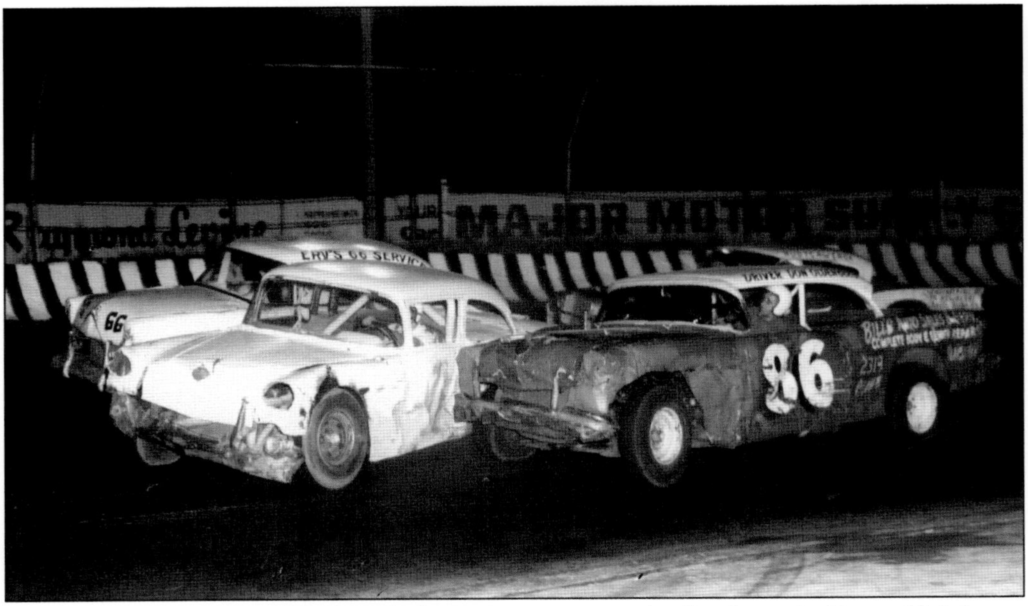

In this 1960 scene, Don Oldenberg (86) is trying to squeeze his Buick inside George Neinhouse (1) and Bob Vickery (66) with Rudy Gawenda (55) trailing the threesome. Oldenberg, the proprietor of a towing and recovery business in Gary, Indiana, won a total of 42 feature races but never won a track championship at Raceway Park, having come close in 1962 by finishing second to Ray Young in the standings. Oldenberg did win back-to-back championships at Chicago's Soldier Field in 1957 and 1958. (Courtesy of Stan Kalwasinski.)

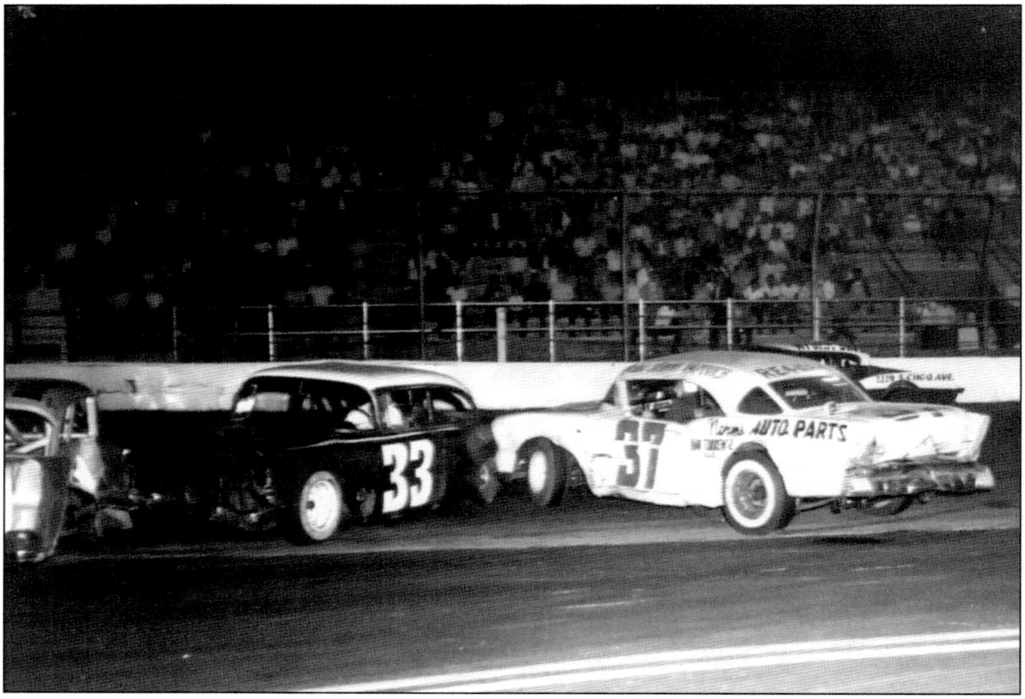

In this 1960 scene, Paul Bauer (33) and Johnny Kapovich (37) wreck on the front stretch while the Studebaker of Ray Young (99) avoids the mess. (Courtesy of Stan Kalwasinski.)

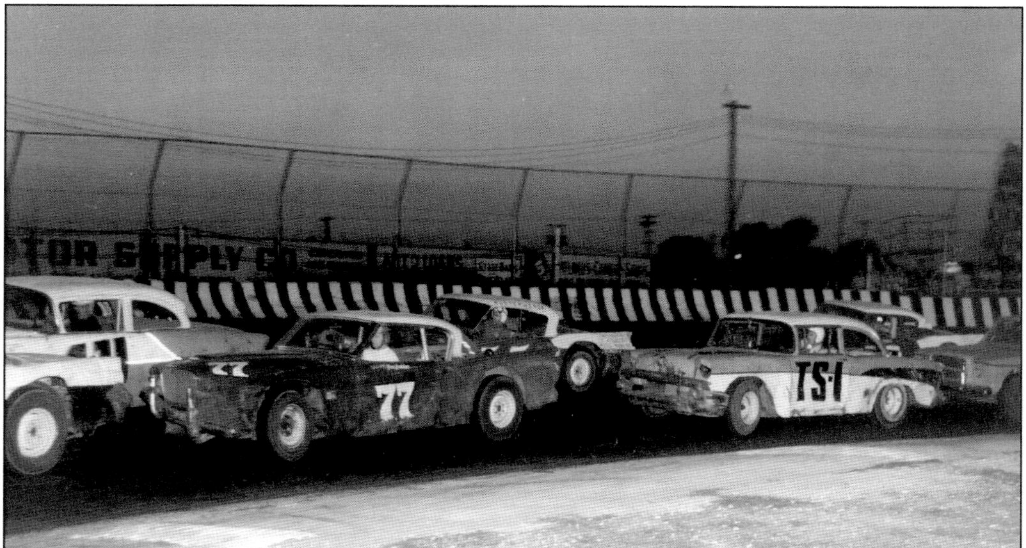

Once again, it is a crowded field in 1960. Visible in turn one are the Oldsmobile of Stanley "Stash" Kullman (4U), Harry Simonsen (TS1) in a Chevrolet, and Bud Koehler (77), Rudy Gawenda (55), Ray Young (99), and Bill Van Allen (6), all of whom are driving Studebakers. (Courtesy of Stan Kalwasinski.)

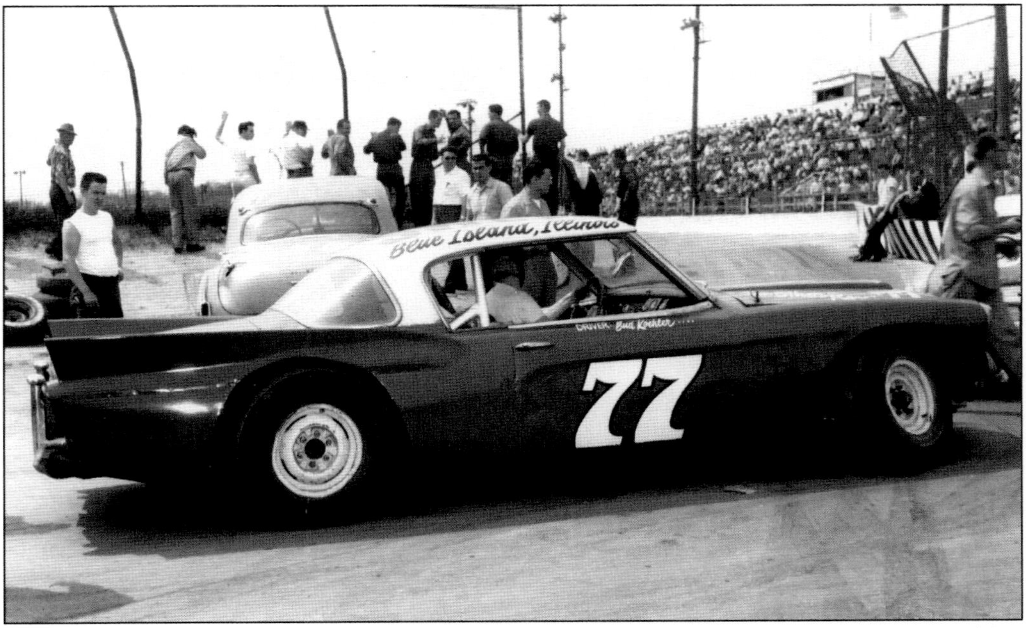

Bud Koehler rolls his Studebaker Hawk (77) out of the pit area on opening day of 1960. Koehler, who ran at Raceway Park for nearly 40 years, was always a fan favorite. During his racing career, Koehler claimed 11 driving championships and won 490 late model feature races in addition to 10 midget feature wins. In 1949, Koehler won both the midget and stock car championships. (Courtesy of Stan Kalwasinski.)

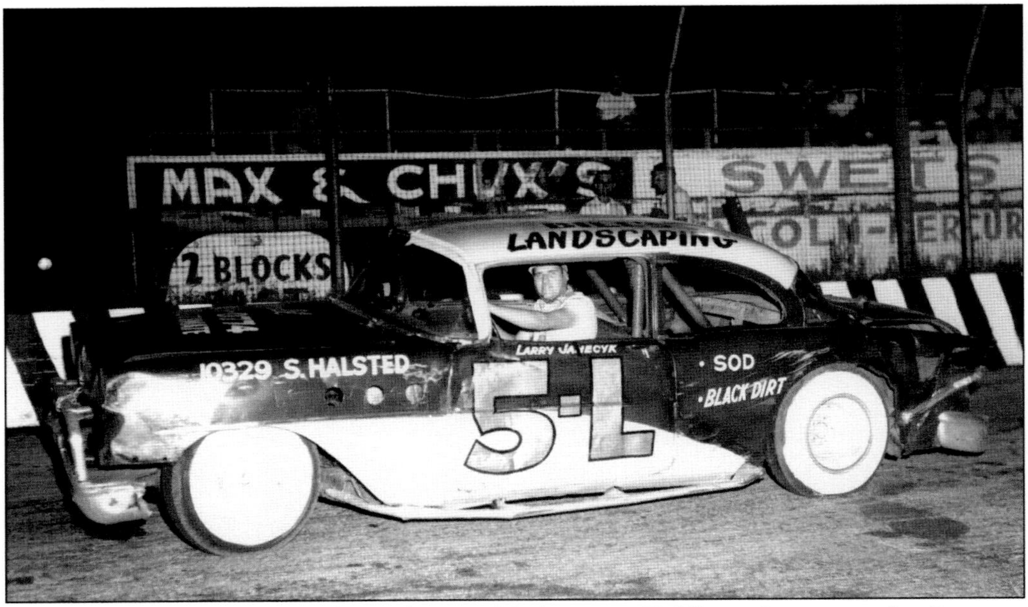

Larry Janecyk (5-L), brother of 1965 late model champion Ted Janecyk, competed at Raceway Park in the late 1950s and early 1960s. Larry is most remembered for his actions during the Fourth of July weekend in 1965. Ted Janecyk and Bob Pronger wrecked during the first of the twin 50s held that day, and after exiting their race cars, they fist-fought each other on the racetrack. Larry climbed the 15-foot-high safety fence separating the track from the grandstands to help his brother beat up Pronger. (Courtesy of Stan Kalwasinski.)

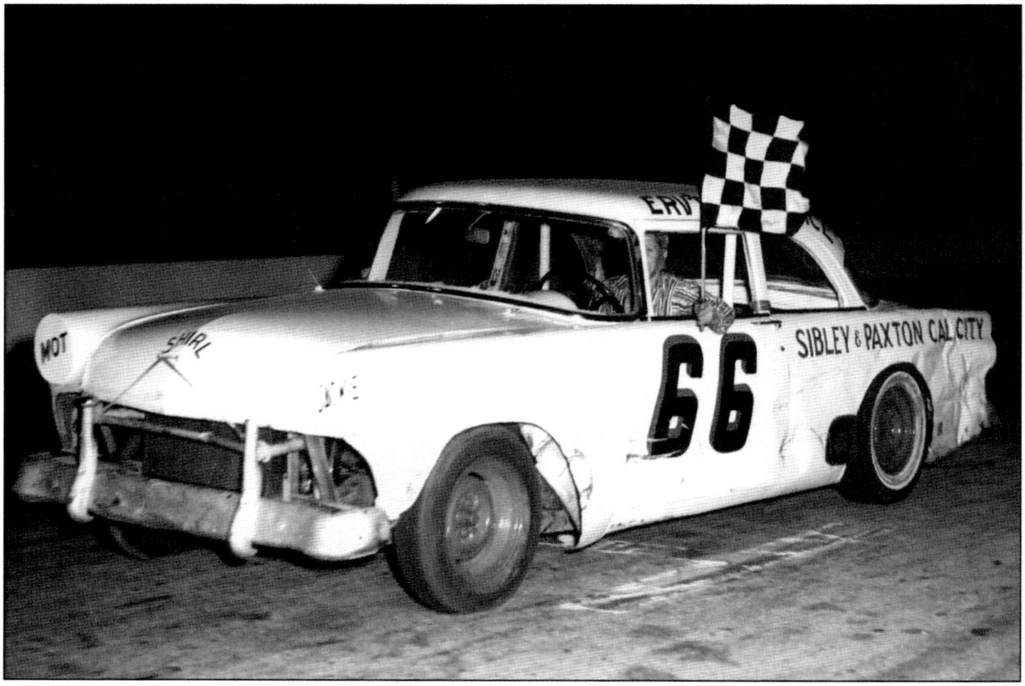

Bob Vickery (66) enjoys a win in the 1960 racing season. Vickery's 1955 Ford was sponsored by Erv's Phillips 66 gas station, located at the corner of Sibley Boulevard and Paxton Avenue in Calumet City, hence the car being numbered 66. (Courtesy of Stan Kalwasinski.)

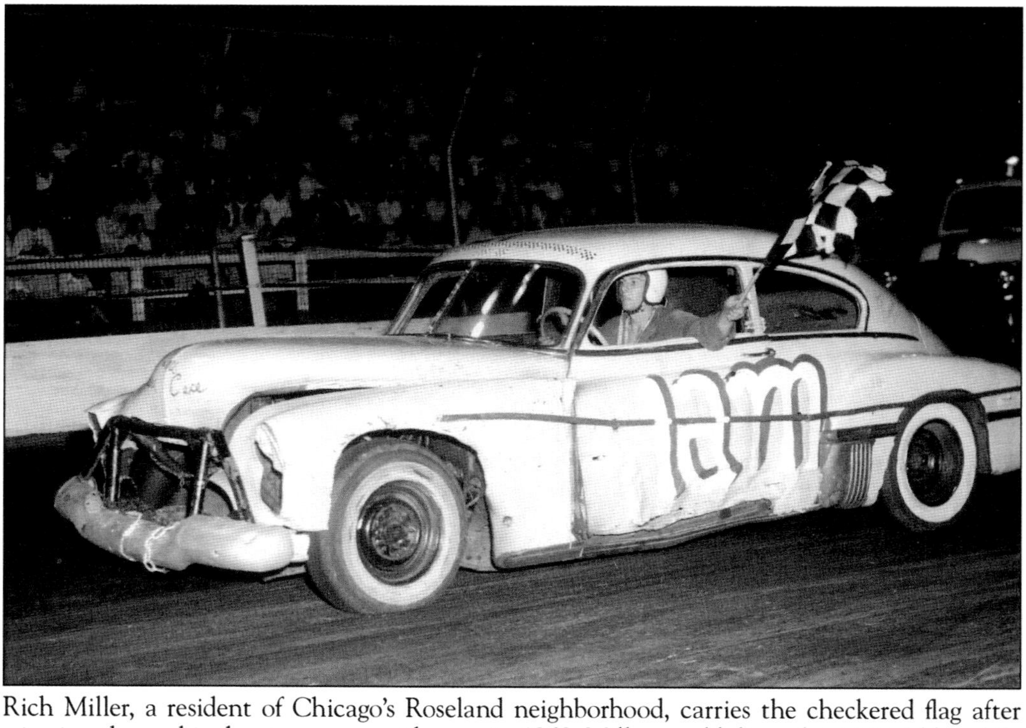

Rich Miller, a resident of Chicago's Roseland neighborhood, carries the checkered flag after winning the rookie division season title race in 1960. Miller would drive this 1949 Oldsmobile to win the 1960 amateur driving championship. (Courtesy of Stan Kalwasinski.)

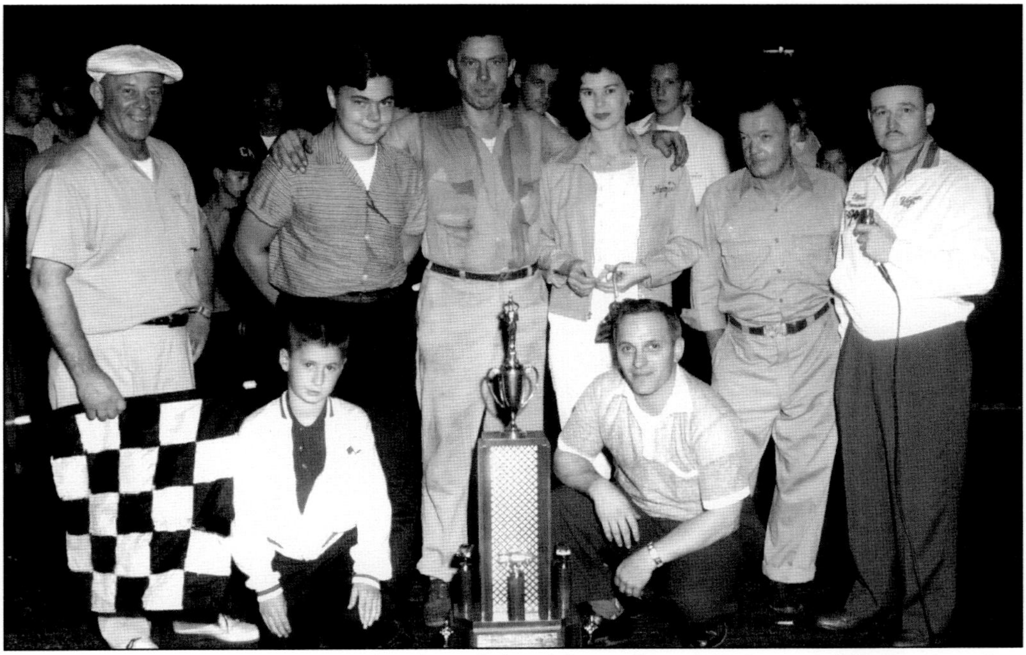

Fan favorite Harry Simonsen (behind trophy) celebrates his 1960 late model championship with his son, Lee (left of Harry), and wife, Marge (right of Harry). Track officials Tom Plouzek (far left) and Smokey Smith (kneeling on the right), along with announcer Wayne Adams (far right) and groundskeeper Clare Duncan (second from right) present Simonsen (TS1) with his championship trophy. (Courtesy of Stan Kalwasinski.)

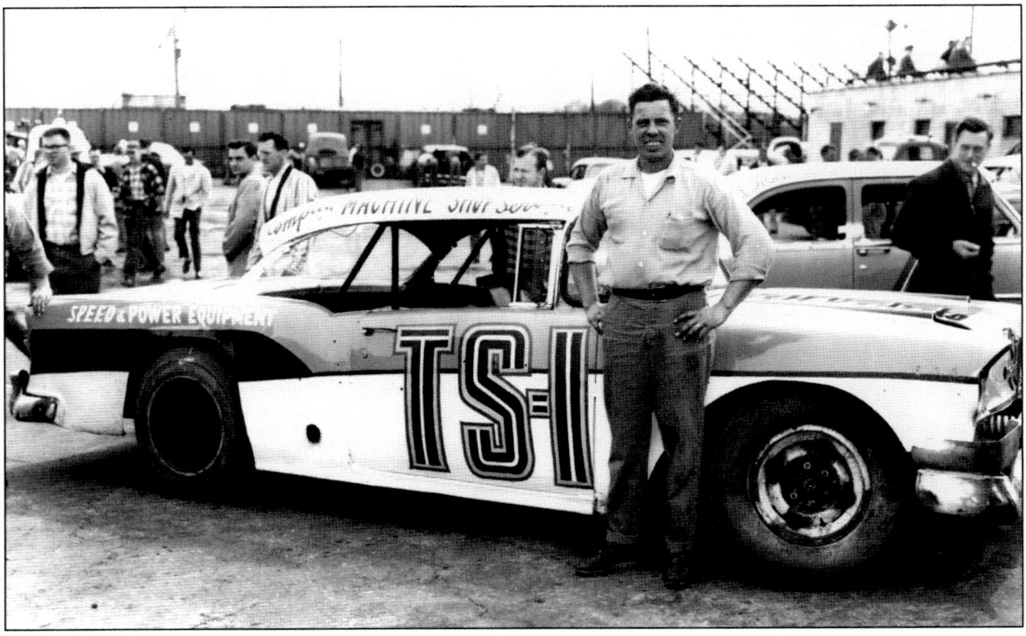

In this 1961 photograph, defending track champion Harry Simonsen poses with his Chevrolet (TS1). Simonsen won his first late model feature race along with the track championship in 1960, a feat that would be repeated 10 years later by George Hill. Ironically, Hill achieved his feat in a Chevrolet purchased from Simonsen. (Courtesy of Stan Kalwasinski.)

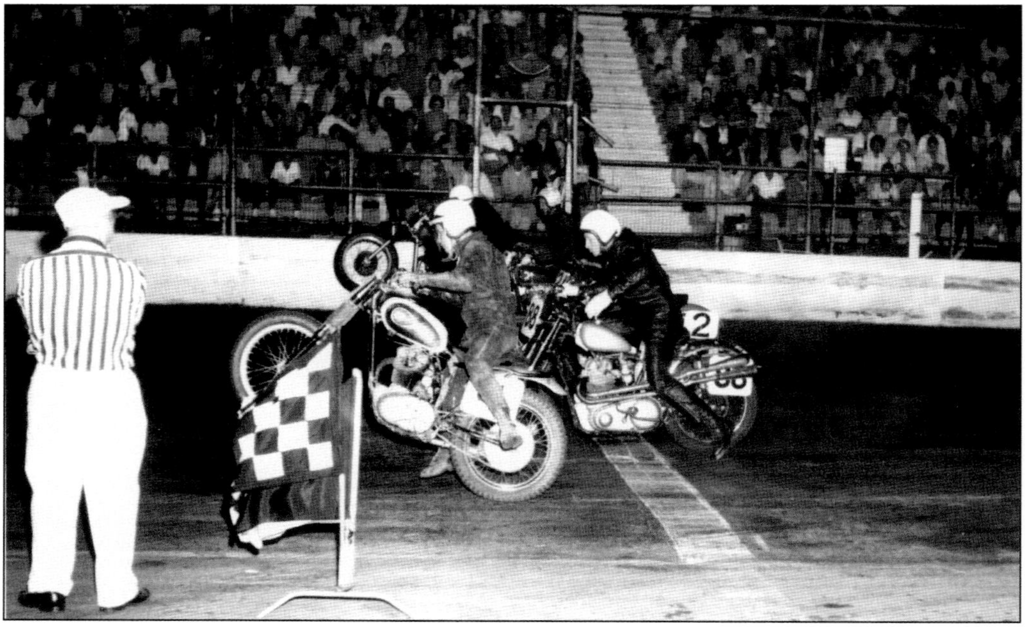

Motorcycles, on both the dirt and paved surfaces of Raceway Park, were on the track's schedule in the 1950s and 1960s. Ready to battle on the asphalt in the early 1960s, a field of motorcycles is ready to jump into action. (Courtesy of Stan Kalwasinski.)

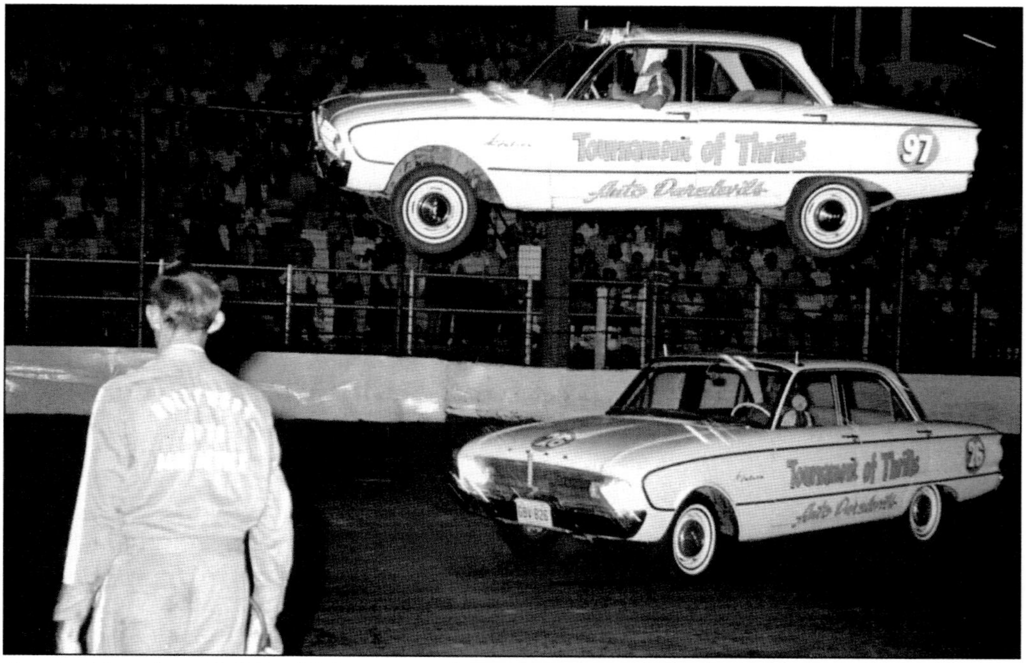

A pair of four-door 1961 Ford Falcons goes through the paces during a Joey Chitwood Tournament of Thrills auto daredevils thrill show at Raceway in July 1961. Over the years, the track presented almost every type of motorized competition imaginable, including various stock car classes, go-karts, demolition derbies, enduros, midgets, hot rods, modifieds, motorcycles, ministocks, and minisprints. The track also hosted events such as exhibition greyhound dog racing and an appearance by the Harlem Globetrotters basketball team. (Courtesy of Stan Kalwasinski.)

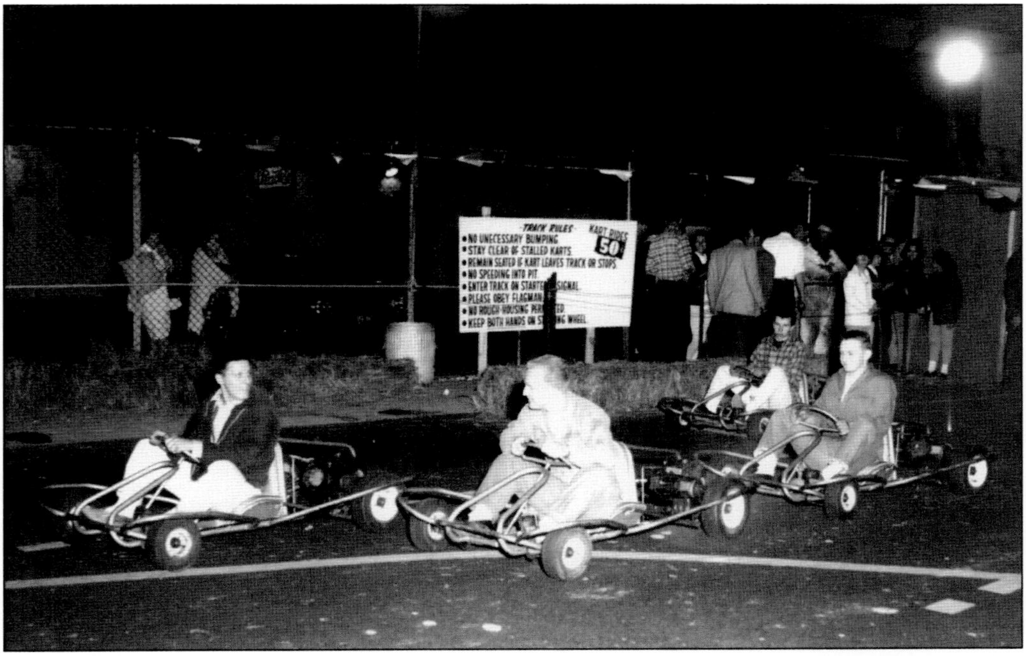

Not only was there plenty of action within the confines of the racetrack, but there was also plenty of entertainment outside of it as well. In this early-1960s photograph, some young fans test their driving skills on the go-karts as they pretend to be some of Raceway Park's top drivers. (Courtesy of Stan Kalwasinski.)

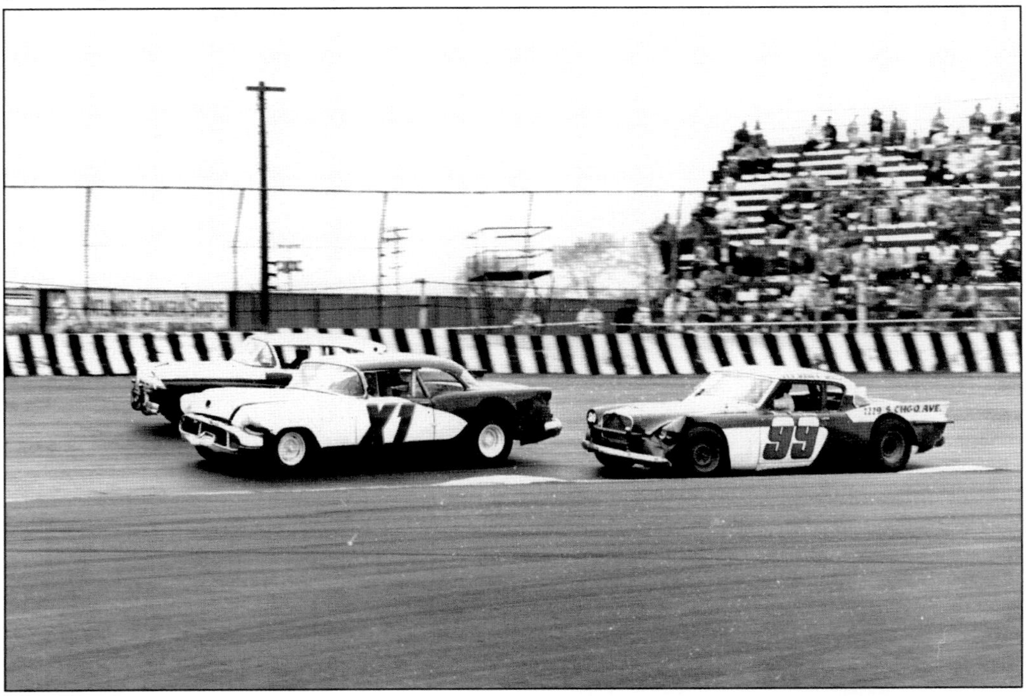

In this 1961 scene, Bill DeGonia (X1) is trying to stay ahead of Ray Young (99) as Louie Panico (75) stays to the outside of the battling duo. DeGonia, a Chicago native, competed at the track as both a driver and car owner. (Courtesy of Stan Kalwasinski.)

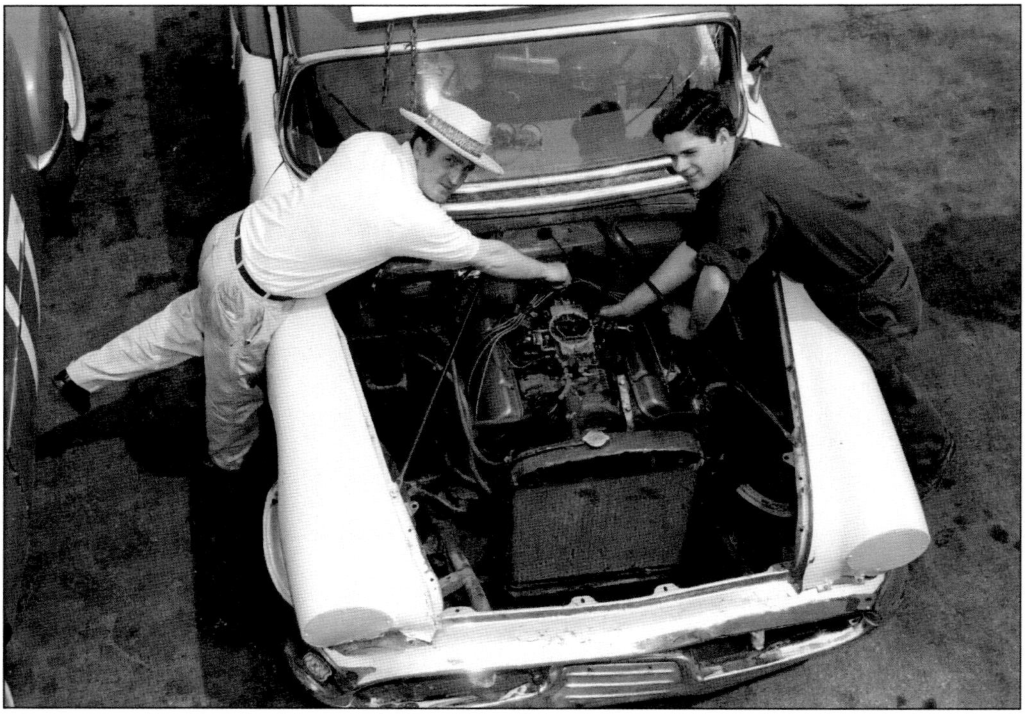

This unique photograph shows two mechanics making preparations to their Oldsmobile prior to the first race of the 1961 season. (Courtesy of Stan Kalwasinski.)

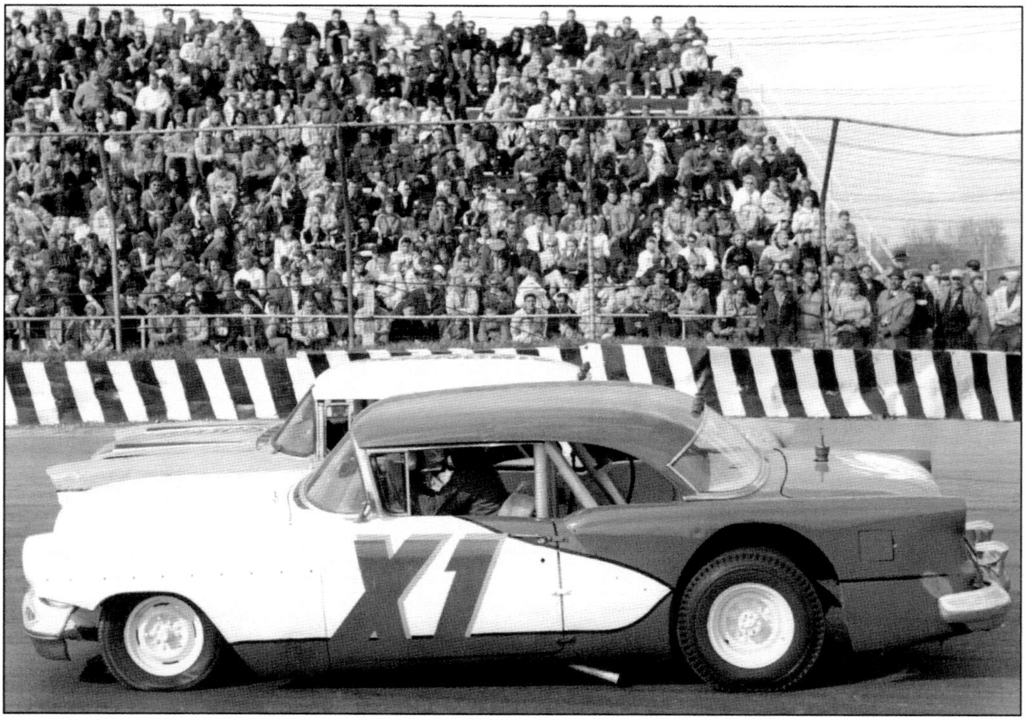

Here is that same Oldsmobile (X1), driven by Bill DeGonia, lined up alongside Harry Simonsen (TS1). The stands are packed on 1961's opening day. (Courtesy of Stan Kalwasinski.)

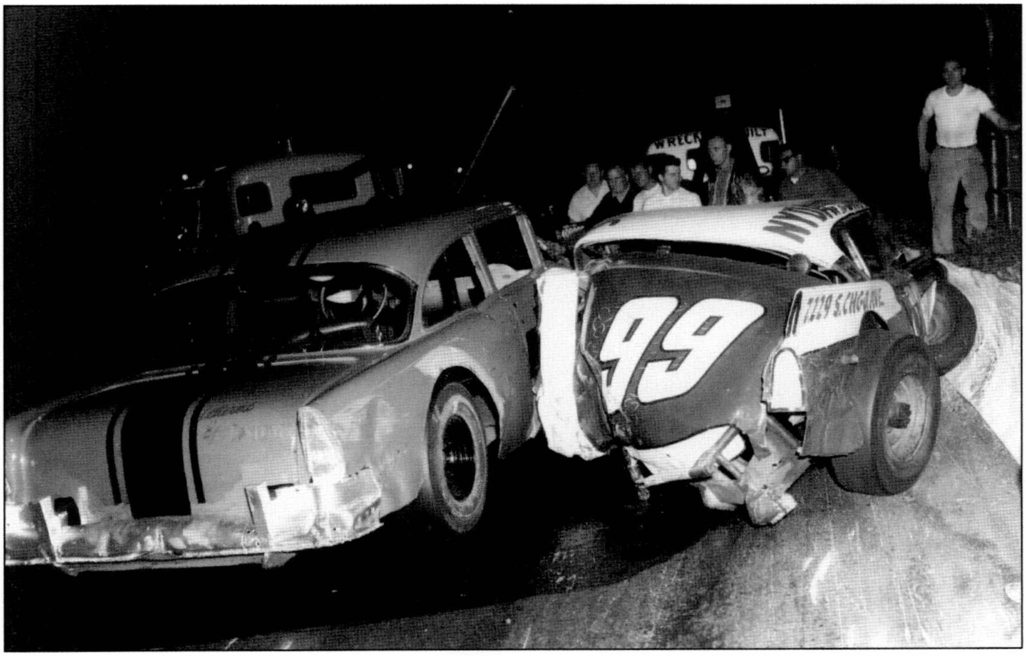

In this 1961 scene, Bob Pronger (1) destroys Ray Young's Studebaker Hawk (99) after Young's car stalled on the backstretch. Although Young was uninjured, Pronger was transported to St. Francis Hospital in Blue Island after suffering a broken leg in the crash. Pronger would recover from the injury to win that year's late model driving championship. (Courtesy of Stan Kalwasinski.)

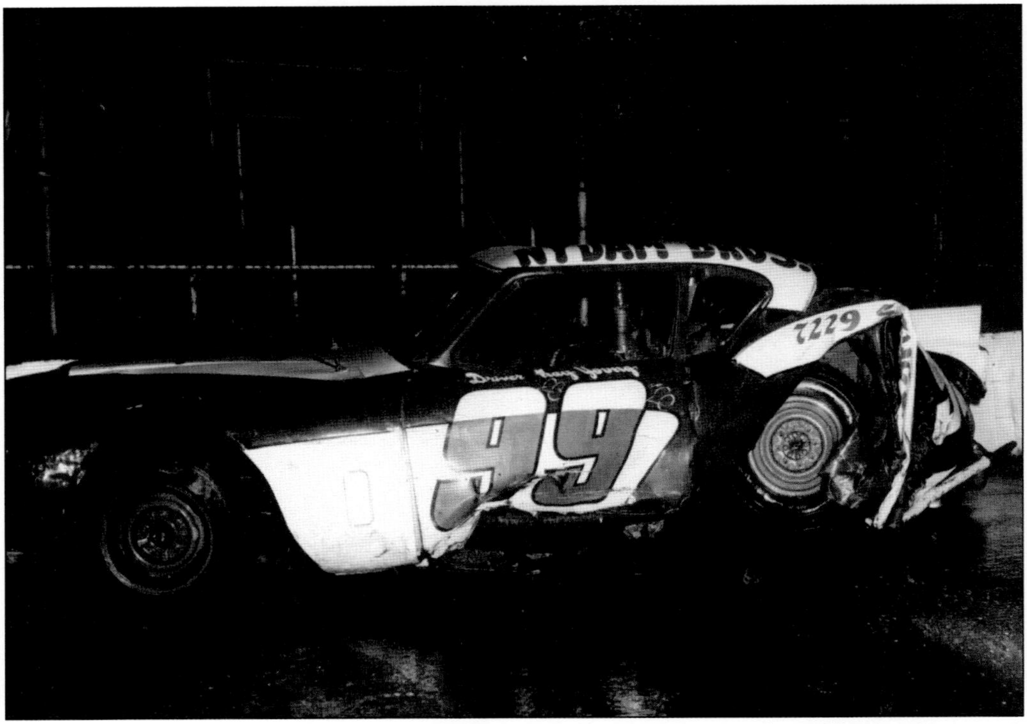

This is what remains of Ray Young's Studebaker (99) after Bob Pronger clipped him on Raceway's backstretch in 1961. (Courtesy of Stan Kalwasinski.)

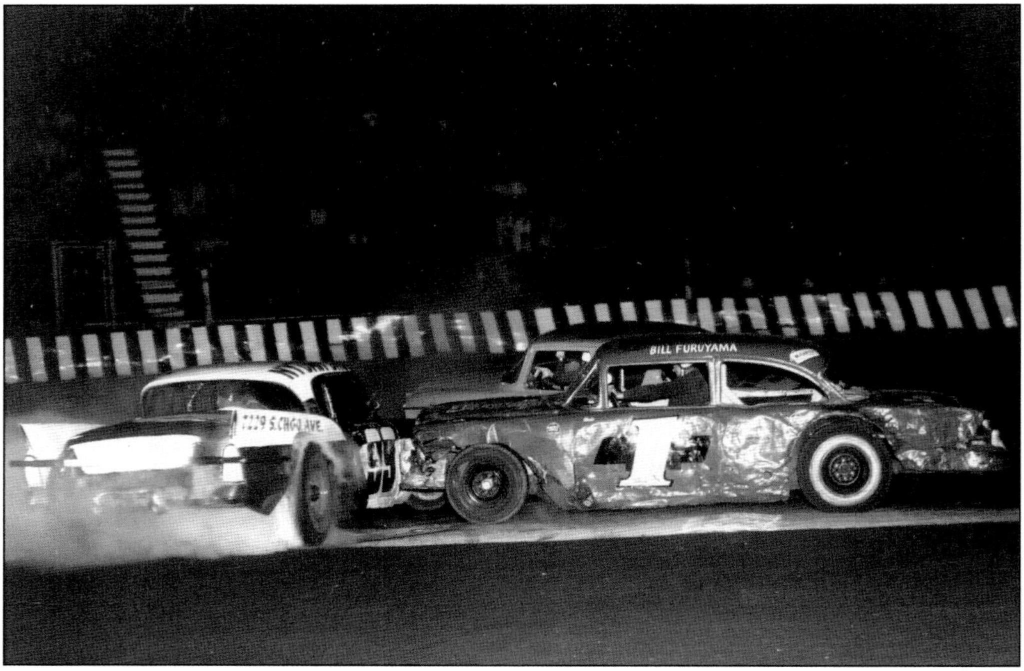

In this 1961 scene, a spinning Ray Young (99) smokes his tires trying to escape Bill Van Allen (6) and Bob Pronger (1),who are bearing down on him in turn two. (Courtesy of Stan Kalwasinski.)

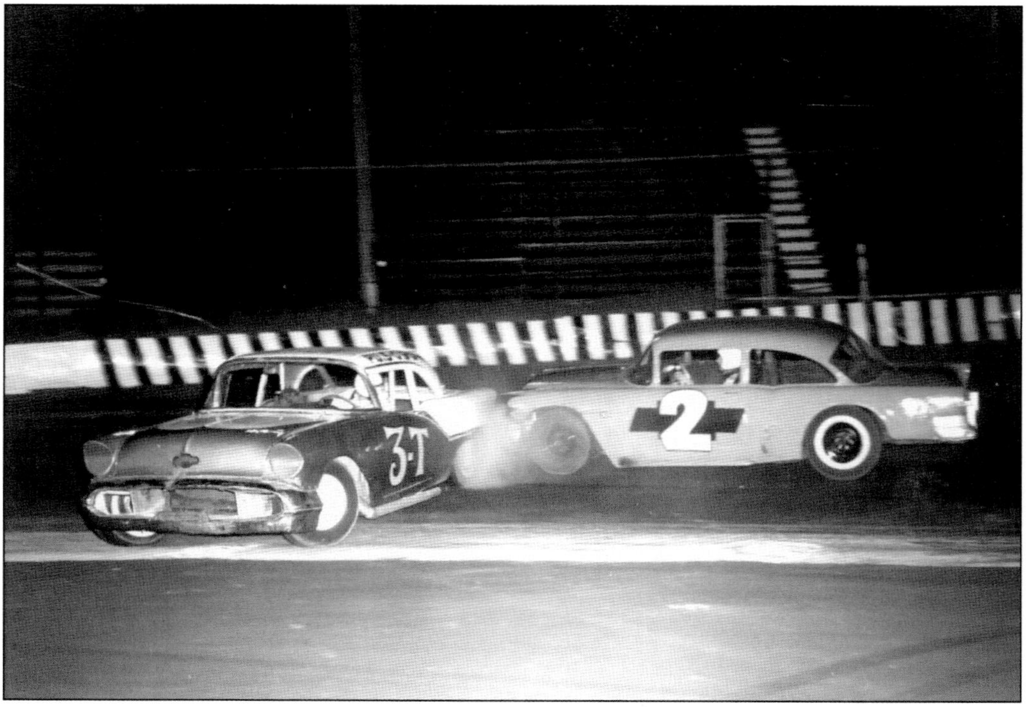

Ted Janecyk (3-T) spins his Oldsmobile coming out of turn two after making contact with Bob Roeber (2). Janecyk, not very happy after beginning the spin, shoots "the look" at his fellow competitor in this 1961 scene. (Courtesy of Stan Kalwasinski.)

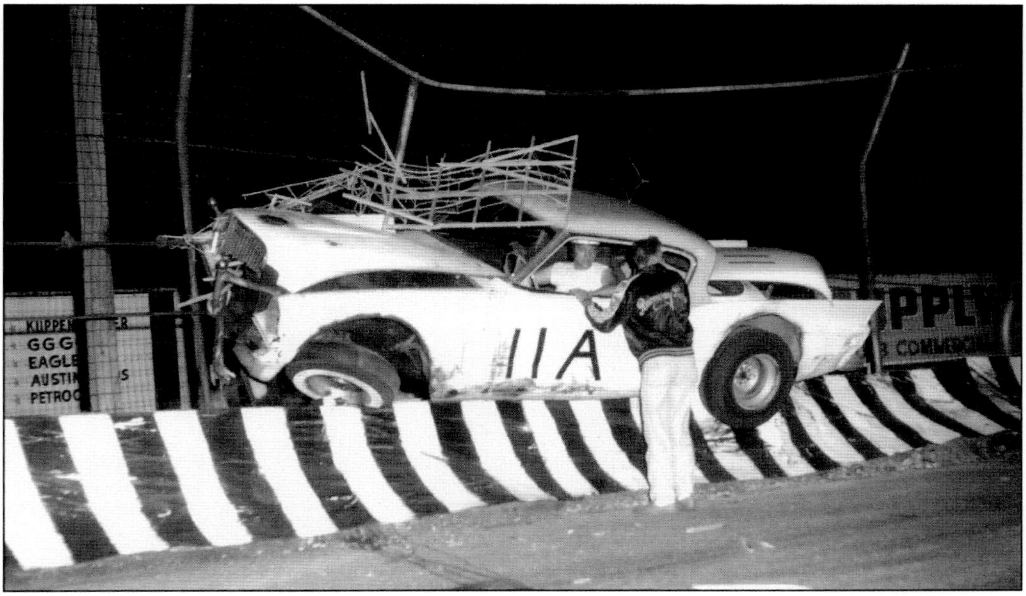

Don Allen (11A) and his Studebaker Hawk rest on the wall after crashing during 1961's Fourth of July racing program. With some fireworks displays resting on his car, Allen is checked out by a track official after his wild ride. Raceway Park featured one of the best fireworks displays in the Midwest, and after Interstate 57 was constructed adjacent to the speedway, motorists on the expressway would pull off onto the shoulder to watch the fireworks. (Courtesy of Stan Kalwasinski.)

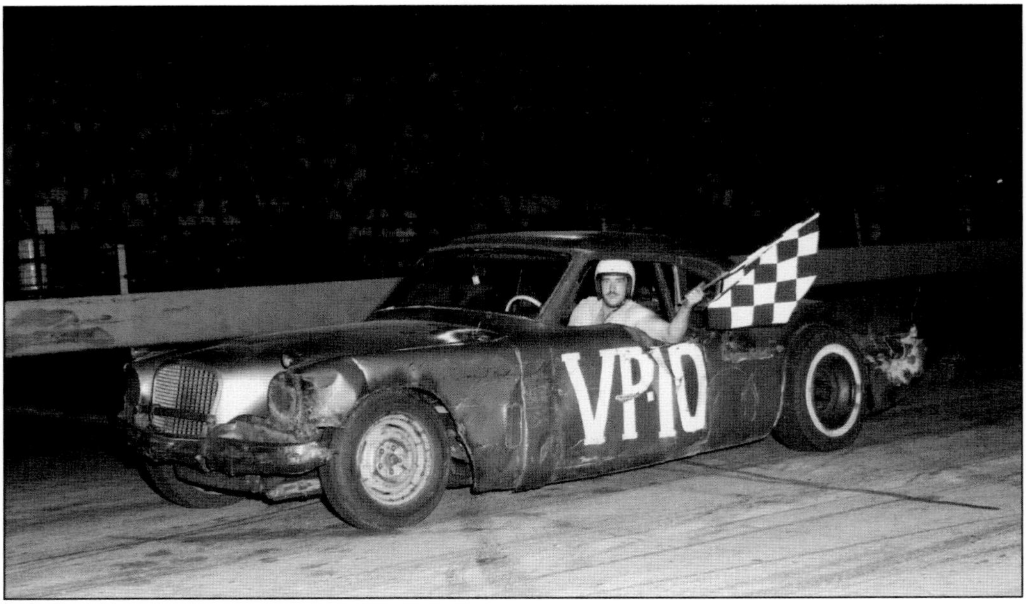

Longtime track statistician George Rowlette, who took over the announcing chores after the retirement of Wayne Adams at the end of the 1989 season, compiled a list of 817 different feature winners of the 6,770 features that were held from 1938 to 2000. Never a feature winner, Floyd Basset (VP10), pictured here in 1964, is among an incredibly long list of race-winning hopefuls who tested their skills at the longtime Chicagoland speed plant known as Raceway Park. (Courtesy of Stan Kalwasinski.)

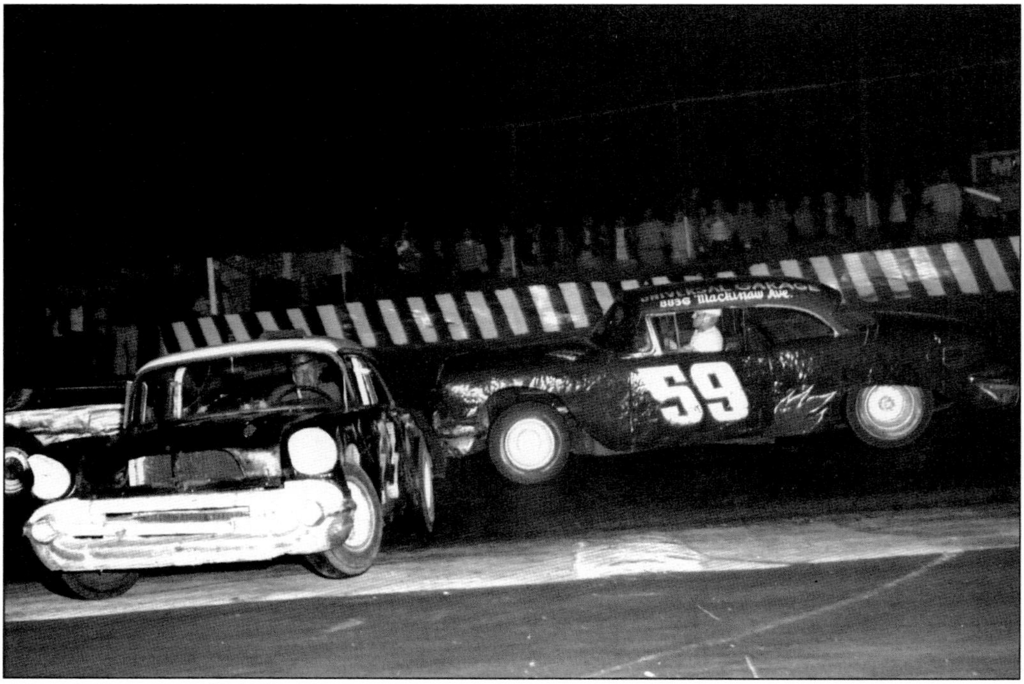

After Bill Cornwall (53), of Harvey, spun entering turn four, Chicago native Erv Dunner (59) guides his Oldsmobile past his fallen comrade in 1961 late model action. (Courtesy of Stan Kalwasinski.)

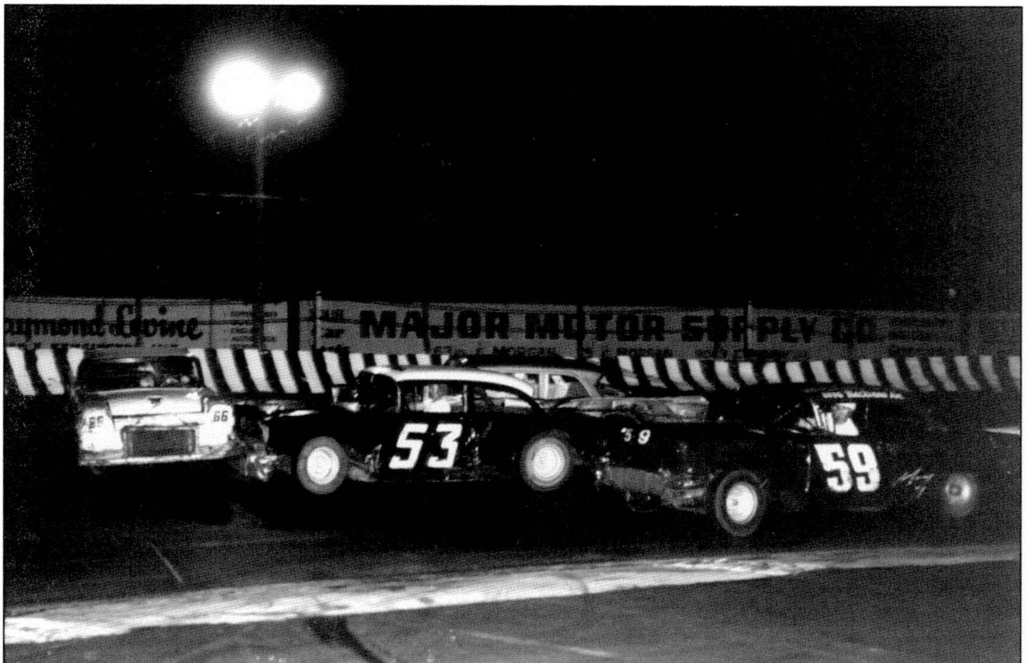

The late model action is hot and heavy in 1961 as Bill Cornwall (53), Johnny Exman (79), and Erv Dunner (59) try to avoid a spinning Bob Vickery (66) in turn two. (Courtesy of Stan Kalwasinski.)

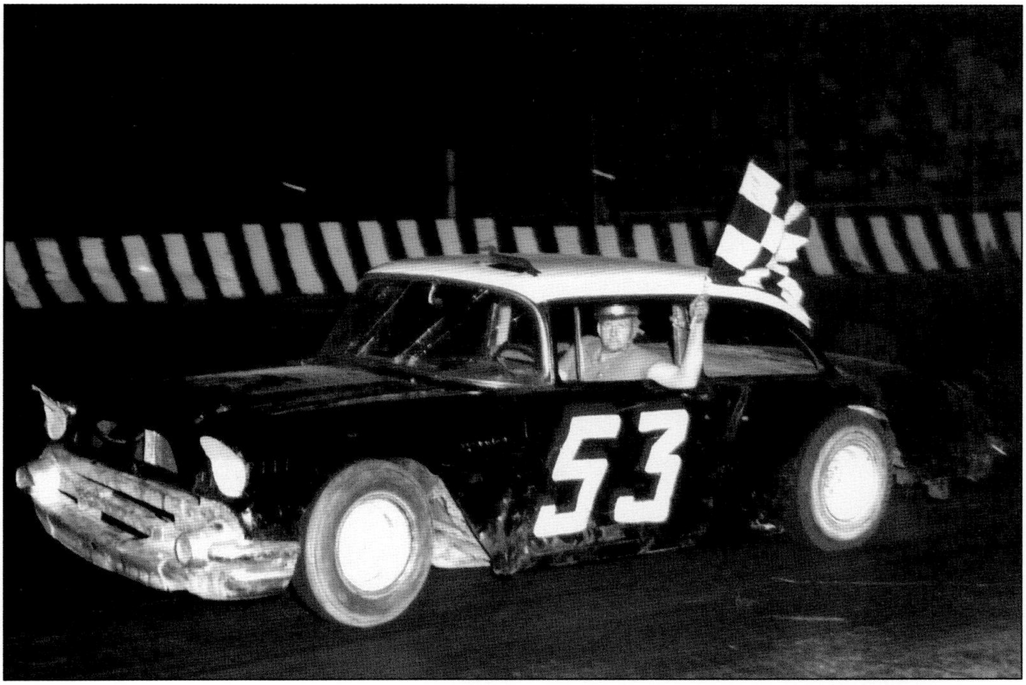

Bill Cornwall (53) takes his 1961 late model ride for a victory lap after another feature victory. Cornwall would win the late model championship two years later. (Courtesy of Stan Kalwasinski.)

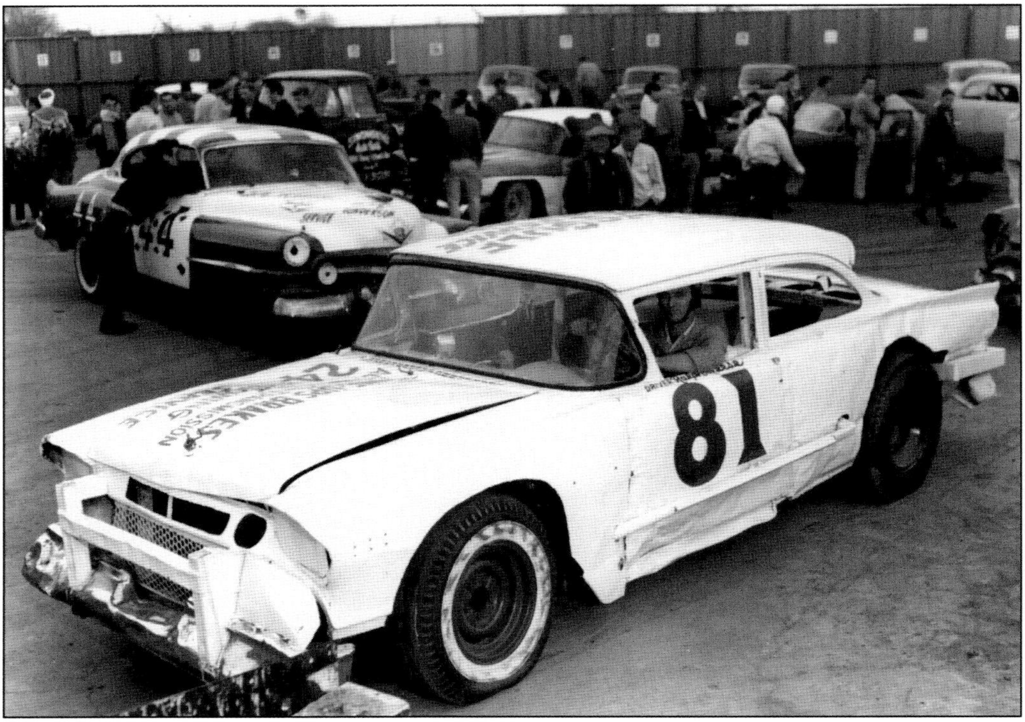

In this 1961 scene, late model driver Ralph Reese (81) is emerging from a crowded pit area as he waits to take his qualifying run. (Courtesy of Stan Kalwasinski.)

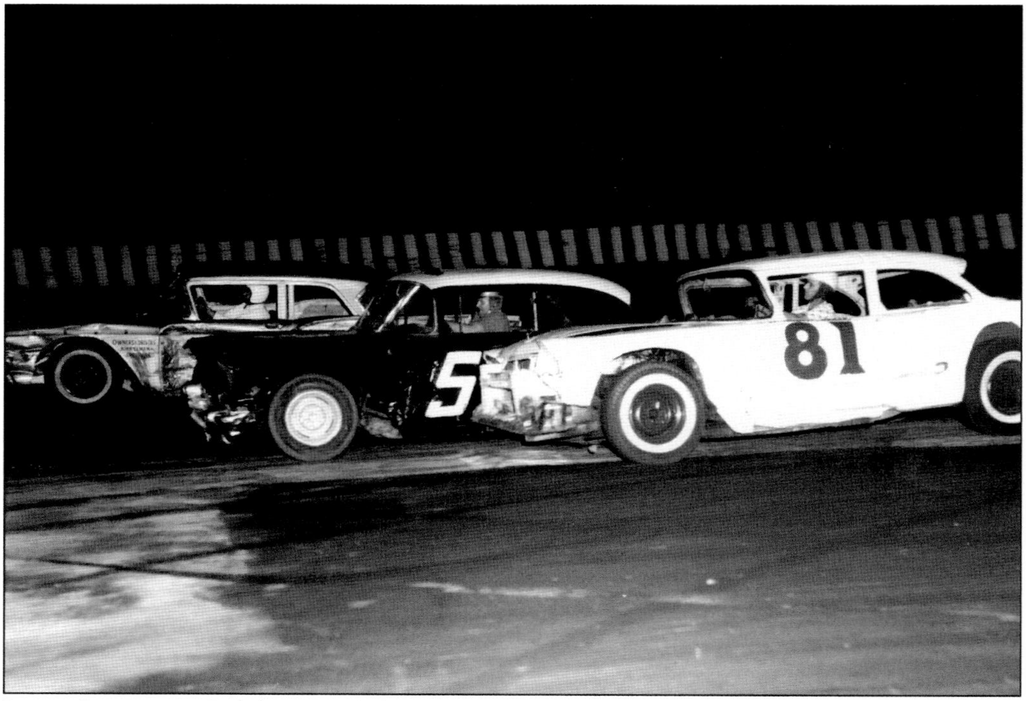

In a tight squeeze, Ralph Reese (81), Bill Cornwall (53), and Johnny Exman (79) battle during 1961 racing action. (Courtesy of Stan Kalwasinski.)

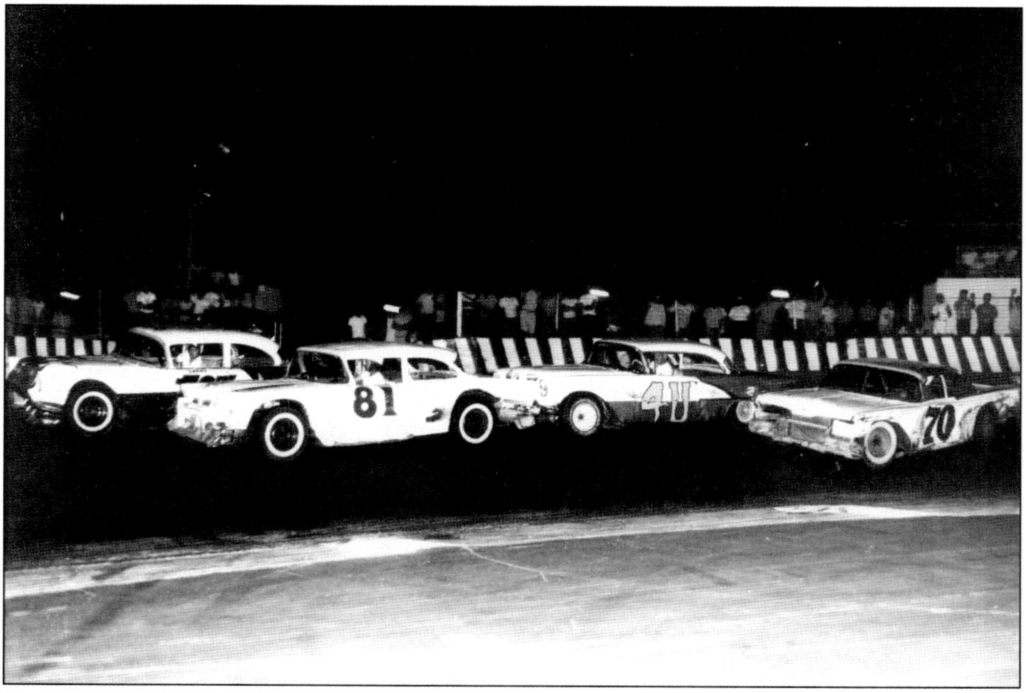

During a 1961 late model feature race, Larry Furst (1st) leads a pack of cars including the Ford of Ralph Reese (81), Stash Kullman's Oldsmobile (4U), and the 1959 Chevrolet of Bob Williams (70). (Courtesy of Stan Kalwasinski.)

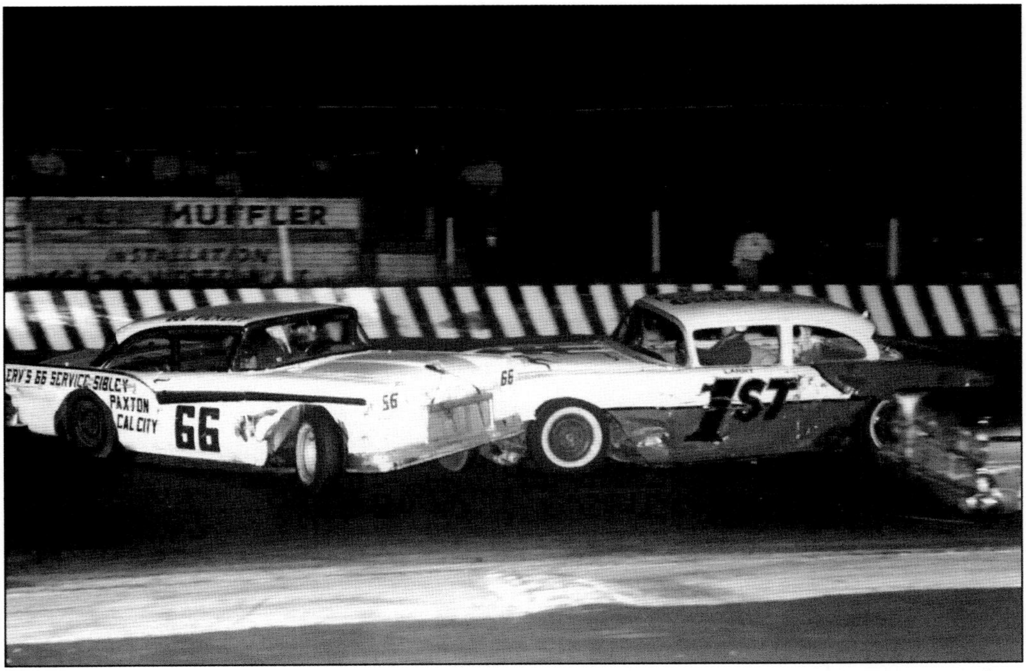

Bob Vickery (66) goes for a spin after making contact with Larry Furst (1st) during a 1961 late model race. (Courtesy of Stan Kalwasinski.)

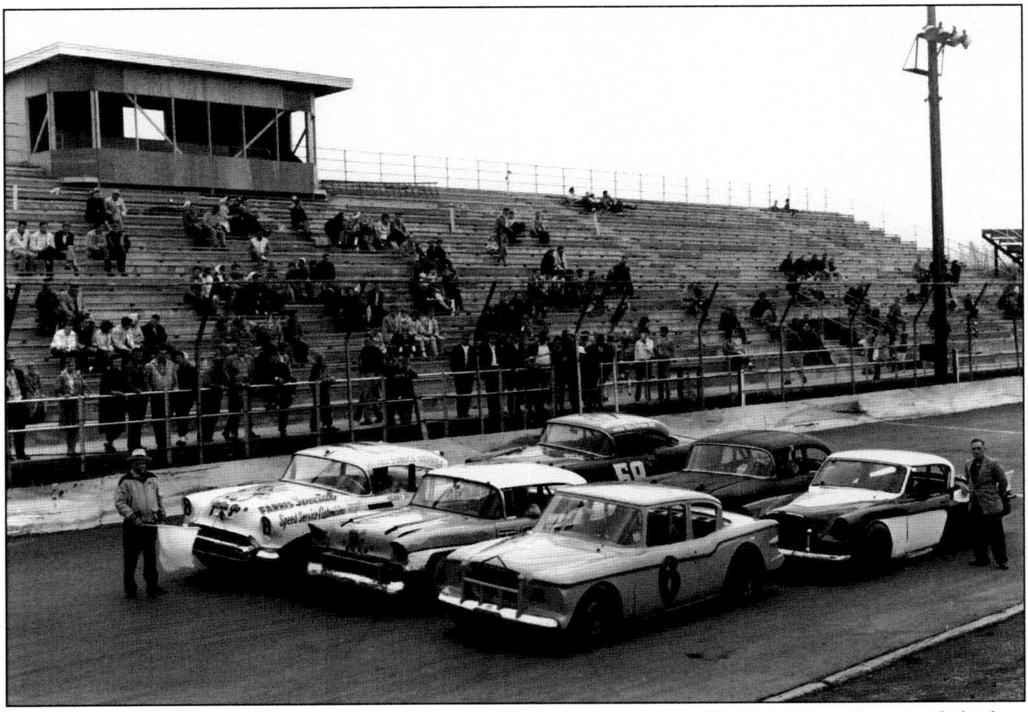

Raceway Park shows off its new grandstand and nearly completed scorers' booth a week before 1961's opening day. The 1960 top points finishers, comprised of Ken Boyer (8), Harry Simonsen (TS1), Bill Van Allen (6), Erv Dunner (59), Bill Cornwall (3), and Ray Young (99), pose for starters Tom Plouzek (left) and Smokey Smith (right). (Courtesy of Stan Kalwasinski.)

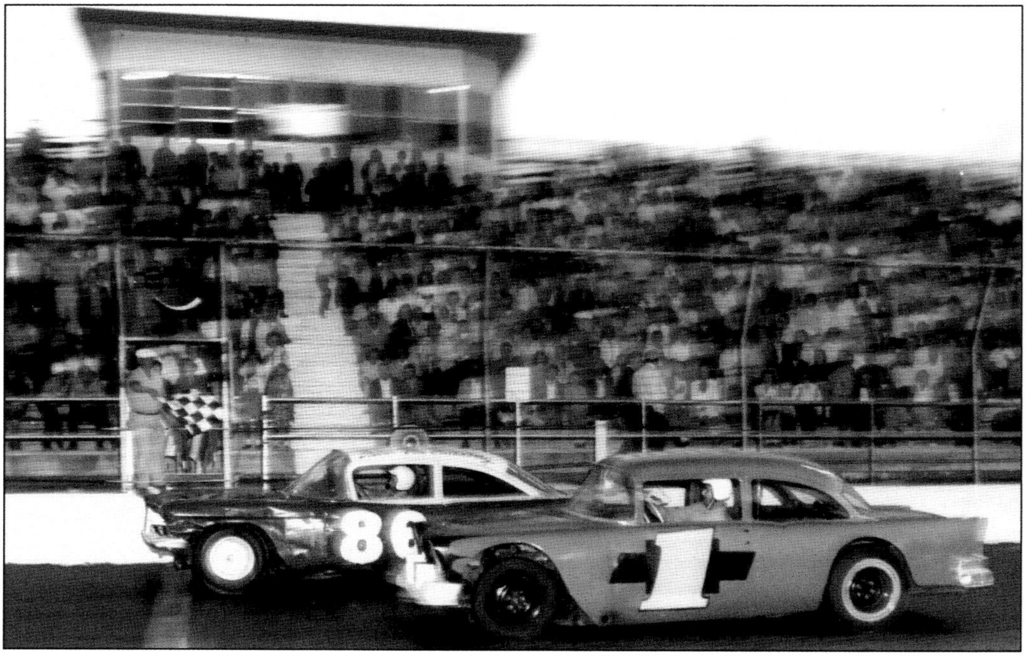

Society of Auto Sport, Fellowship, and Education (SAFE) NASCAR convertible champion of 1955, Don Oldenberg (86), a resident of Hammond, Indiana, nips 1961 late model champion Bob Pronger at the start/finish line for the victory. The crowd is on its feet as starter Tom Plouzek drops the checkered flag on the pair in this 1961 view. (Courtesy of Stan Kalwasinski.)

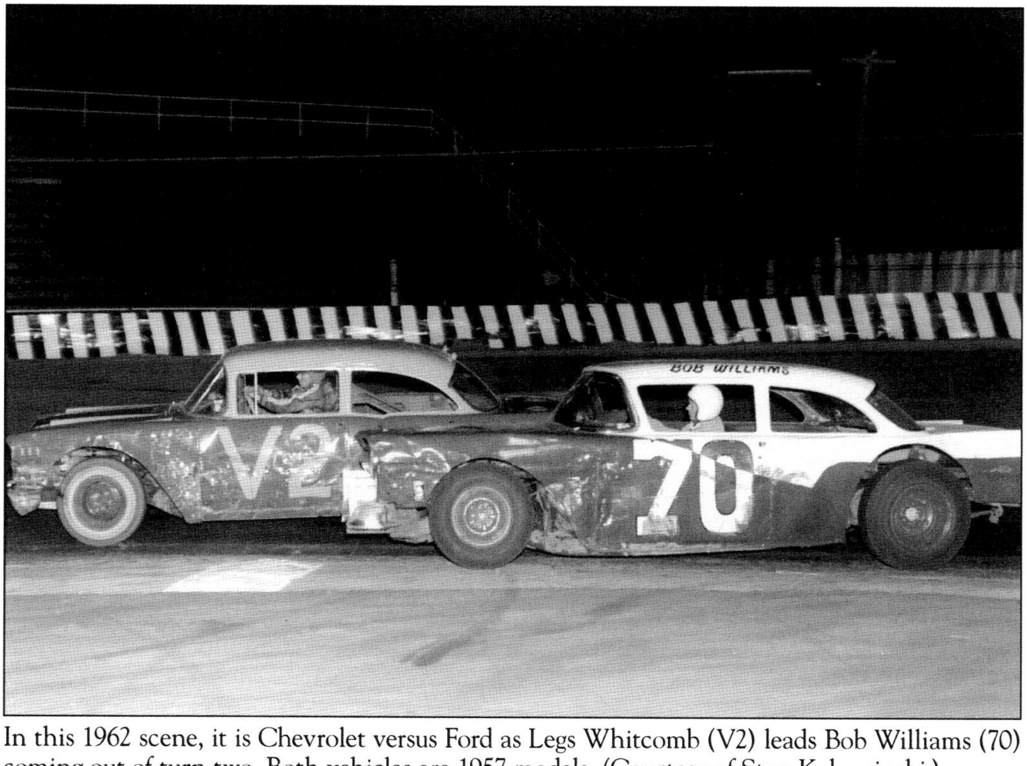

In this 1962 scene, it is Chevrolet versus Ford as Legs Whitcomb (V2) leads Bob Williams (70) coming out of turn two. Both vehicles are 1957 models. (Courtesy of Stan Kalwasinski.)

Bob Pronger picks up another win and another trophy during the 1961 season. Pronger would go on to win the late model championship that year. (Courtesy of Stan Kalwasinski.)

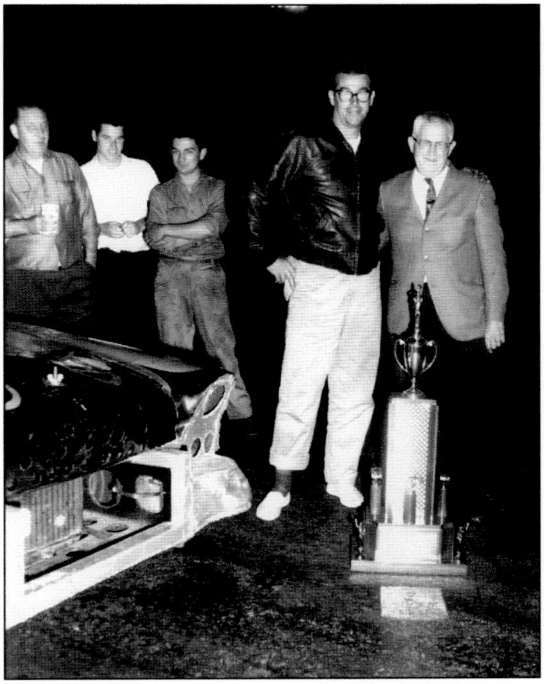

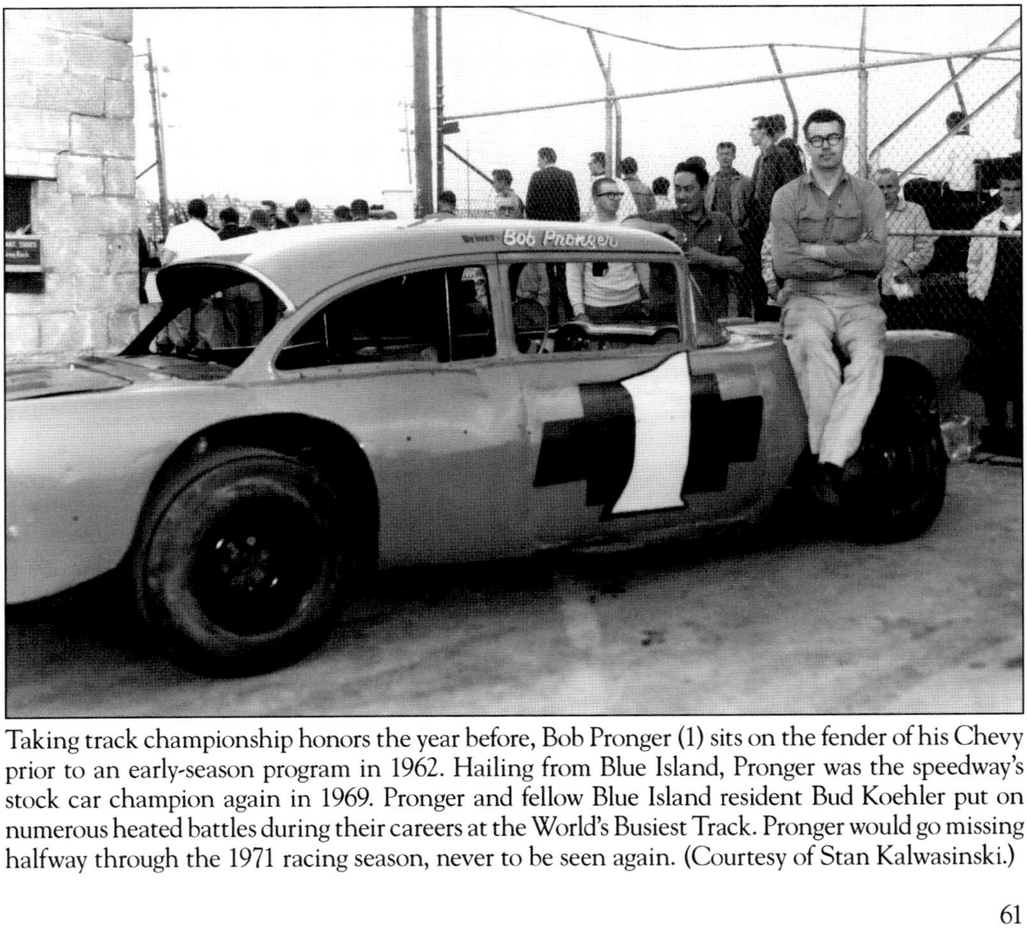

Taking track championship honors the year before, Bob Pronger (1) sits on the fender of his Chevy prior to an early-season program in 1962. Hailing from Blue Island, Pronger was the speedway's stock car champion again in 1969. Pronger and fellow Blue Island resident Bud Koehler put on numerous heated battles during their careers at the World's Busiest Track. Pronger would go missing halfway through the 1971 racing season, never to be seen again. (Courtesy of Stan Kalwasinski.)

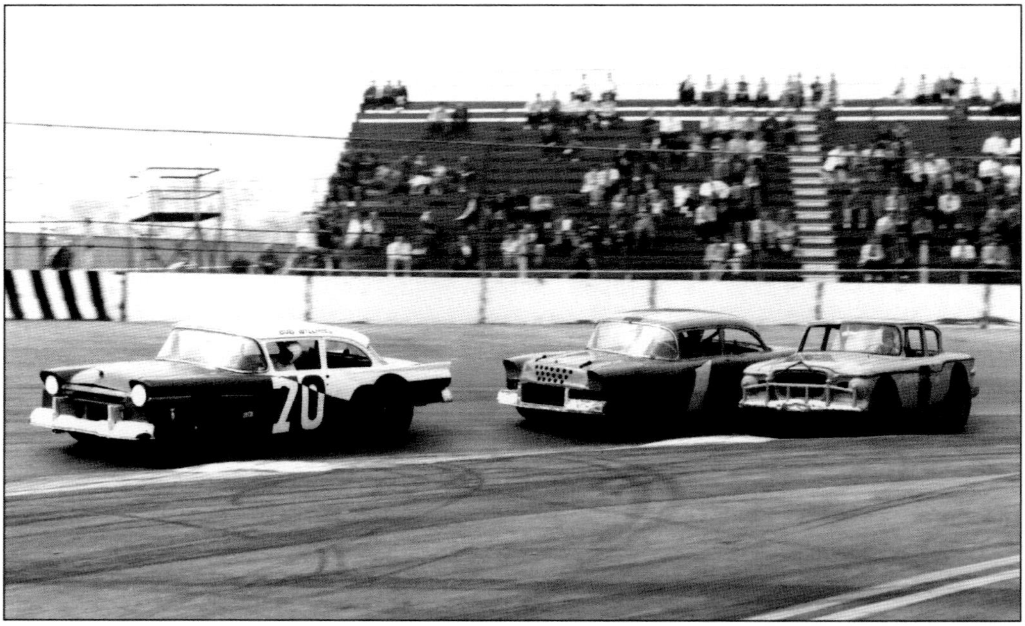

The action heats up in 1962 as Bob Williams (70) leads Bob Pronger (1) and Bill Van Allen (6) through turn one. Van Allen quit running at Raceway midway through the 1962 season after several disputes with track owner Pete Jenin. Van Allen competed elsewhere during 1963 and made a brief comeback at Raceway in 1964, before leaving for good. (Courtesy of Stan Kalwasinski.)

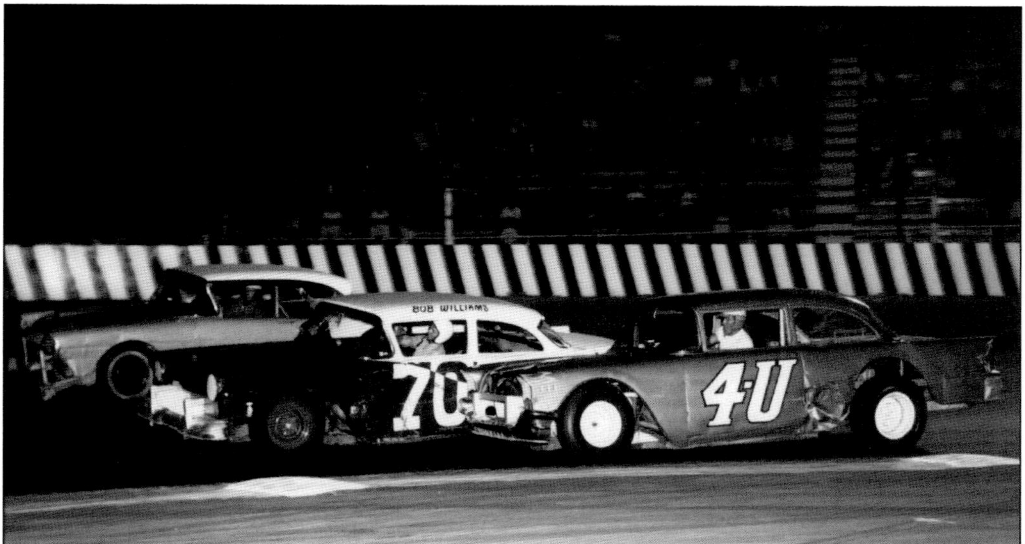

Late model champion of 1959, Bob Williams (70) pushes his 1957 Ford past the 1957 Chevrolet of Stash Kullman (4U) during a 1962 late model feature race. In the final race of the season, Kullman "flew" his Chevrolet over the turn-one wall after breaking a driveshaft. Kullman hopped the retaining wall and landed on top of four cars owned by spectators in the general admission parking lot, a good 75 feet from the racetrack itself. Although Kullman was uninjured, his wife fainted after viewing the wreck and was rushed to St. Francis Hospital in Blue Island. (Courtesy of Stan Kalwasinski.)

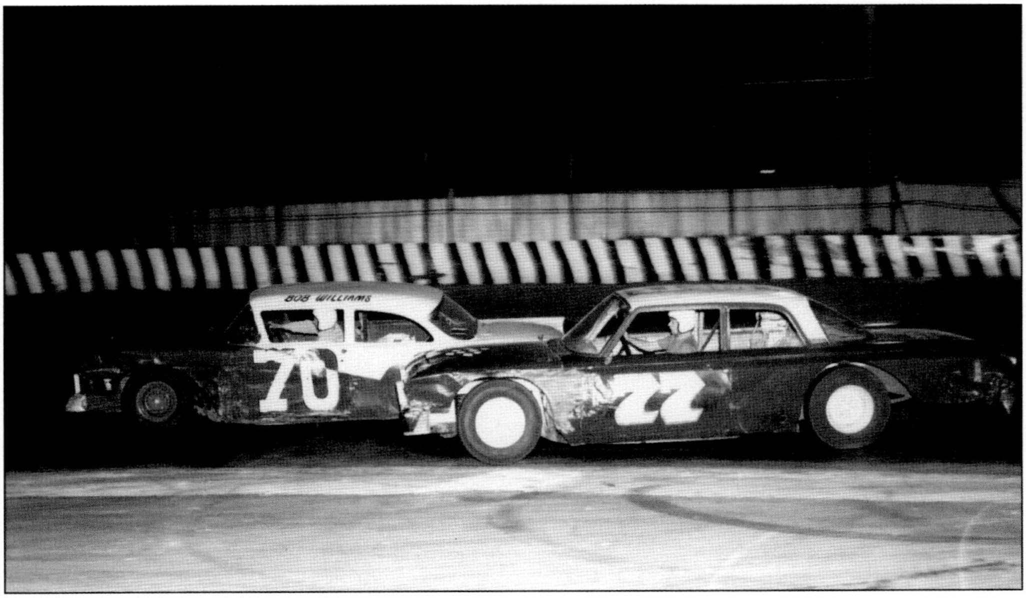

Action in 1962 finds Bob Williams (70) and Bud Koehler (77) battling. Williams and Koehler were definitely archrivals at the speedway, dating back to 1950 when the pair tangled with Koehler's freshly prepared 1949 Ford, crashing and ending up on its roof. Year after year, the duo would race each other hard night after night, with the 1959 season pretty much being the climactic year of the feud. Williams won the track championship that year after Koehler was suspended by track officials for rough driving. (Courtesy of Stan Kalwasinski.)

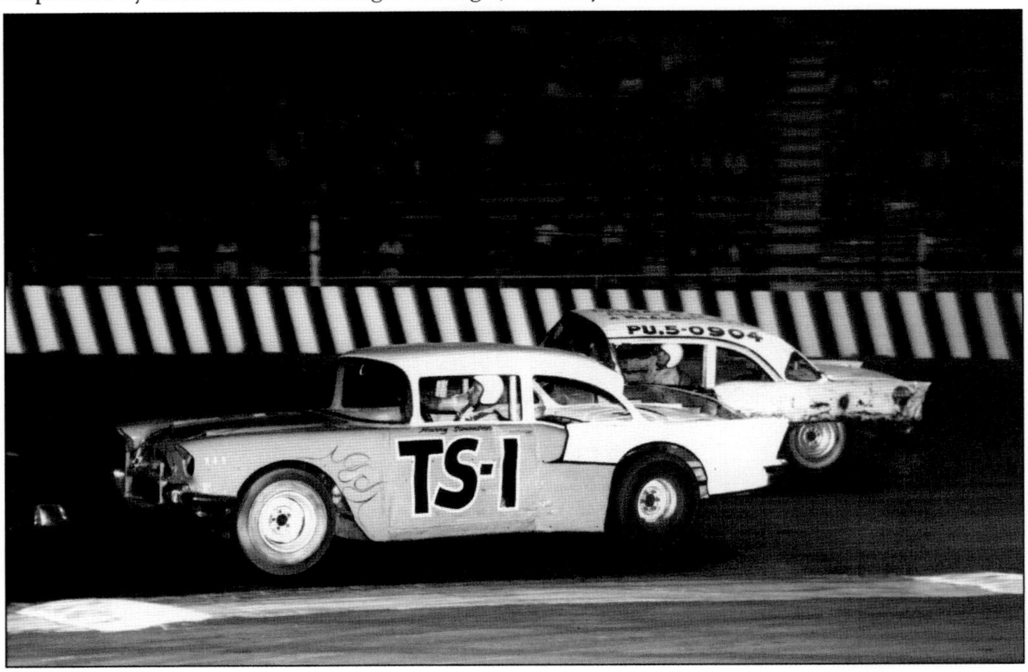

Harry Simonsen's Chevrolet (TS1) and Ted Janecyk's Oldsmobile (3-T) get down to business in 1962 late model action. Simonsen was the proprietor of an auto parts store on Stoney Island Avenue on Chicago's South Side, whereas Janecyk was (and still is) an over-the-road truck driver. (Courtesy of Stan Kalwasinski.)

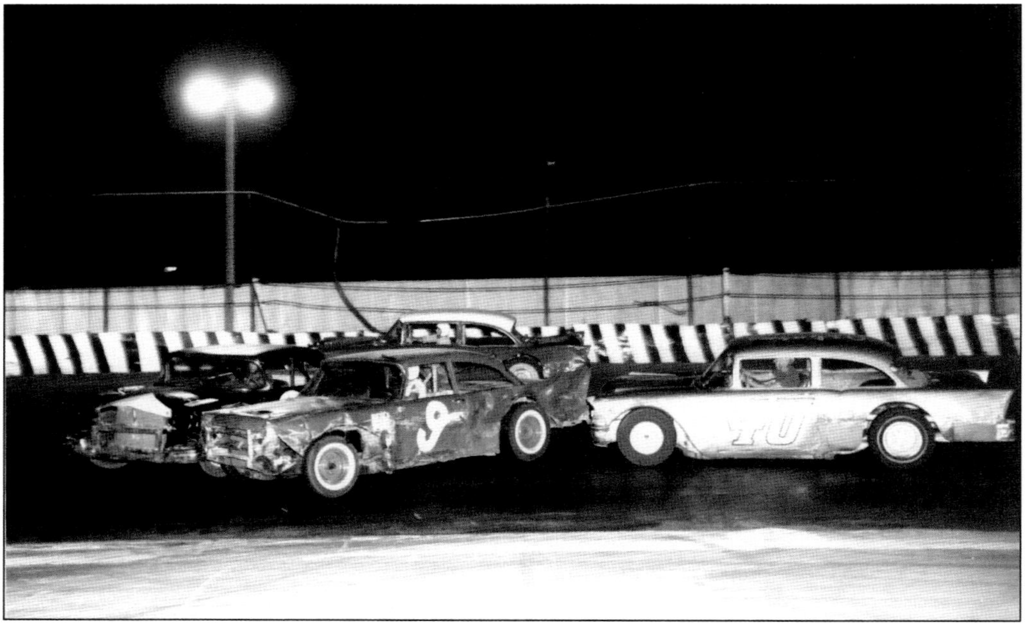

The action was usually rough and ready, with drivers battling every inch of the way. This 1962 photograph shows Jerry Kemperman (9) a bit sideways with Dennis Rubino (15) in pretty much the same position. Stash Kullman (4U) is just about ready to "nail" Kemperman's spinning car, with Ted Janecyk (1) trying to maneuver around everyone on the outside. (Courtesy of Stan Kalwasinski.)

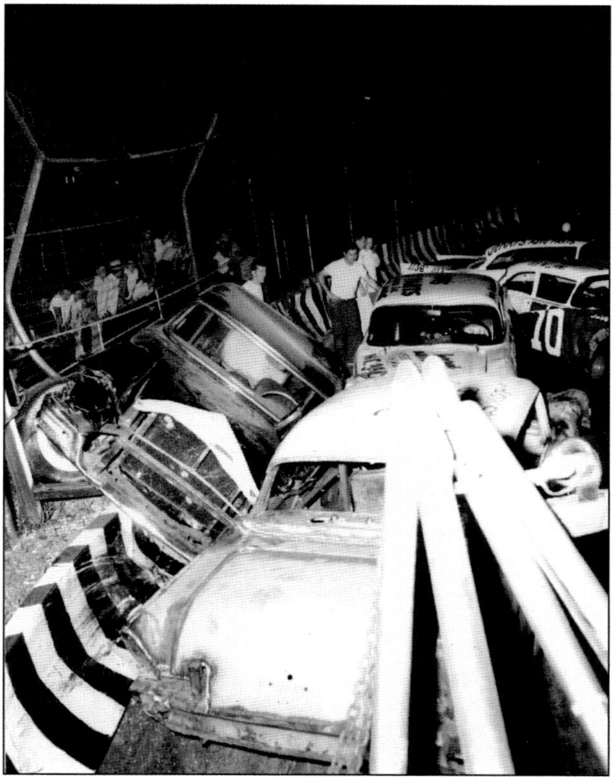

A view from the back of a tow truck shows a bunch of late model cars pretty much done for the night in 1962. Dennis Perzely's car (21D) is in the foreground with Dennis Rubino's car (15) on the wall. Johnny Kapovich's ride (37) and Bob Williams's (70) are among the other cars involved in a typical multicar wreck. (Courtesy of Stan Kalwasinski.)

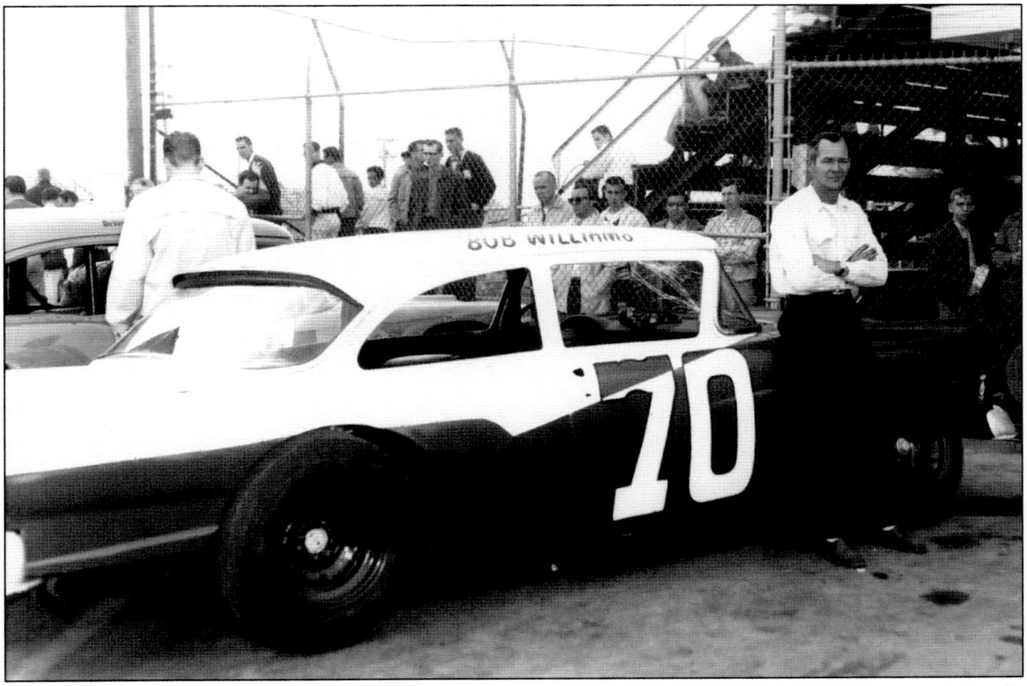

Late model track champion in 1959, Bob Williams (70) poses with his 1962 late model ride as intrigued and curious fans watch the action in the pits through the fence. (Courtesy of Stan Kalwasinski.)

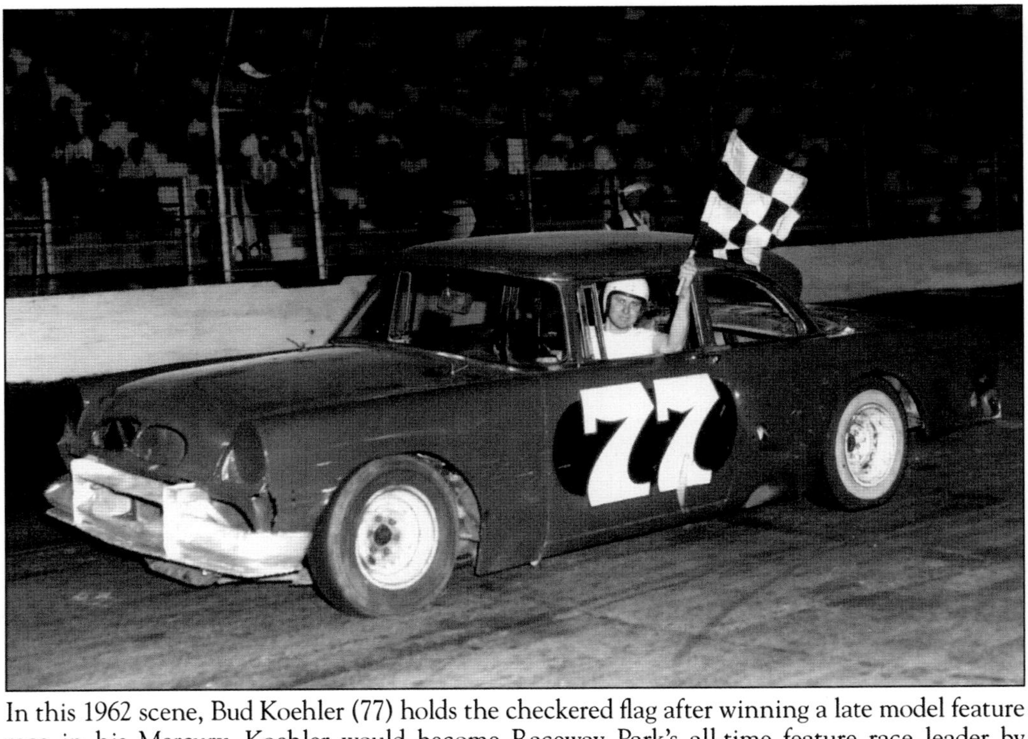

In this 1962 scene, Bud Koehler (77) holds the checkered flag after winning a late model feature race in his Mercury. Koehler would become Raceway Park's all-time feature race leader by winning 490 late model features along with 10 midget features. (Courtesy of Stan Kalwasinski.)

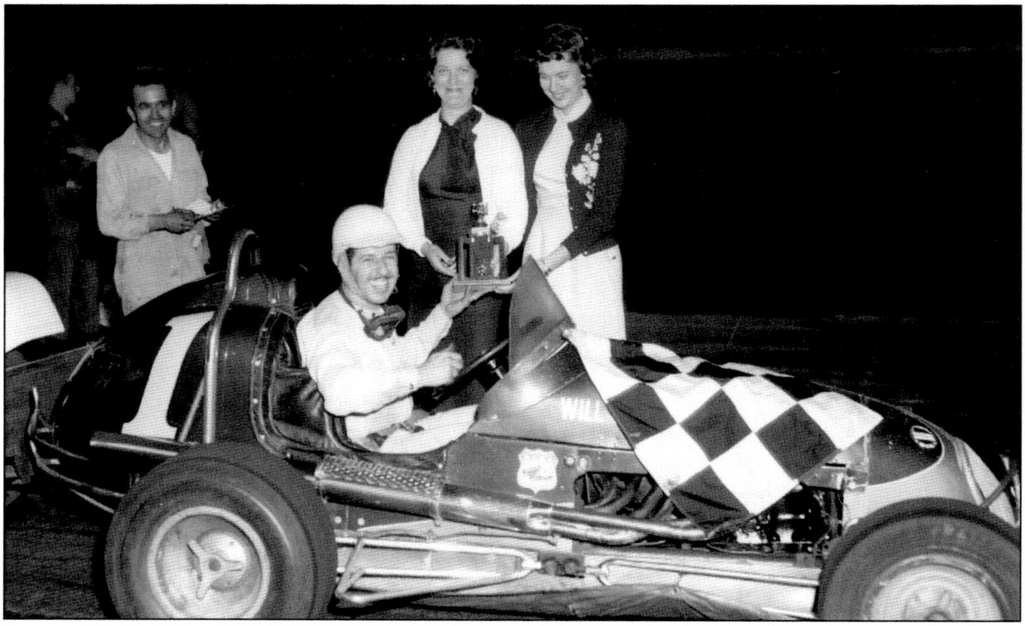

Danny Kladis (1) accepts his trophy from two unidentified presenters after winning a United Auto Racing Association (UARA) midget race in 1962. Kladis, a longtime area open-wheel racer, won the track's first stock car race, a 300-lap contest on October 31, 1948. Kladis borrowed a military jeep from a local recruiting station, whitewashed it, and then used its four-wheel-drive option to score a victory over Bill Van Allen. (Courtesy of Stan Kalwasinski.)

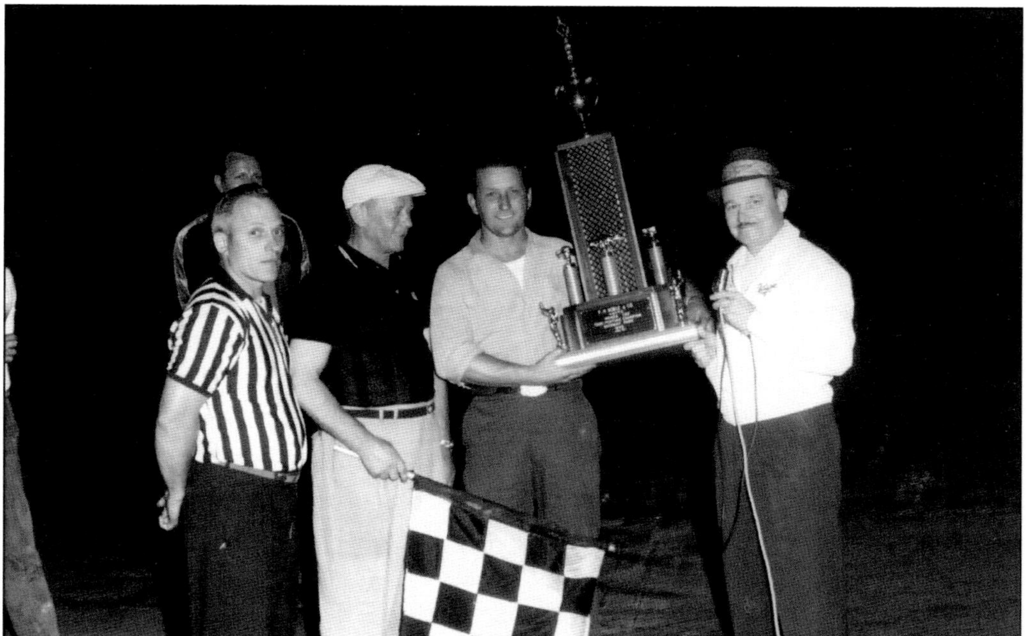

The year 1962 was a great year for Ray Young, second from right, a tobacco-chewing truck driver from Whitwell, Tennessee. Here Young accepts his F. H. Noble and Company trophy for winning a 1962 Monza 120. Sharing the smiles are, from left to right, Smokey Smith, Tom Plouzek and Wayne Adams. (Courtesy of Stan Kalwasinski.)

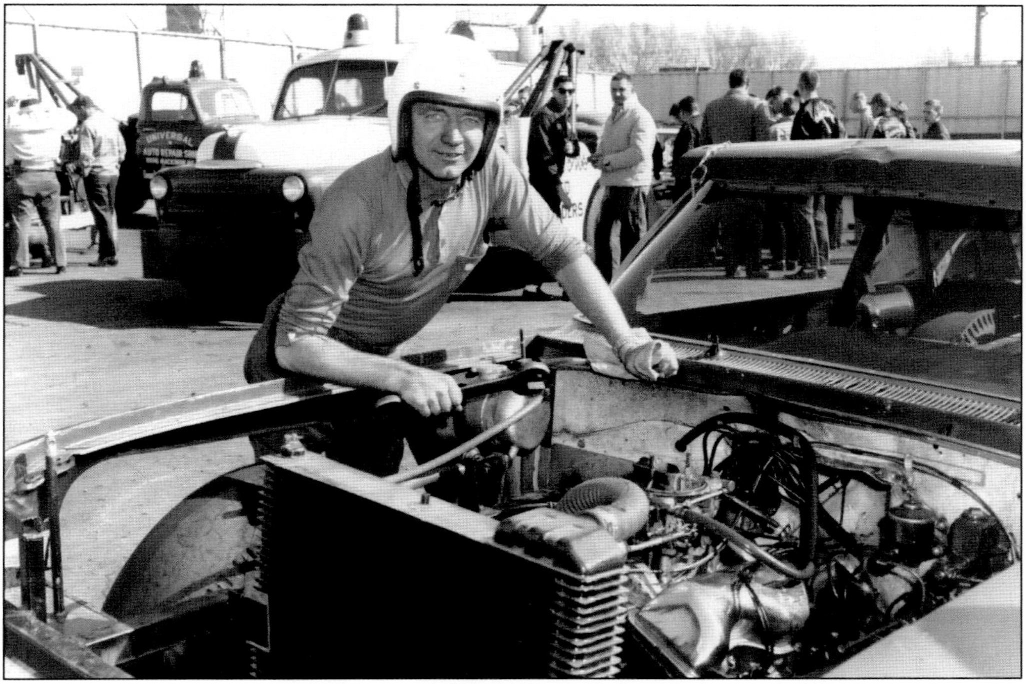

Ted Janecyk works underneath the hood of his Chevrolet between races on 1963's opening day. The Chevrolet 409-cubic-inch motor was not up to peak performance, as Janecyk was shut out of the win column that day. (Courtesy of Stan Kalwasinski.)

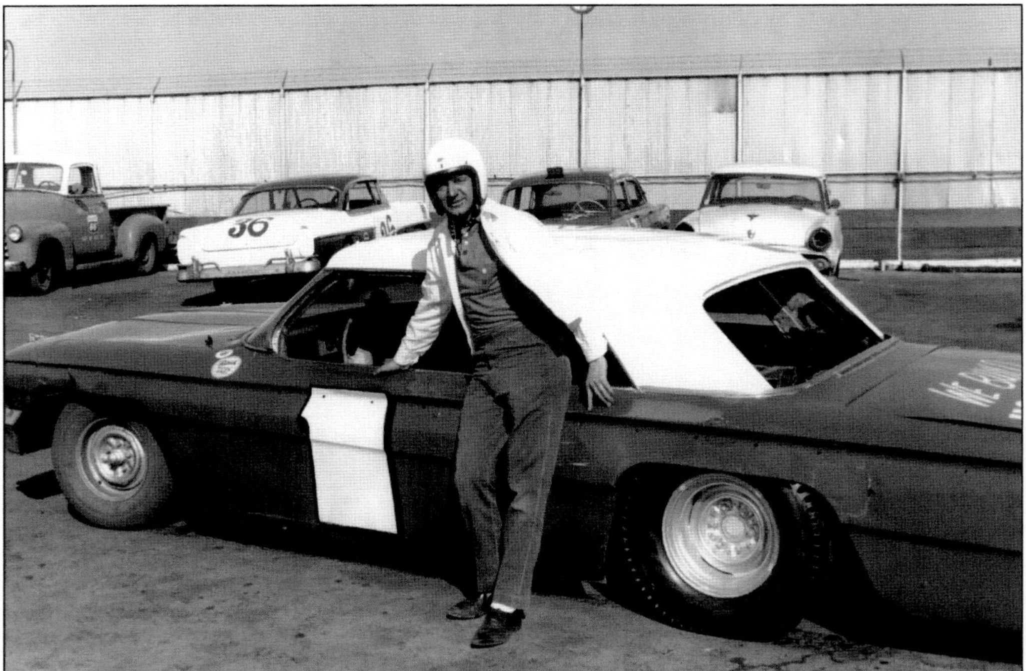

Ted Janecyk, who lived directly across the street from the racetrack's main entrance, was the 1965 late model champion. Janecyk began racing in 1952, and in this 1963 scene, he poses with his Bill Koenig–owned 1962 Chevrolet (1). (Courtesy of Stan Kalwasinski.)

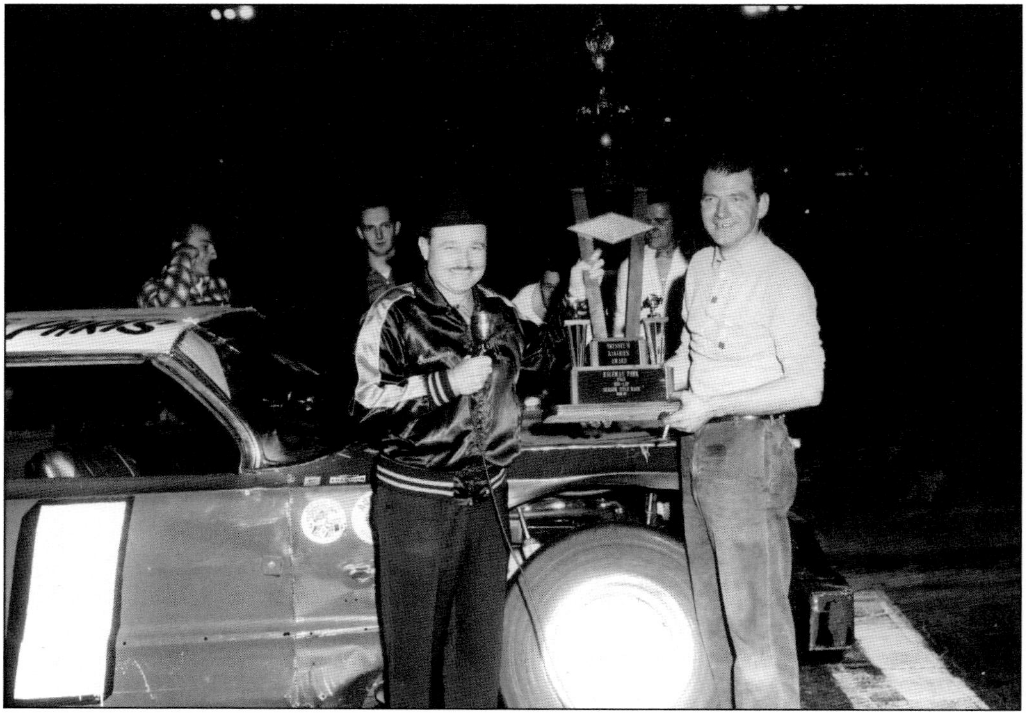

After winning the 1963 100-lap season title race, Ted Janecyk (1) is all smiles as he receives the Dressel's Bakeries trophy from track announcer Wayne Adams. (Courtesy of Stan Kalwasinski.)

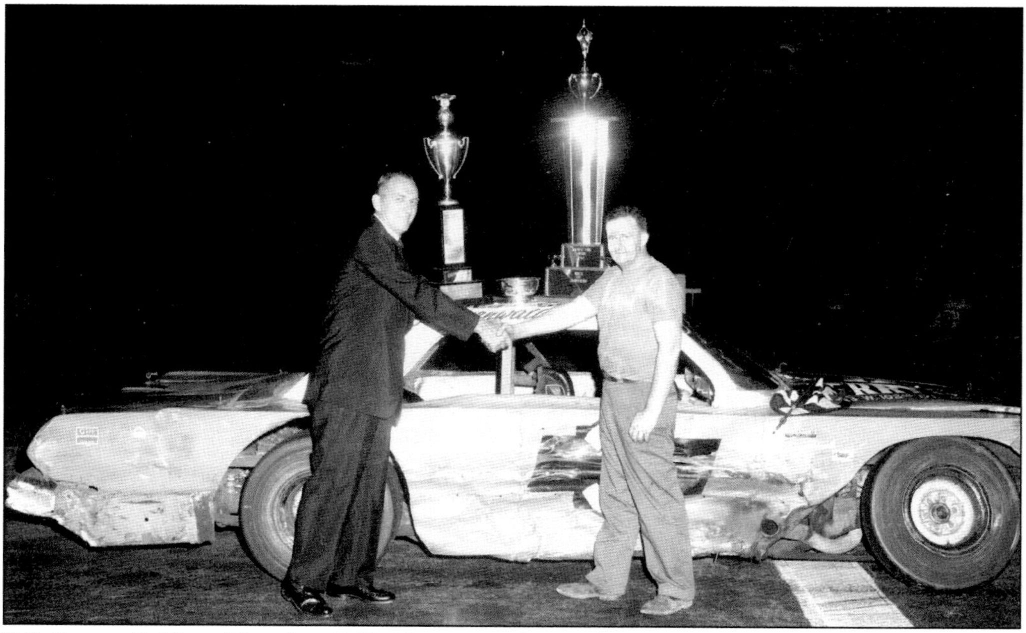

Bill Cornwall (3) and his fast 1963 Chevy was the combo to beat in stock car racing action at the track in 1963. Eighteen feature wins were among Cornwall's racing laurels that season, as he went on to win his first and only track title at the Pete Jenin/Jimmy Derrico–promoted speedway. Cornwall is shown picking up some trophies after an overall Monza Classic 120 victory during his title-winning season. (Courtesy of Stan Kalwasinski.)

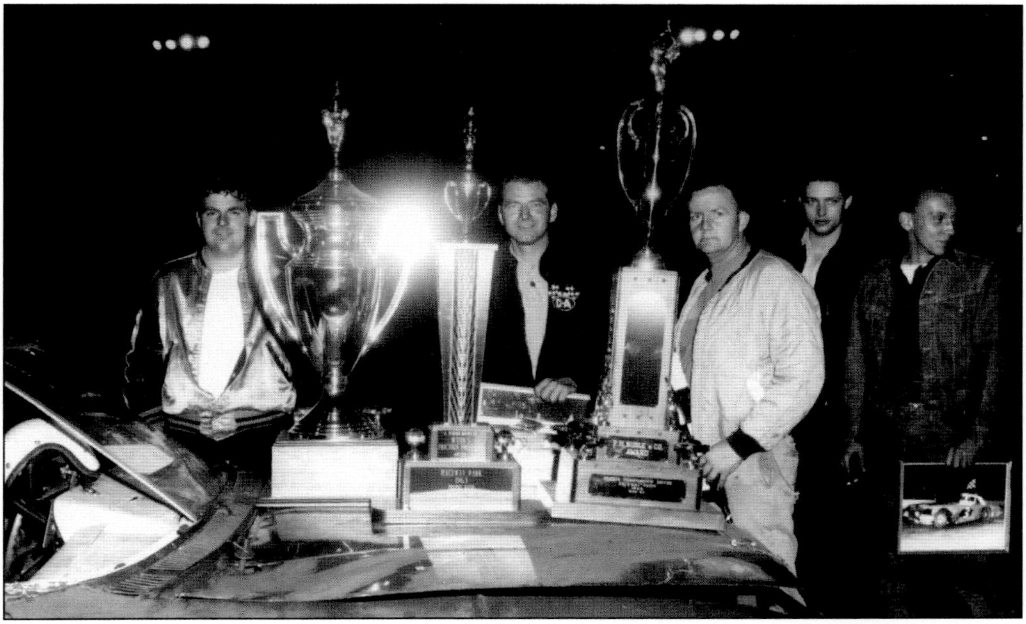

Jerry Kemperman, Ted Janecyk, and Bill Cornwall (seen from left to right) receive recognition for their 1963 racing successes. Kemperman was the winner of the 1963 300 Lap Classic, Janecyk won the most late model trophy dash races, and Cornwall was the late model driving champion. Cornwall and Janecyk were the top two drivers that season, and Cornwall was able to nudge out Janecyk for the points championship. (Courtesy of Stan Kalwasinski.)

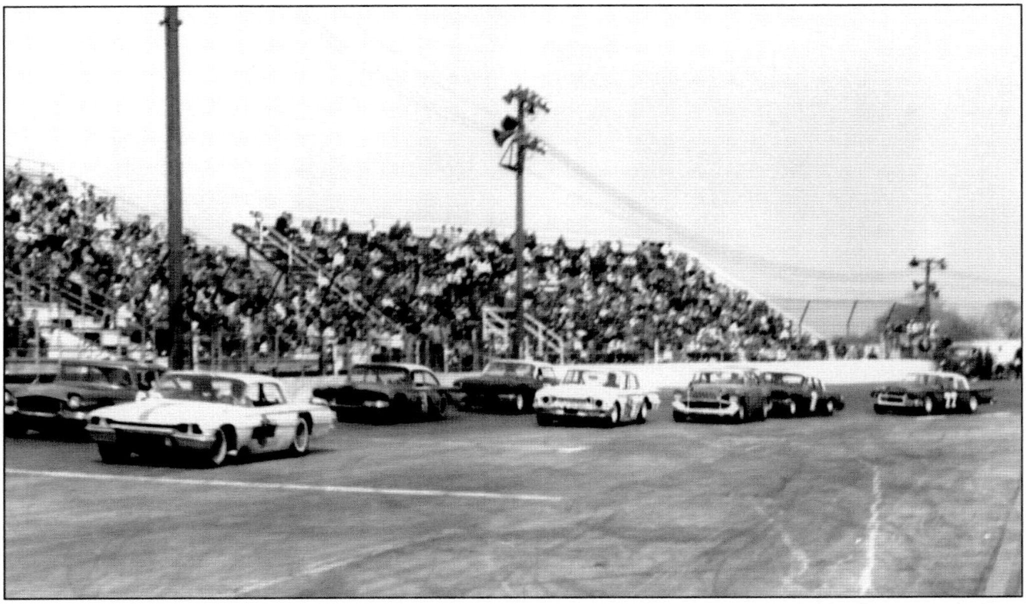

The first fast car heat race of the 1963 season saw Rich Miller leading a field of cars including Bob Alonso (68), Bill Cornwall (3), Bill Johnson (55), Legs Whitcomb (V2), Ted Janecyk (1), Dennis Rubino (15), and Bud Koehler (77). Whitcomb would sweep the opening-day program, but his luck would not last much longer. After selling his 1957 Chevrolet to Larry Middleton, Whitcomb would win only one more late model feature race in his career, another victim of the opening-day jinx. (Courtesy of Stan Kalwasinski.)

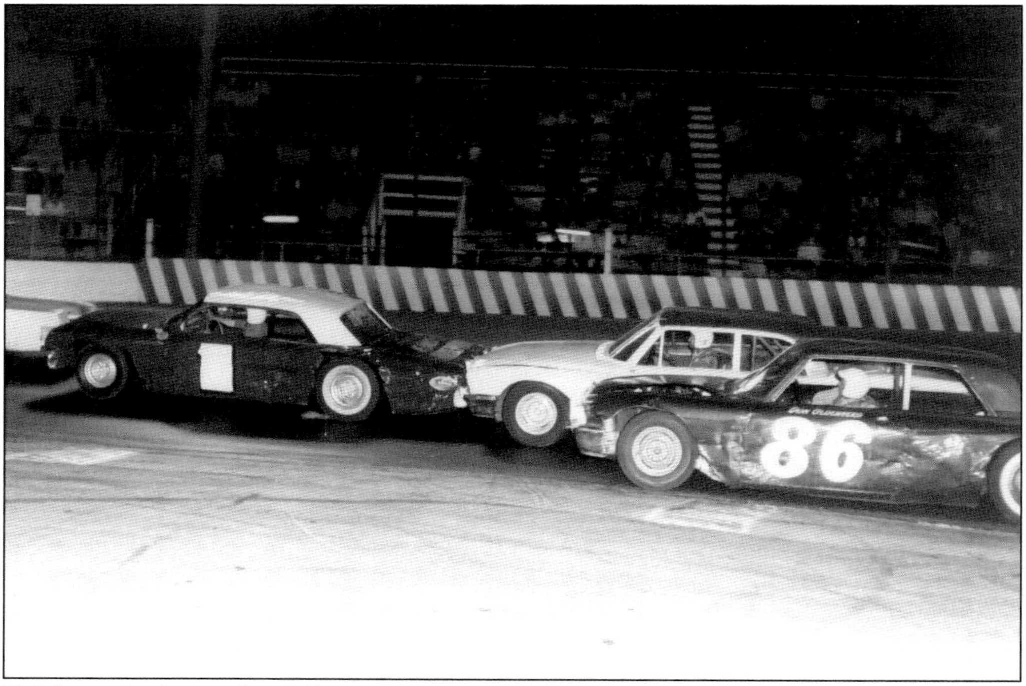

Ted Janecyk, driving his Bill Koenig–owned 1962 Chevrolet (1), leads the 1960 Ford of Bill Johnson (55) and the 1962 Ford of Don Oldenberg (86) out of turn four and toward the start/finish line in this 1963 scene. (Courtesy of Stan Kalwasinski.)

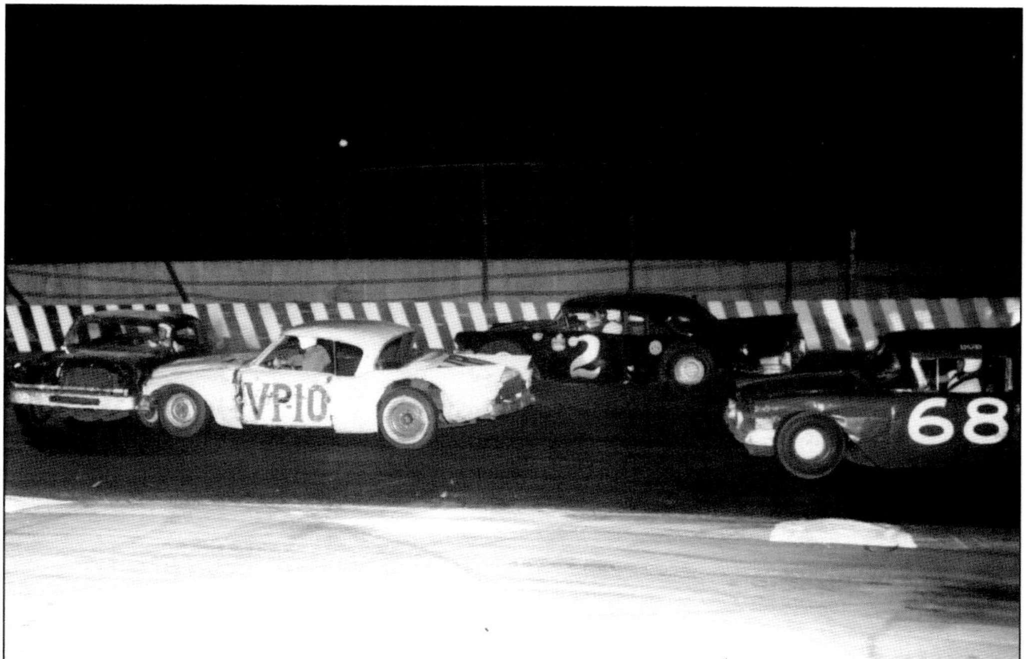

Late model action in 1963 finds Floyd Bassett (VP-10), Dick Kozelka (2), and Bob Alonso (68) taking different paths to try to avoid an unidentified spinning competitor. (Courtesy of Stan Kalwasinski.)

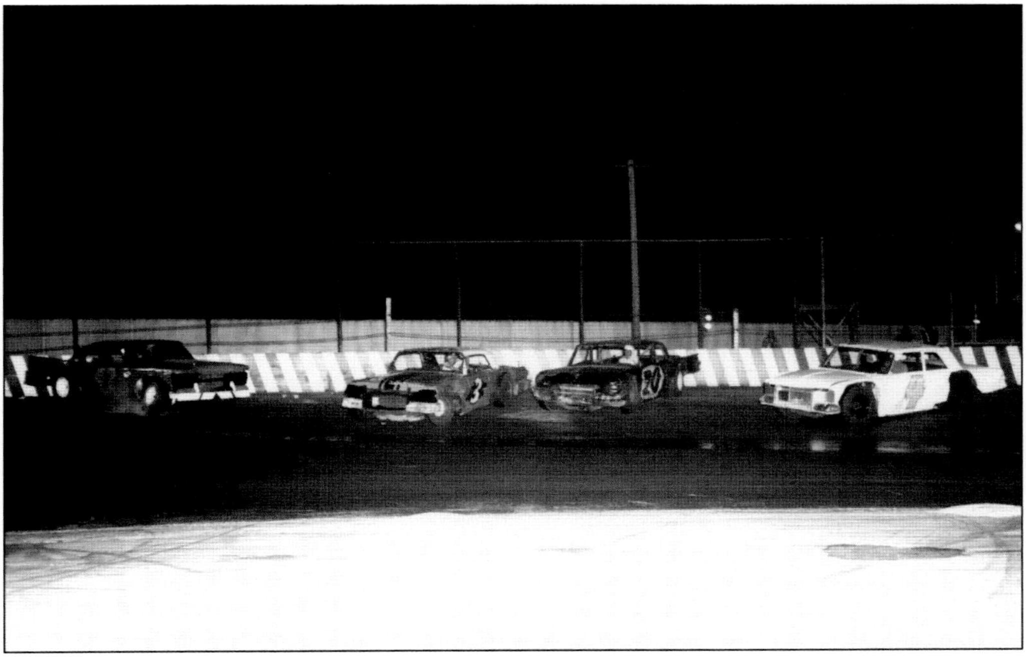

In this 1963 scene, Rich Hill's Plymouth (42) blows a radiator hose in turn one, resulting in a wet track and Bill Cornwall (3), Bob Williams (70), and Bob Pronger (4) sliding toward the wall. Cornwall would recover from this mishap to win the 1963 late model driving championship. (Courtesy of Stan Kalwasinski.)

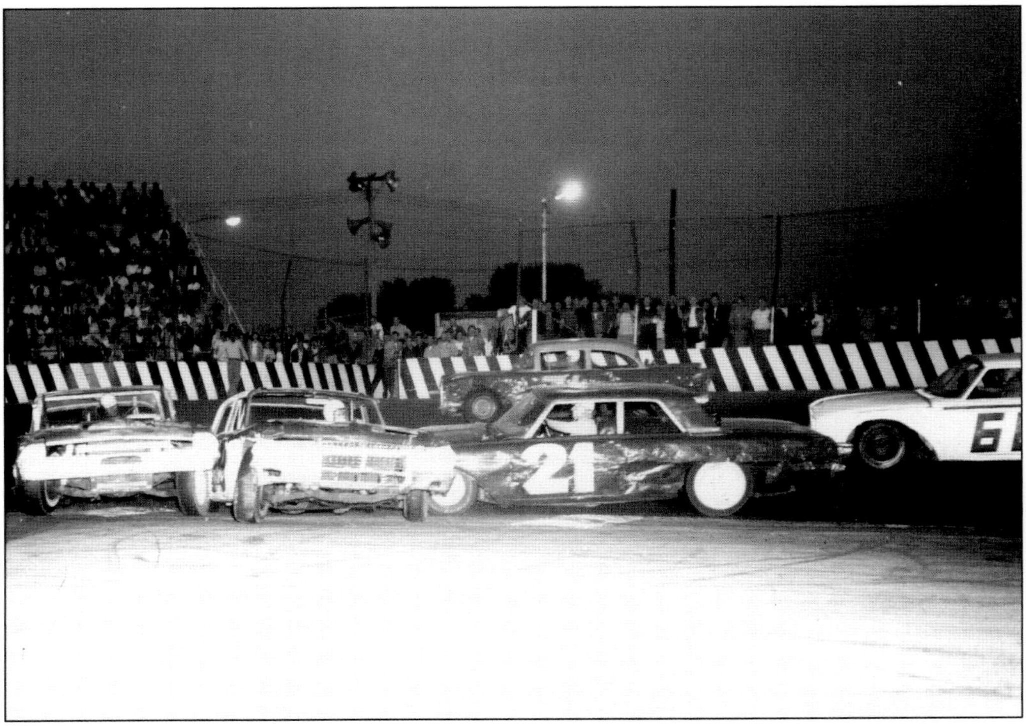

In this 1963 scene, Bob Slepski (21) cannot avoid two spinning cars as Larry Middleton (71) and Bob Vickery (66) manage to avoid the turn-four tangle. (Courtesy of Stan Kalwasinski.)

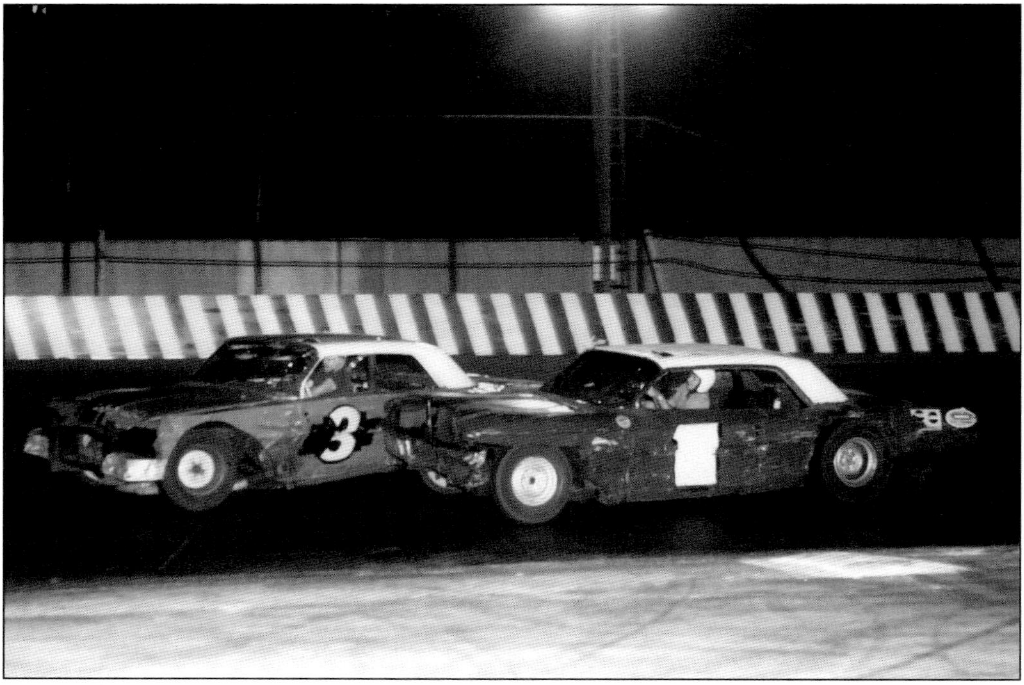

One of the best rivalries ever witnessed at Raceway Park involved Bill Cornwall (3) and Ted Janecyk (1) in 1963. Cornwall came home with the late model driving championship in 1963, and Janecyk would win it two years later. (Courtesy of Stan Kalwasinski.)

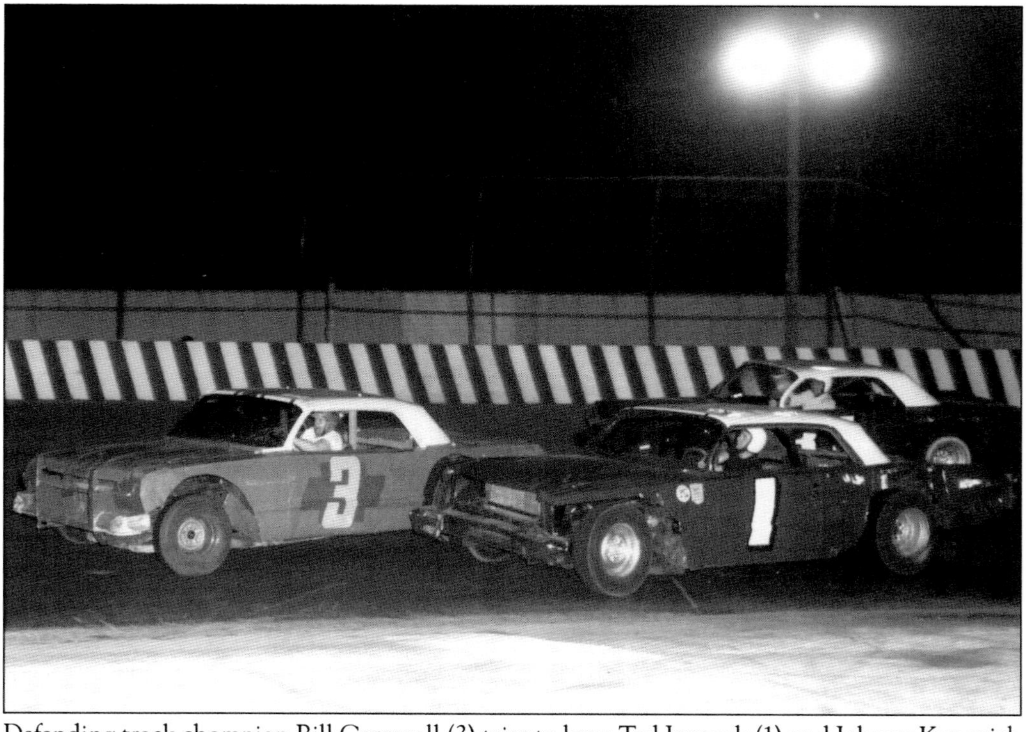

Defending track champion Bill Cornwall (3) tries to keep Ted Janecyk (1) and Johnny Kapovich (37) behind him during 1964 racing action. (Courtesy of Stan Kalwasinski.)

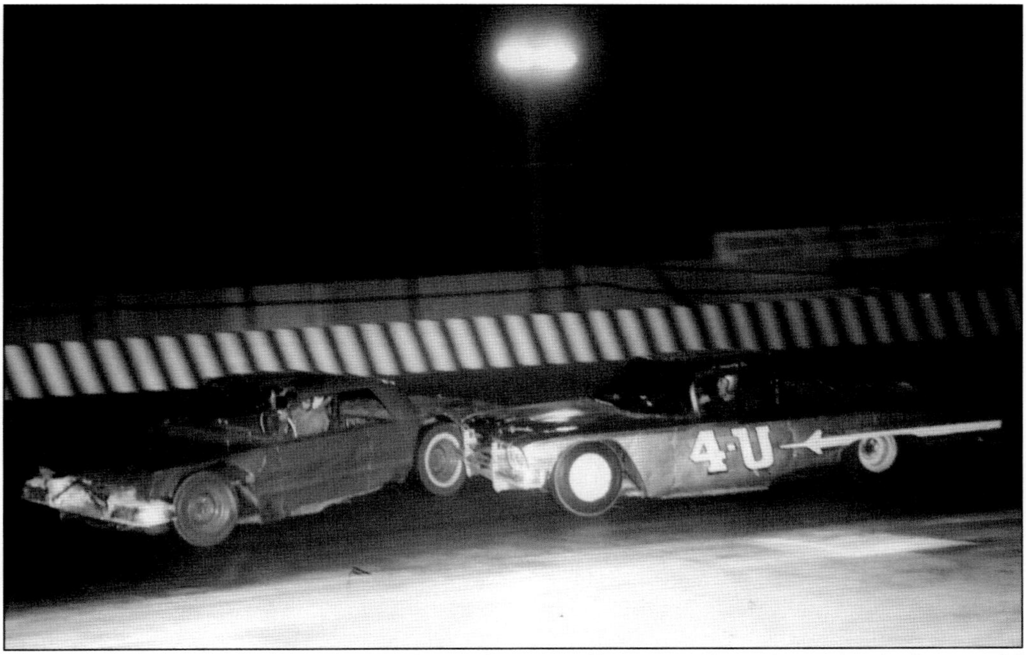

In this 1964 scene, Stash Kullman (4U) gets the nose of his 1960 Chevrolet under the late model ride of Jerry Kemperman (9). To pass competitors at the racetrack, one had to use their front bumper to move the car in front of them out of the way, as demonstrated above. (Courtesy of Stan Kalwasinski.)

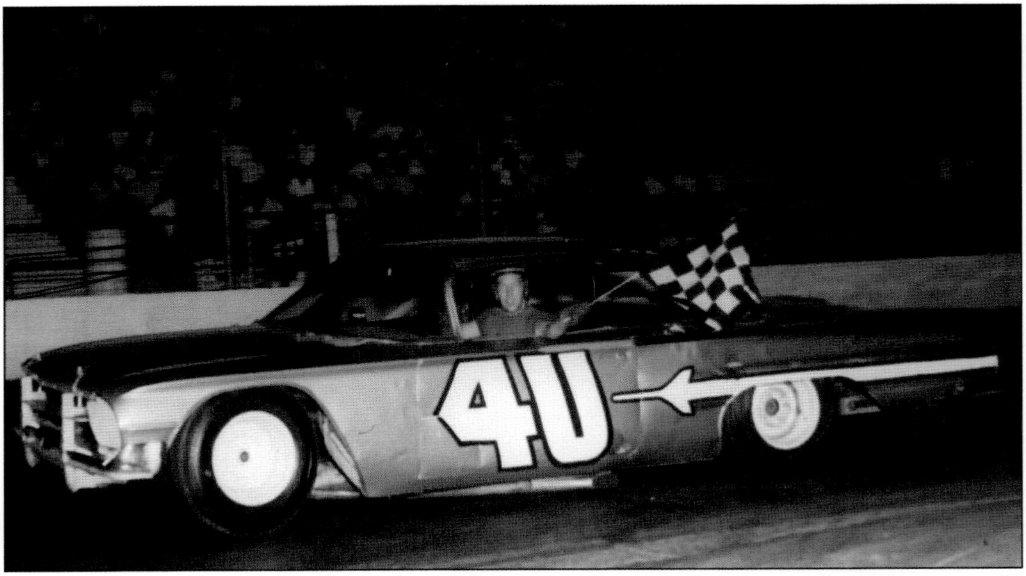

Stash Kullman's cars were always neat, detailed, clean, and well maintained. Kullman usually drove Chevrolets painted a shade of pink and trimmed in white, silver, and black. This 1963 example of his 1960 Chevrolet Impala (4U) shows the Stash Kullman touch. Kullman got his start in racing after winning the title to a race car during a dice game at a bar in Calumet City. In Kullman's first race, the steering wheel fell off his car and into his hands, resulting in a wreck with Johnny Schipper. After the cars were towed from the racing surface, Schipper began a fistfight with the rookie driver. (Courtesy of Stan Kalwasinski.)

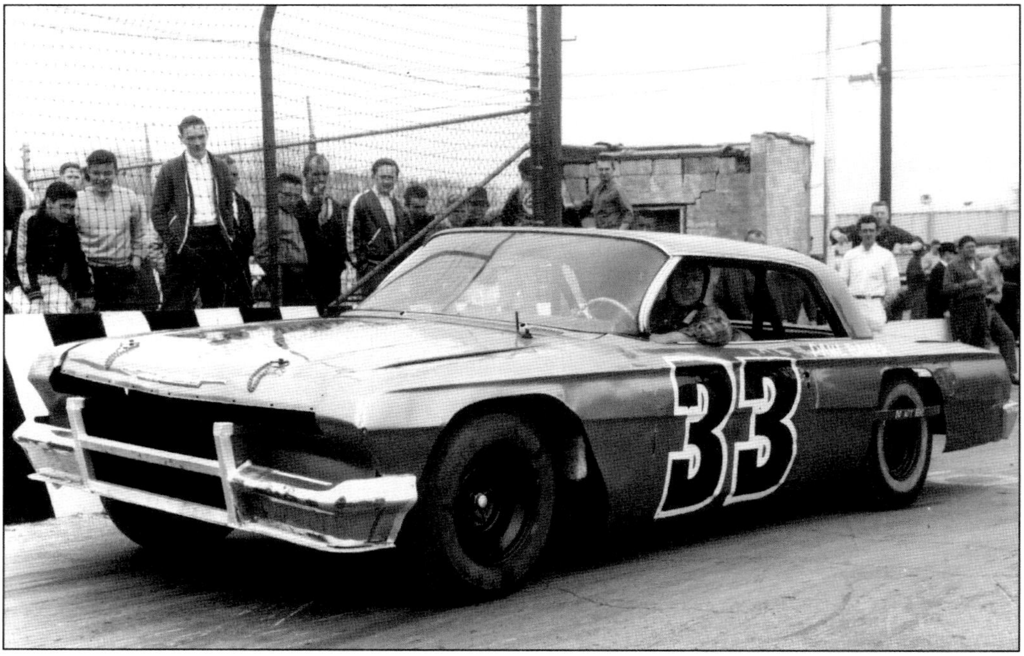

Paul Bauer (33), of Garden Homes, inches his 1962 Chevrolet onto the racetrack on 1964's opening day. Although he never won a track championship, Bauer was almost always at the front of the field in his more than 15 years of service at Raceway Park, and he even competed on the USAC tour in the early 1970s. (Courtesy of Stan Kalwasinski.)

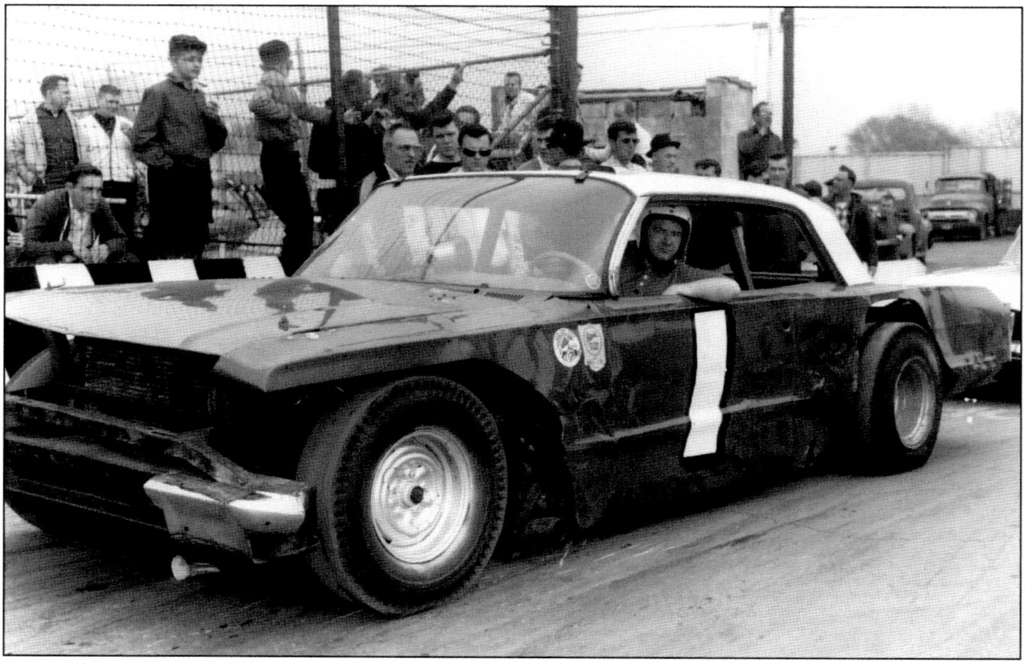

Living directly across the street from Raceway Park, Ted Janecyk (1) started racing at the speedway in 1953 with a 1941 Buick numbered 3T. Janecyk, shown here in 1964, is ready to qualify Bill Koenig's Chevy for an early-season event. Janecyk, the 1965 late model track champion, brought home 96 feature wins during his long driving career. (Courtesy of Stan Kalwasinski.)

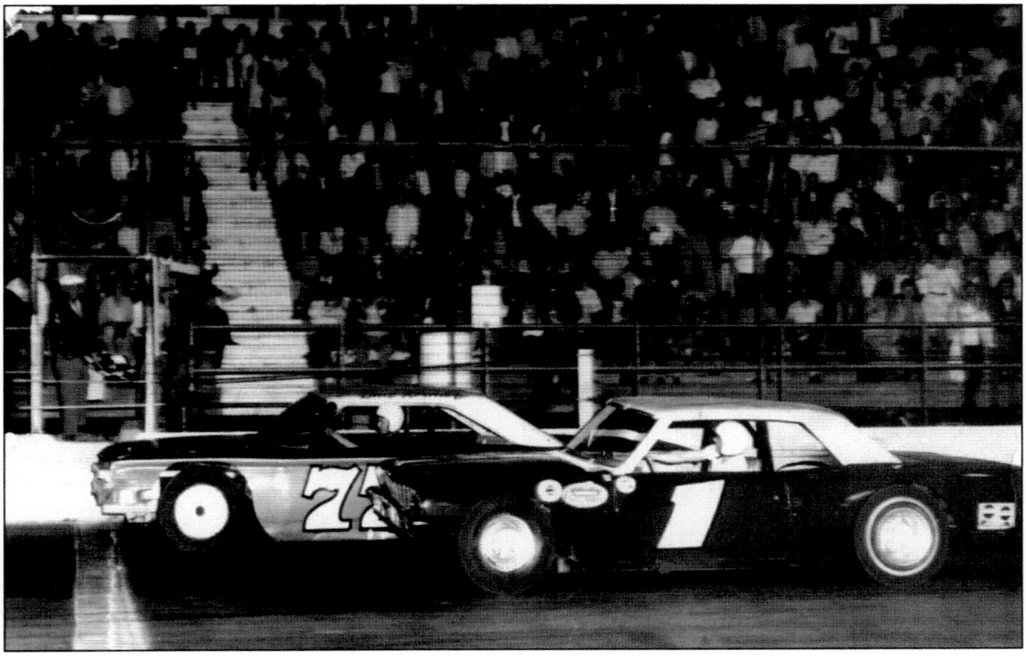

Bud Koehler (77) beats his rival Ted Janecyk (1) by only a couple of feet during a 1965 late model feature race. The crowd, a packed house, is on its feet as they watch this close race. Scenes like this were commonplace at Raceway Park during the 1950s, 1960s, and 1970s. (Courtesy of Paul Beck.)

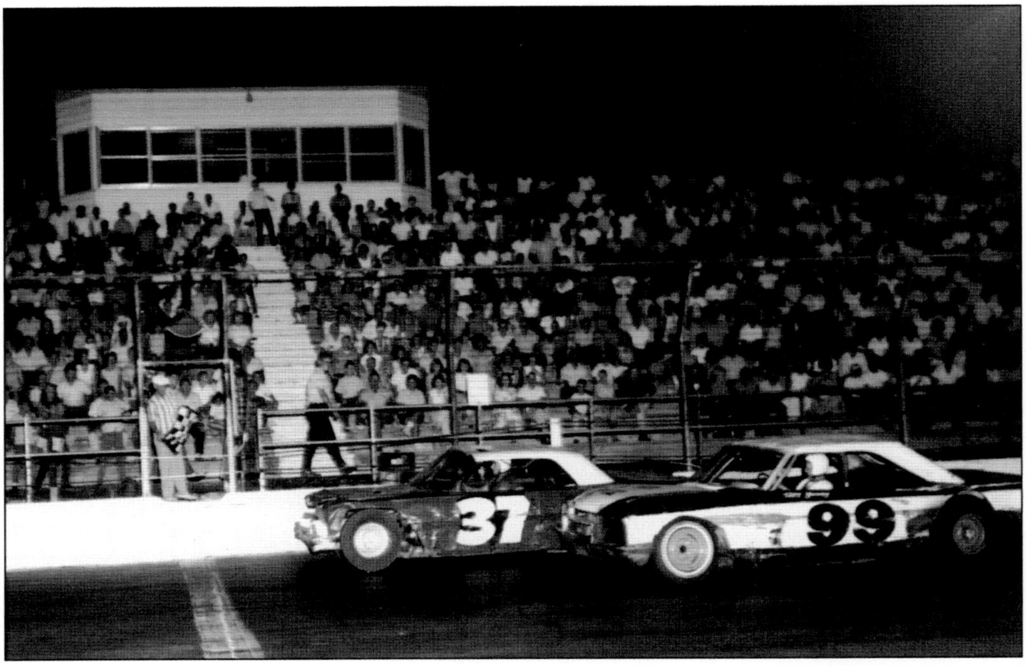

Johnny Kapovich in the Bill Koenig–owned 1963 Chevy (37) holds off Ray Young's 1964 Ford (99), taking starter Tom Plouzek's checkered flag in this 1964 scene. Kapovich wound up fourth in the final standings that year, with Young as the runner-up to champion Bud Koehler. (Courtesy of Stan Kalwasinski.)

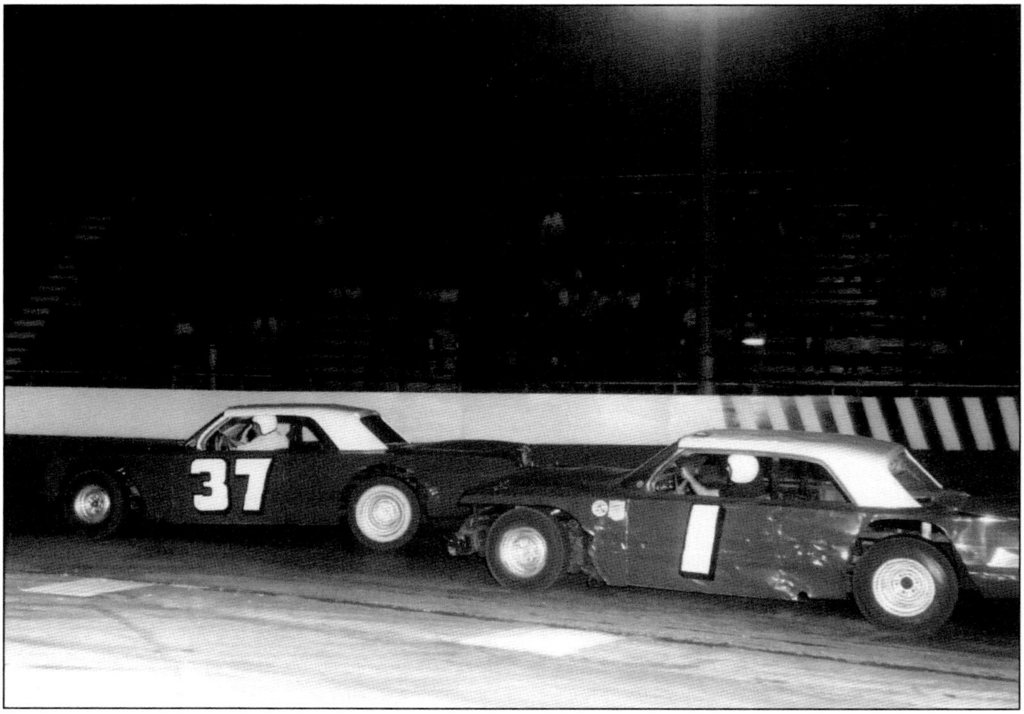

Bill Koenig provided cars for two top drivers in 1964. Johnny Kapovich (37) leads Ted Janecyk (1) in their nearly identical 1963 Chevrolet Impalas. (Courtesy of Stan Kalwasinski.)

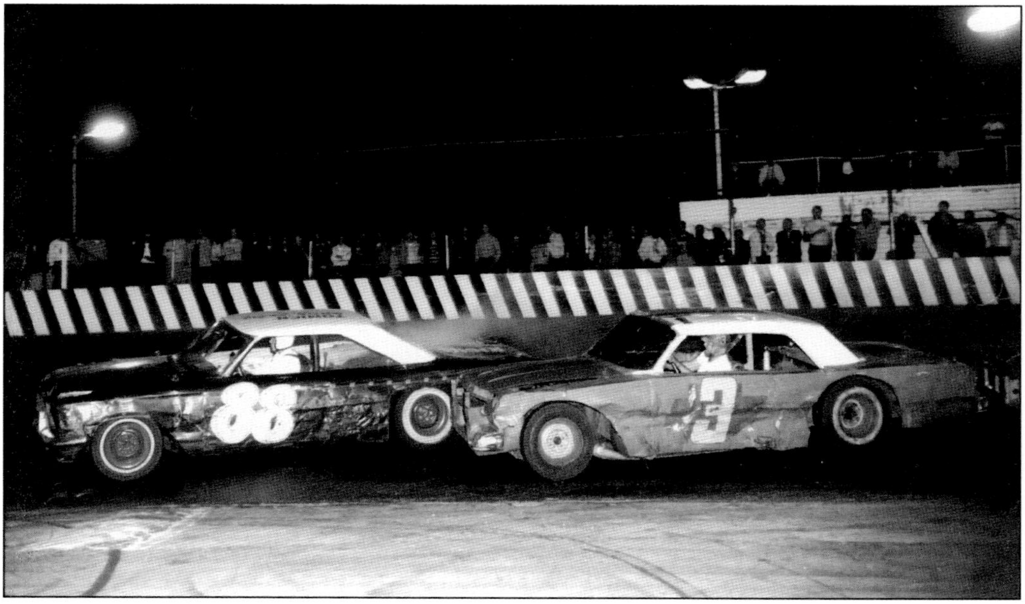

Jimmy Wray (88) feels the pressure from defending late model champion Bill Cornwall (3) during a 1964 racing program. Wray competed for just a handful of seasons in the 1960s, whereas Cornwall's career dated back to 1949. Cornwall's track championship honors in 1963 included 18 feature wins. Cornwall totaled 57 feature wins before his driving days at Raceway Park ended in the mid-1960s. (Courtesy of Stan Kalwasinski.)

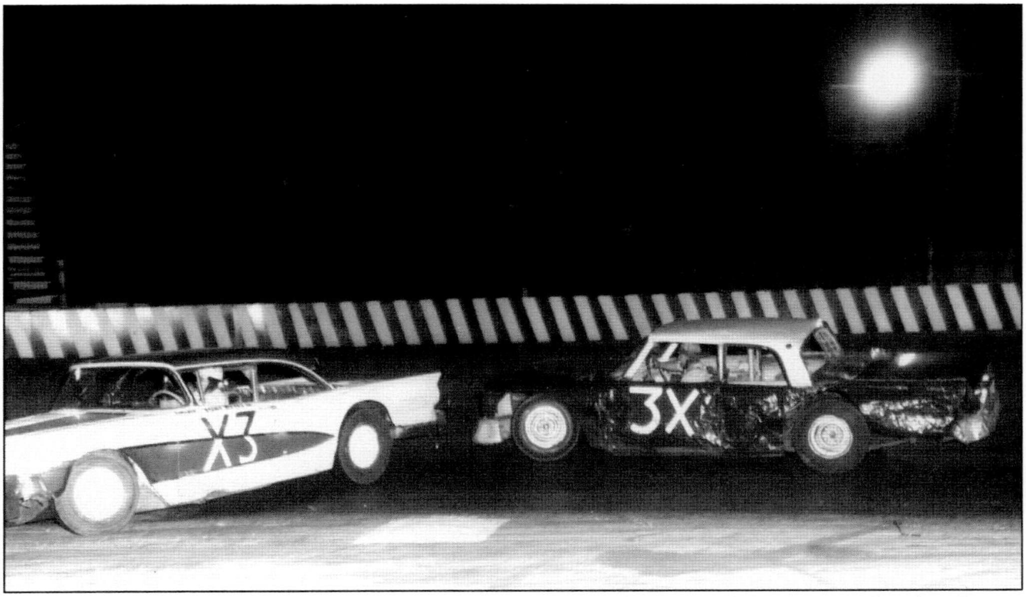

Sometimes the car numbers would get a little confusing, but a loyal fan knew who the drivers were. Tony Reyes (X3) starts to spin as cigar-chewing Johnny Schipper (3X) tries to avoid the spinning car during the 1964 season. Schipper was the police chief of Phoenix, a south suburb of Chicago. (Courtesy of Stan Kalwasinski.)

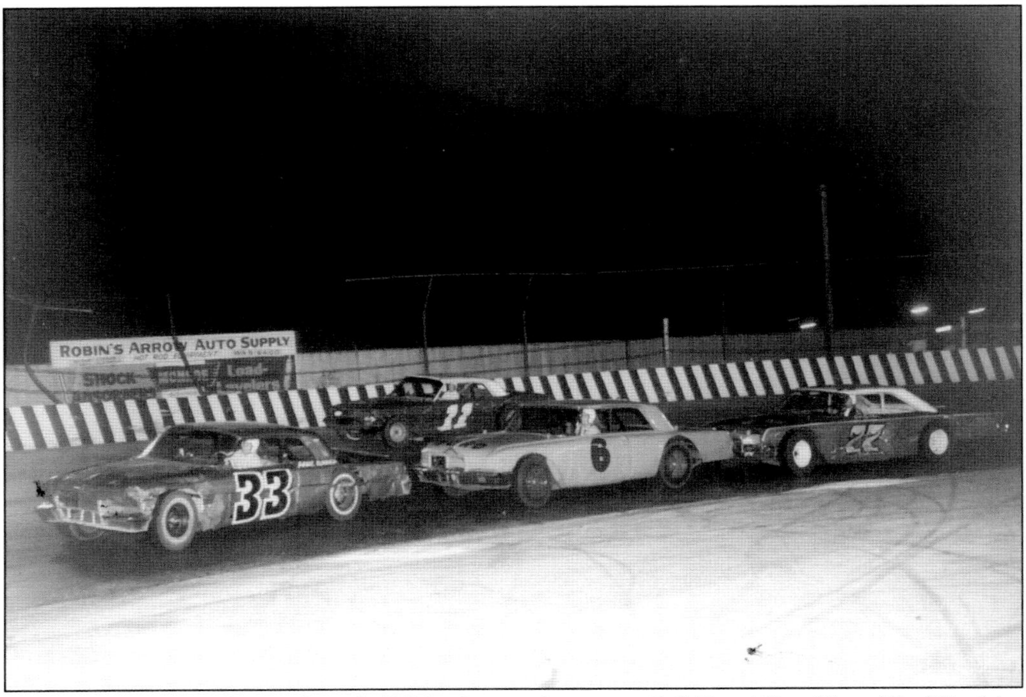

In this 1964 scene, Johnny Slowiak (33) leads past champions Bill Van Allen (6) and Bud Koehler (77), while Chuck Koenig (11) moves to the high side to let the faster cars pass him. (Courtesy of Stan Kalwasinski.)

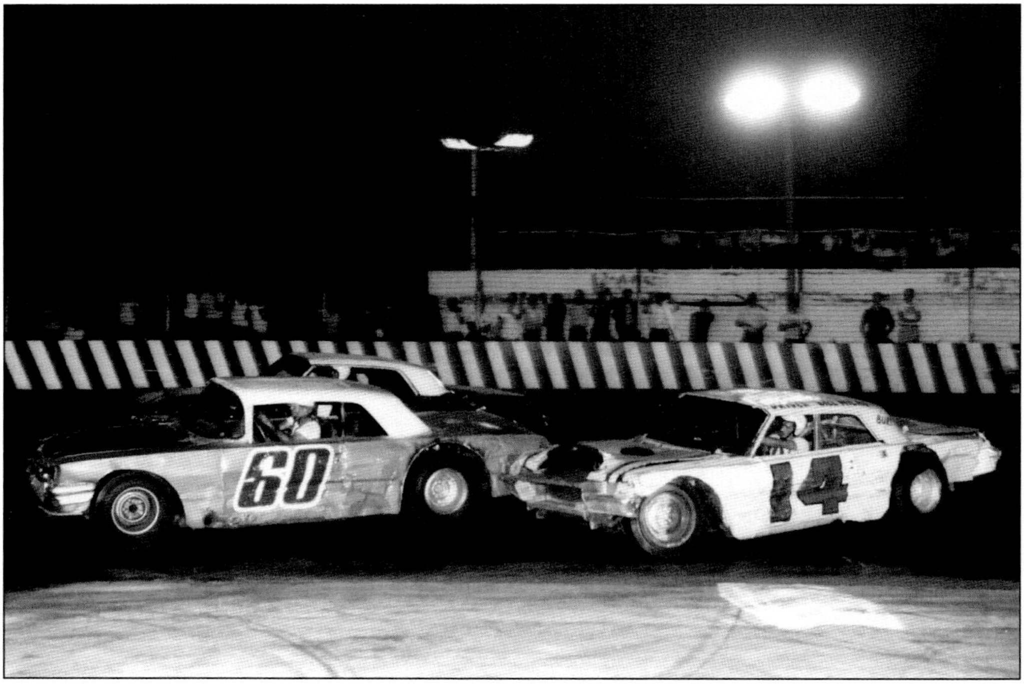

Johnny Squardo (60) and Bill Milan (14) have their hands full as the pair battle during 1964 late model action. Onlookers in the pits watch the battle from behind the safety fence. (Courtesy of Stan Kalwasinski.)

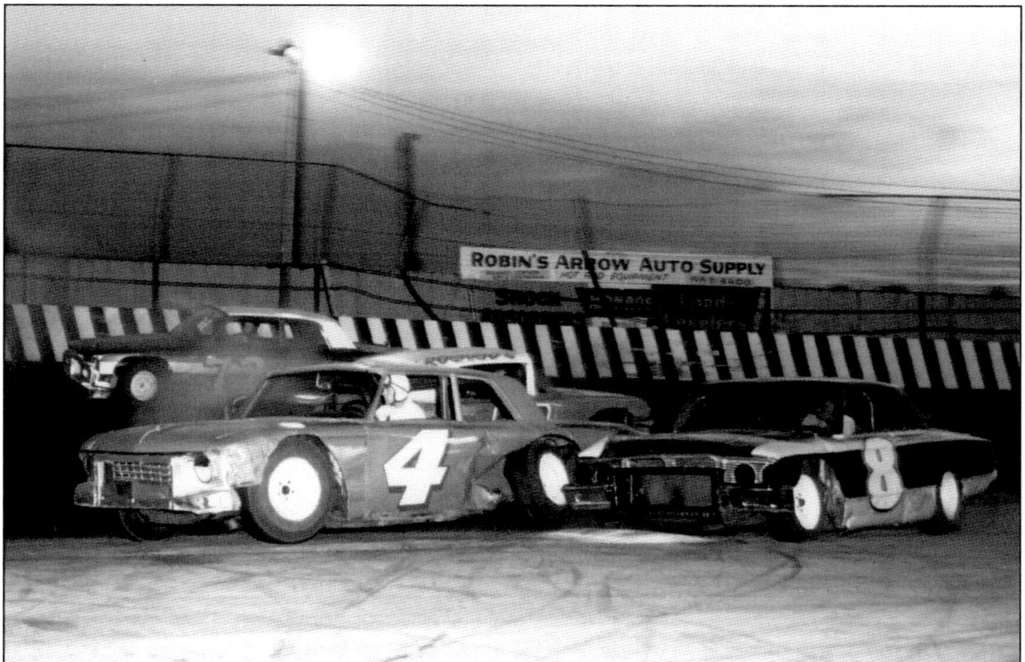

Norm Weltmeyer (8) gets into the left rear tire of George Neinhouse (4) as the pair try to slide inside of a spinning Johnny Squardo (60). George Young (72), brother of two-time track champion Ray Young, goes to the outside to avoid the wreck. (Courtesy of Stan Kalwasinski.)

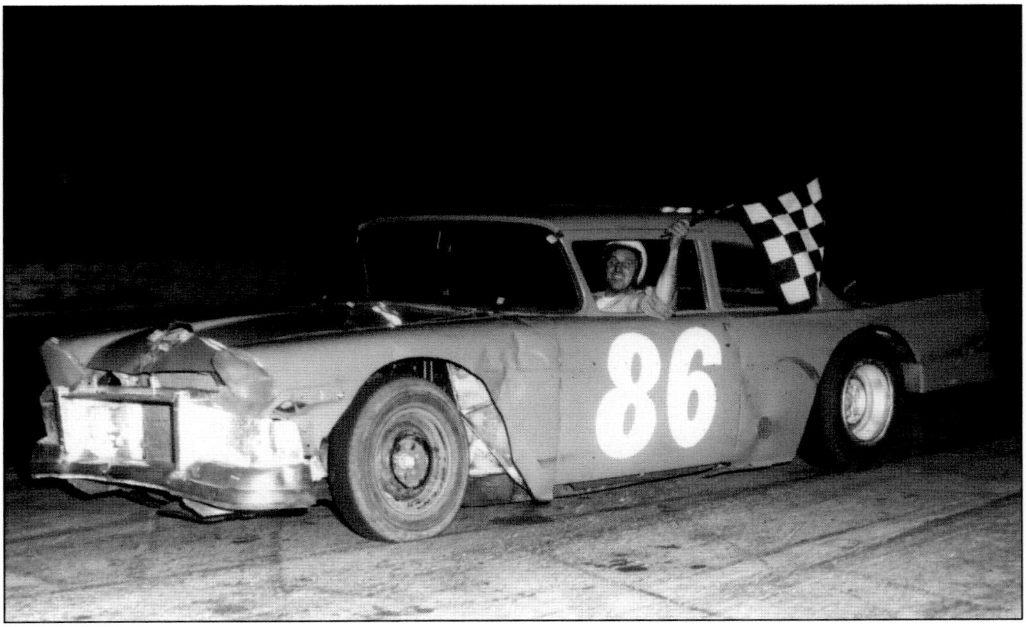

Don Oldenberg (86) was always among the front-running drivers at the track, with his first feature win dating back to 1950. Oldenberg competed in NASCAR and other national circuits in the 1950s, and he was crowned the 1955 national convertible champion of SAFE Circuit of Champions All Stars. Oldenberg and his rapid-running 1958 Ford are shown here after a 1964 victory. (Courtesy of Stan Kalwasinski.)

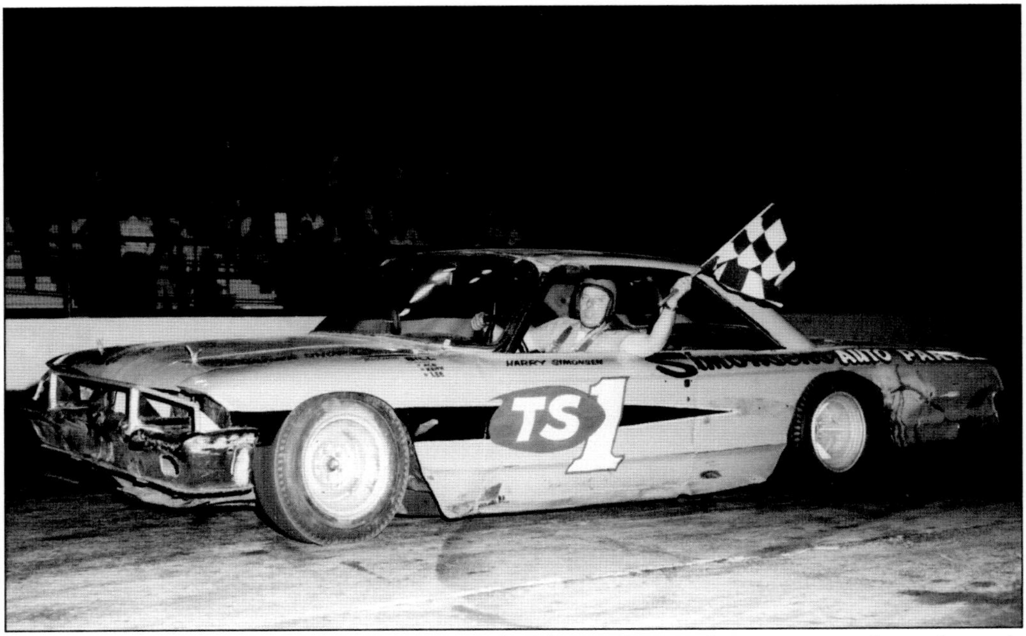

A Chicago auto parts dealer, Harry Simonsen (TS1) was always a front runner and popular with the fans. Simonsen was the track's late model champion in 1960 after a season-long battle with Bill Van Allen and others. Simonsen and his 1964 Ford are shown here with the checkered flag after a 1964 win. Simonsen's son Lee would begin competing in the late models around this time. (Courtesy of Stan Kalwasinski.)

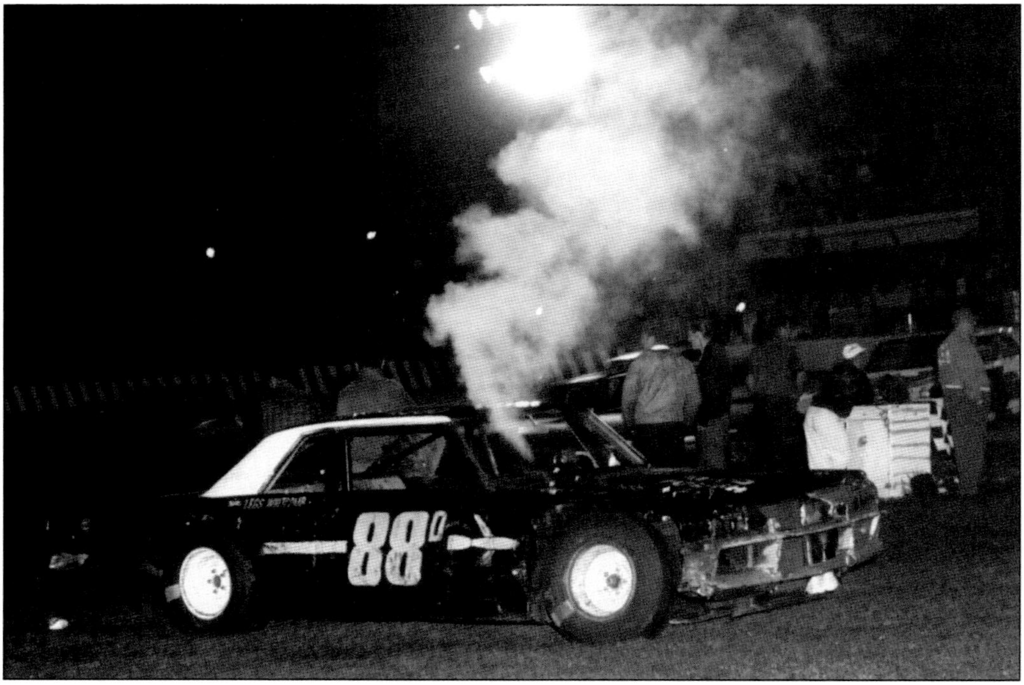

Although the action at Raceway would heat up as the night progressed, sometimes the cars would as well. Legs Whitcomb (88D) has parked his Oldsmobile Rocket 88 in the infield after succumbing to an overheated engine in this 1964 race. (Courtesy of Stan Kalwasinski.)

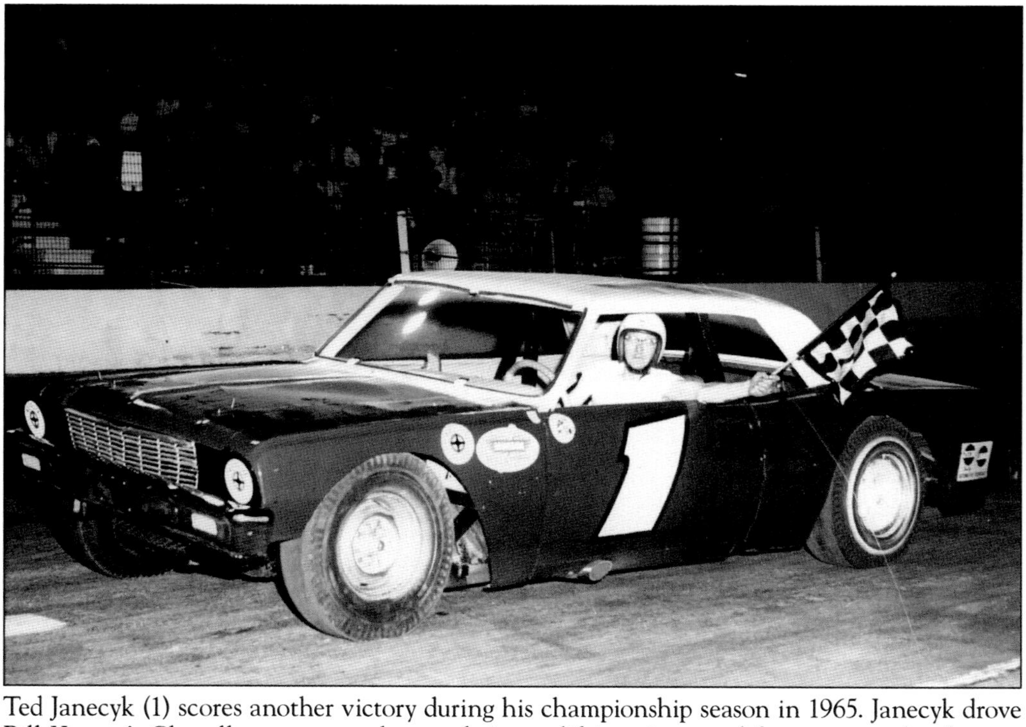

Ted Janecyk (1) scores another victory during his championship season in 1965. Janecyk drove Bill Koenig's Chevelle to new track records in qualifying times and feature wins, but he was replaced behind the wheel the following year by Bud Koehler. (Courtesy of Paul Beck.)

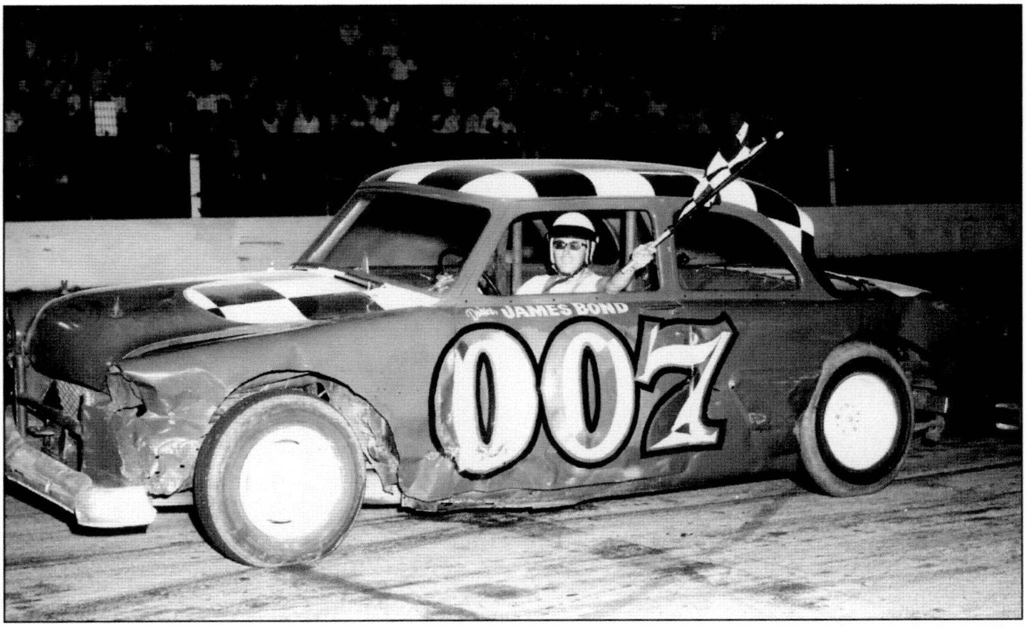

Blue Island sign painter and stock car lettering artist Dan Colyer competed at the track from the 1960s into the 1980s. Not wanting to let his mother know he was racing, Colyer drove under a number of aliases, including Boris Badenoff (or Badenov), James Bond, and, later in his career, Danny Duke. Colyer (007) is shown here in "James Bond trim" after scoring a win in his amateur division Ford in 1965. (Courtesy of Stan Kalwasinski.)

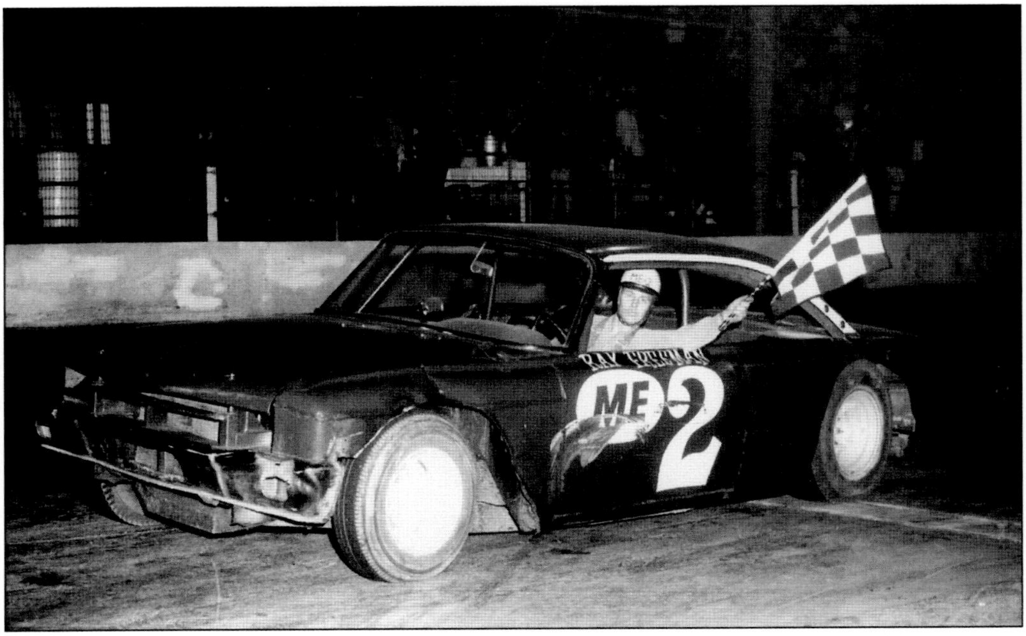

Ray Freeman of Crete was the track's late model champion in 1971. Freeman and his Camaro battled most of the year for the season championship honors with perennial track titlist Bud Koehler. Freeman, who began racing in the claiming division, won the track's annual 300 Lap Classic in 1968. Freeman is shown here in 1966 in one of his first late model cars (ME2), a Ford fastback. (Courtesy of Stan Kalwasinski.)

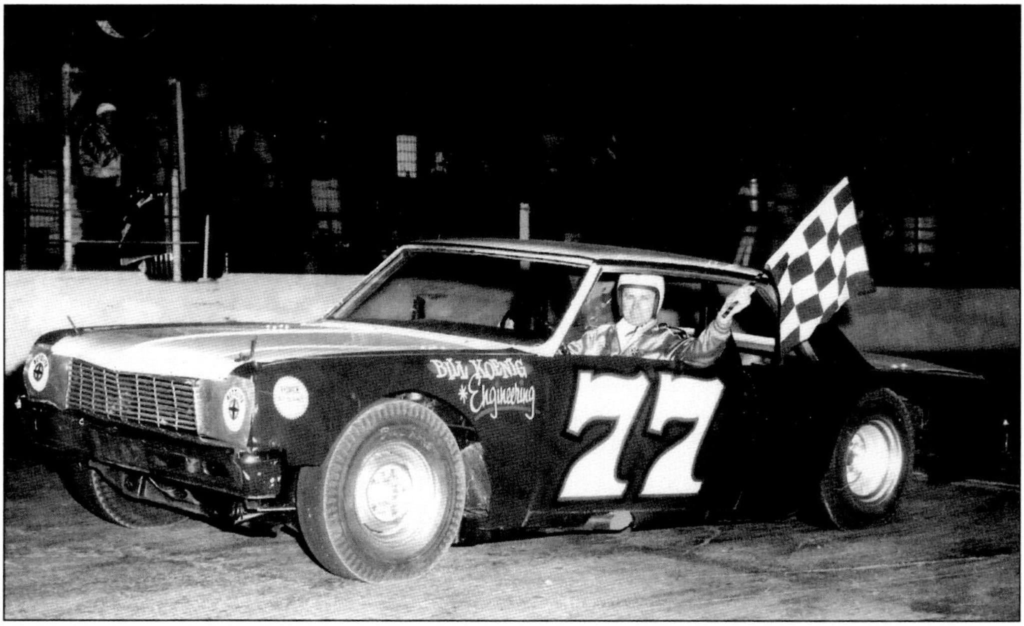

The track's perennial favorite, Bud Koehler (77) joined forces for the first time in 1966 with car owner Bill Koenig. The "K&K duo" made off with the late model track championship that year with Koehler winning 28 features. Koenig's front-running Chevelle carried Koehler to a record 30 wins in 1967. The Koehler/Koenig combo would win a total of six Raceway Park championship titles. (Courtesy of Stan Kalwasinski.)

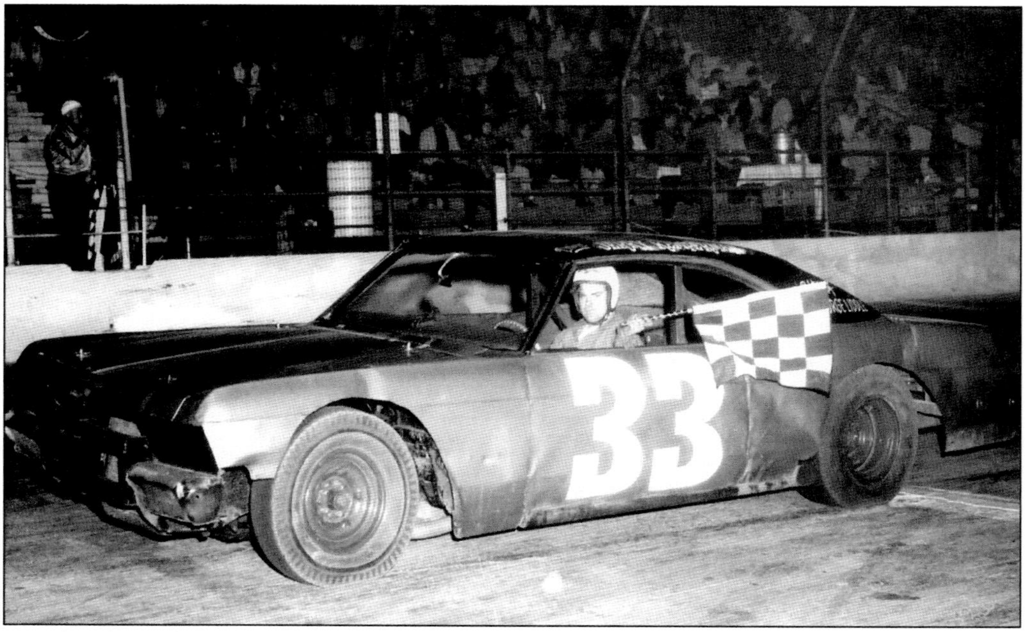

A railroad switchman for the Grand Trunk Western, Jerry Kemperman (33) won the 1968 track championship and 107 late model feature wins in his storied career. Shown here in 1966 with Paul Bauer's full-size 1966 Chevy, Kemperman whistled around Raceway Park at a tune of 12.70 seconds in this stock car on August 20, 1966, setting a new qualifying track record. (Courtesy of Stan Kalwasinski.)

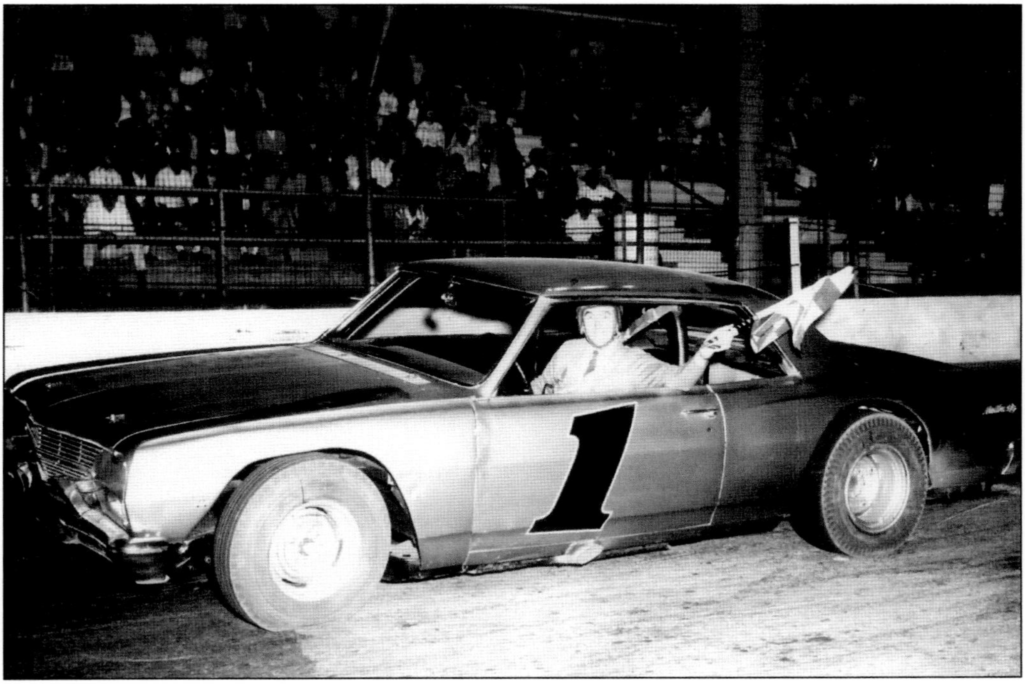

Bob Pronger (1) usually found a way to win. In this 1966 scene, he carries the checkered flag in his own car. The previous year, Pronger won four feature races in a row driving four different race cars. Now that is an amazing feat! (Courtesy of Stan Kalwasinski.)

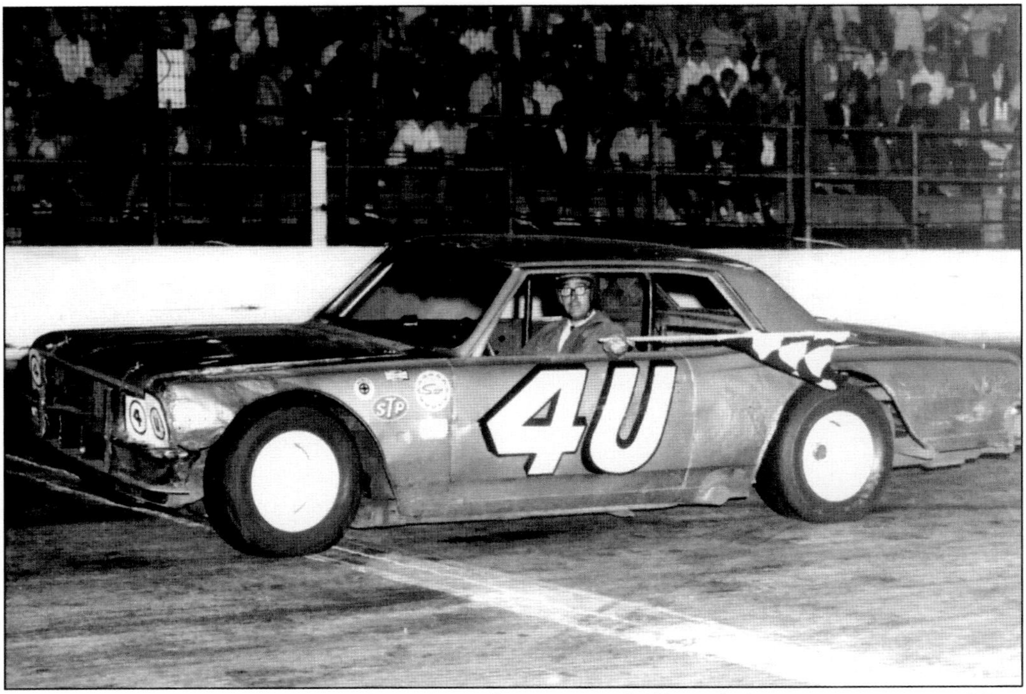

In 1967, Bob Pronger purchased Stash Kullman's car (4U) and drove it to victory. Note Pronger's driving uniform in both photos—a white dress shirt with a black necktie. (Courtesy of Stan Kalwasinski.)

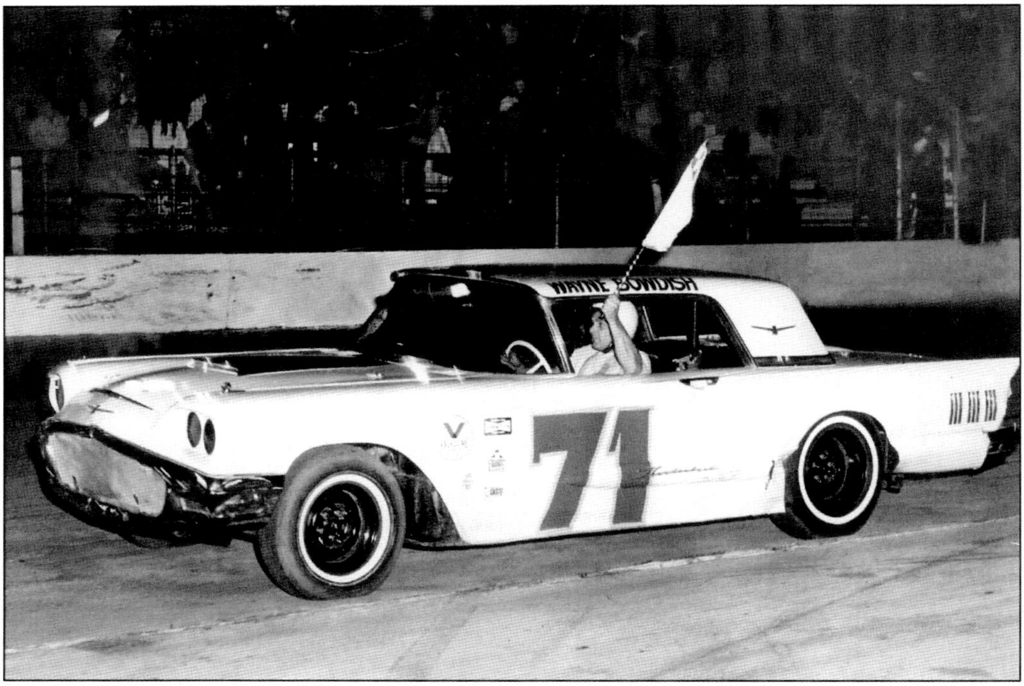

Wayne Bowdish (71) had a pretty, neat-looking Ford Thunderbird in competition in the novice division in 1967. Bowdish, a resident of Markham, was the track's rookie division champion in 1961. Records show that Bowdish won a career total of 24 non–late model feature races. (Courtesy of Stan Kalwasinski.)

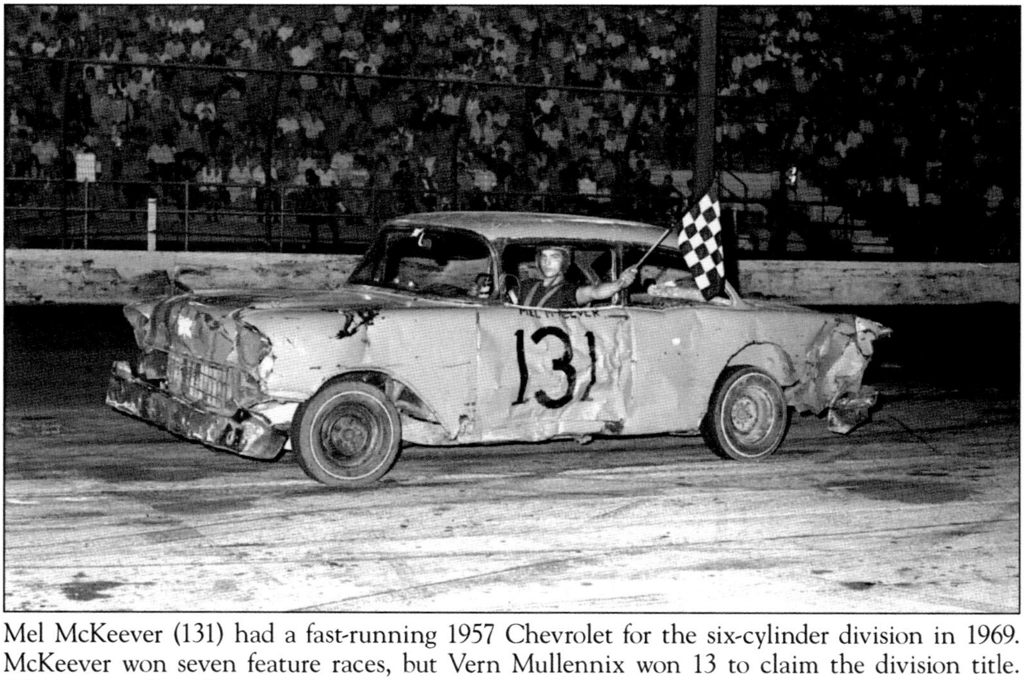

Mel McKeever (131) had a fast-running 1957 Chevrolet for the six-cylinder division in 1969. McKeever won seven feature races, but Vern Mullennix won 13 to claim the division title. (Courtesy to Stan Kalwasinski)

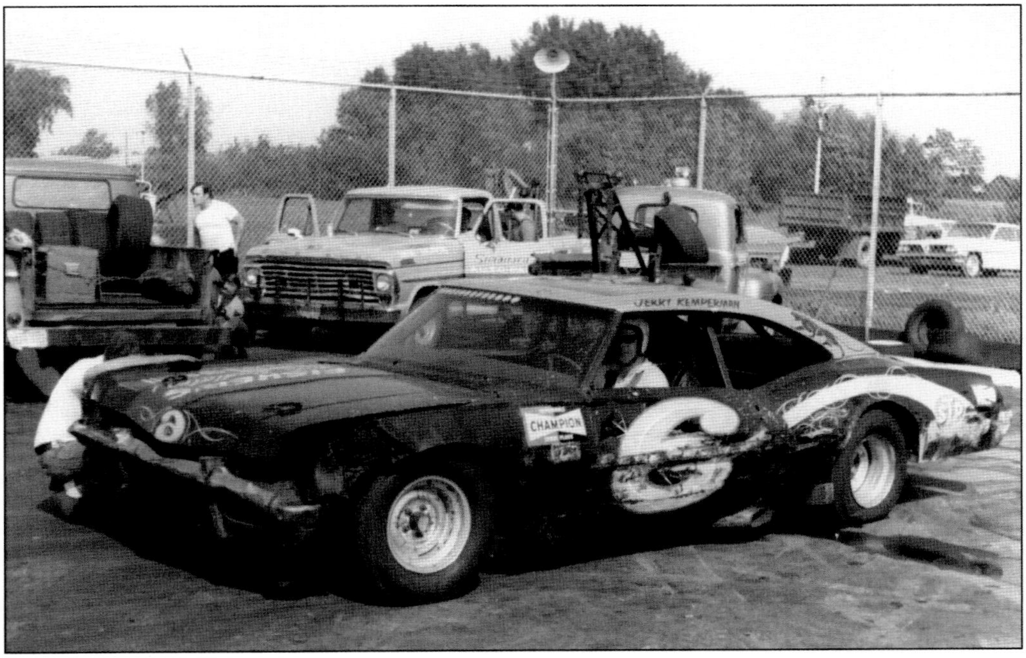

Ready to compete in the season finale, Jerry Kemperman sits in his Dave Roulo–prepared Chevrolet before the start of a Sunday-afternoon feature race. Another resident of Blue Island, Kemperman claimed late model track championship honors in 1968 and was always among the guys to beat when he competed at his home track. (Courtesy of Stan Kalwasinski.)

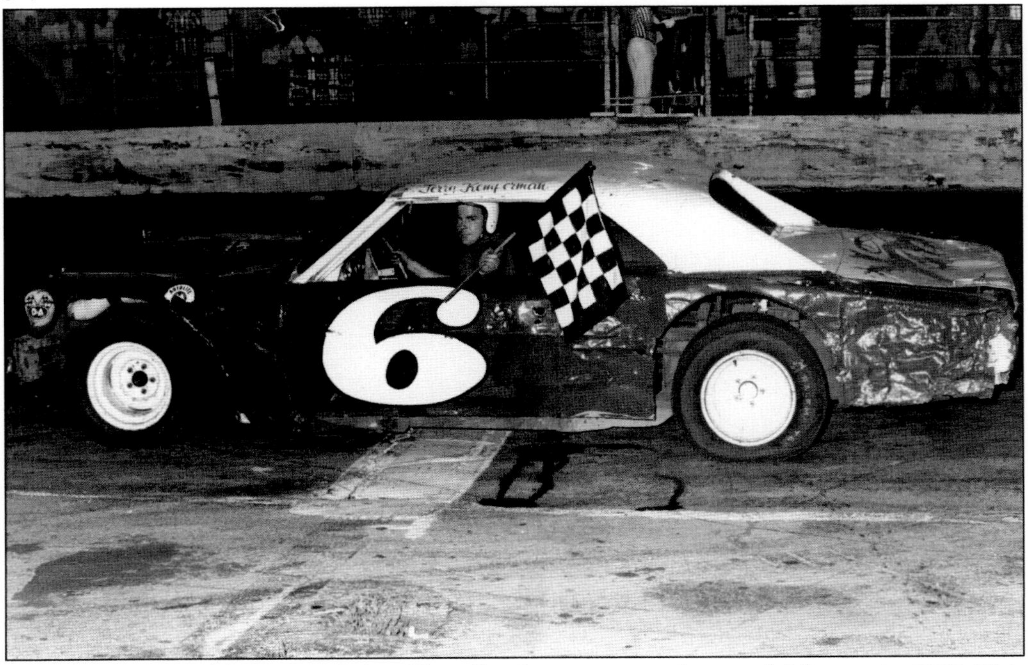

Jerry Kemperman (6) poses with his Chevelle after winning a late model feature in 1969. This car was the Bill Koenig–owned machine formerly driven by Bud Koehler, and the number 77 can still be seen bleeding through a fresh coat of red paint on the driver's door. (Courtesy of Stan Kalwasinski.)

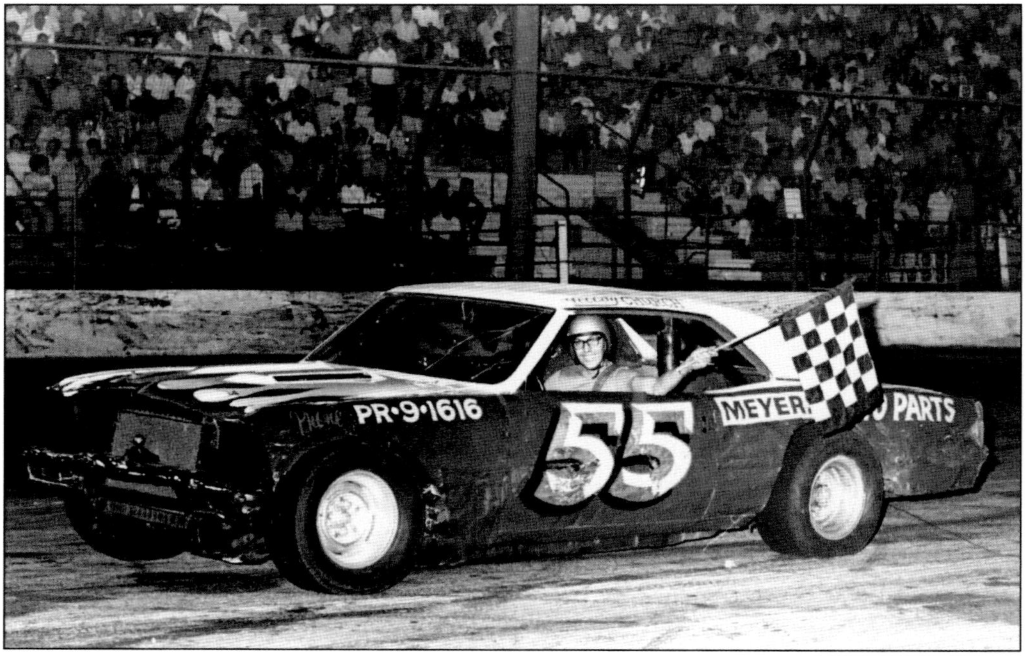

Returning from military service, Woody Church (55) purchased a ready-to-race Chevelle and returned to the racing action in 1969. Starting his racing career in 1965, Church, who raced Fords for most of his career, carries the checkered flag after a win during the 1969 season. (Courtesy of Stan Kalwasinski.)

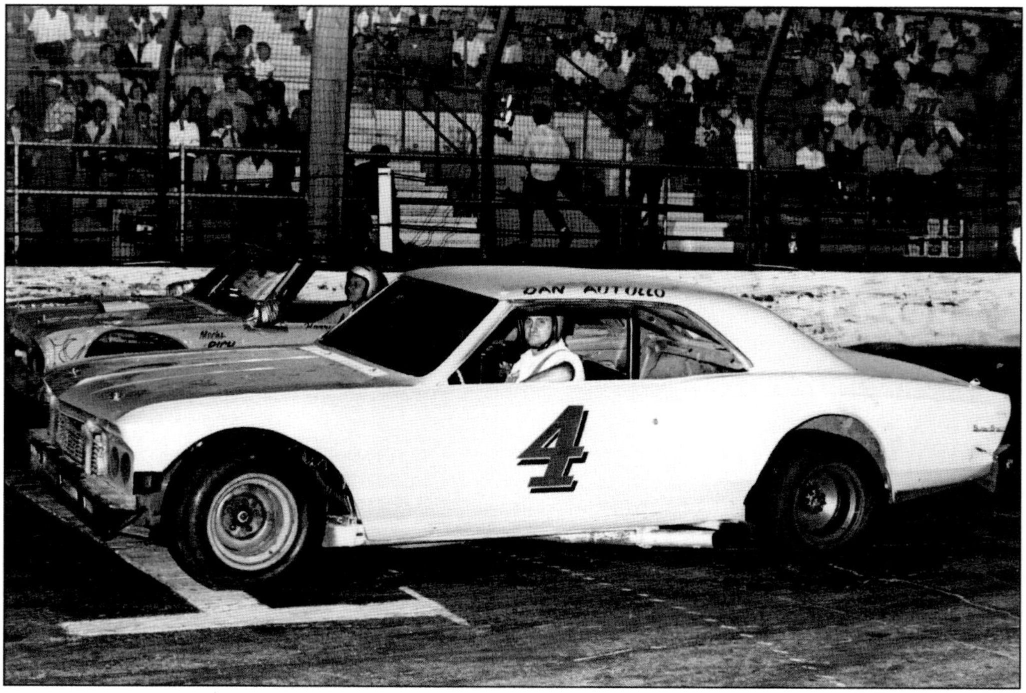

Chicago natives Dan Autullo (4) and Harry Simonsen (TS1) await the start of a 1969 late model race. Meister Brau beer, a Chicagoland favorite, was served at Raceway Park, as witnessed by the cases stacked near Tex, one of Raceway's beer vendors. (Courtesy of Stan Kalwasinski.)

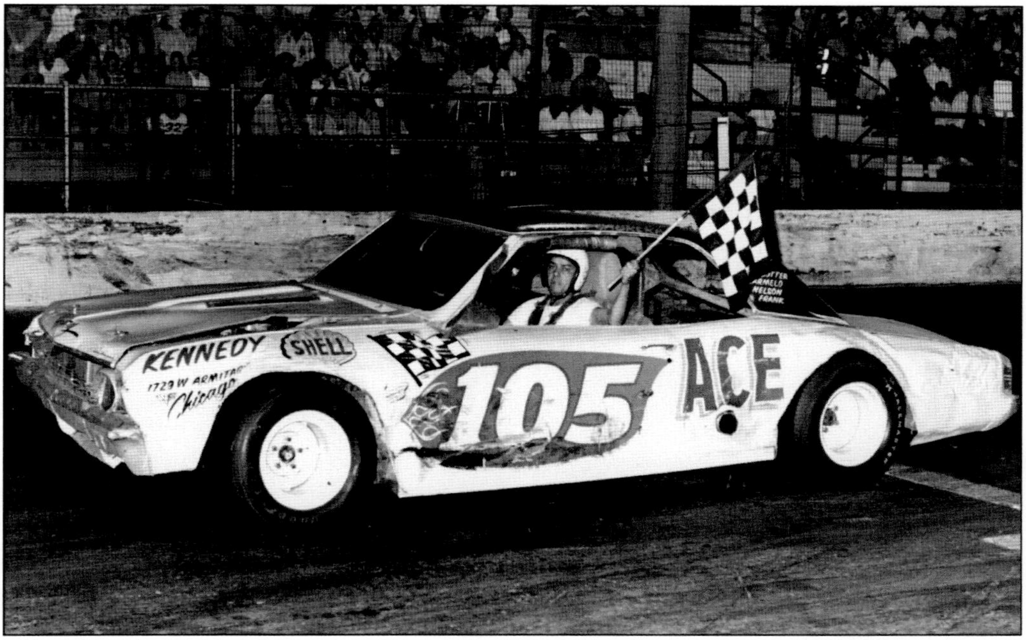

Frank Cabrera (105, above) celebrates a late model heat race victory in 1969. The celebration would not last long, as during the feature race, Cabrera would t-bone the car of rookie driver Howie Gast (7, below), fatally injuring Gast. Gast was a rookie late model driver in a car formerly driven by Lee Schuler. Gast spun out between turns one and two facing traffic and was struck by Cabrera while attempting to turn his car around. Although three midget drivers died during wrecks at Raceway Park, Gast was the only stock car driver to be killed at the racetrack. (Courtesy of Stan Kalwasinski.)

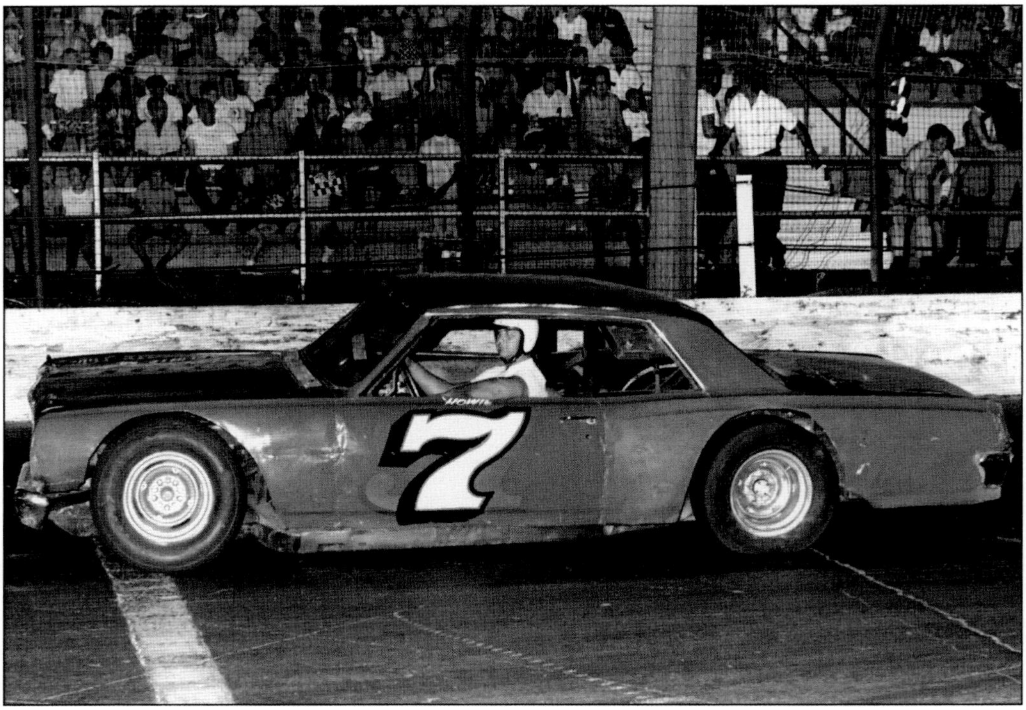

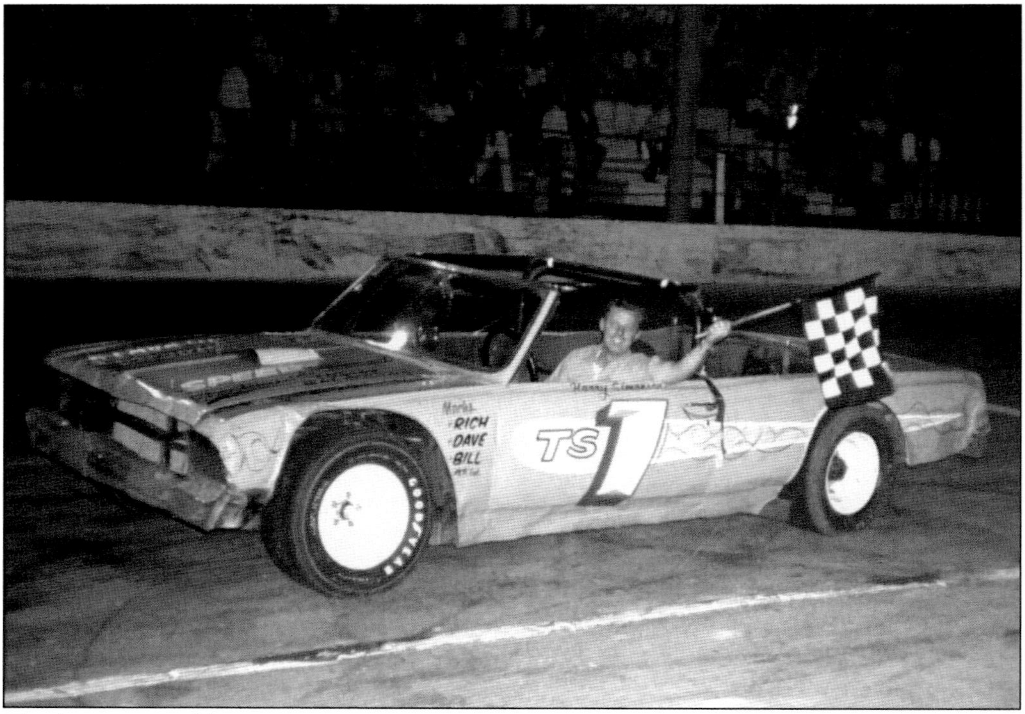

The last convertible in competition at Raceway Park was this Chevelle belonging to Harry Simonsen (TS1) in 1969. (Courtesy of Stan Kalwasinski.)

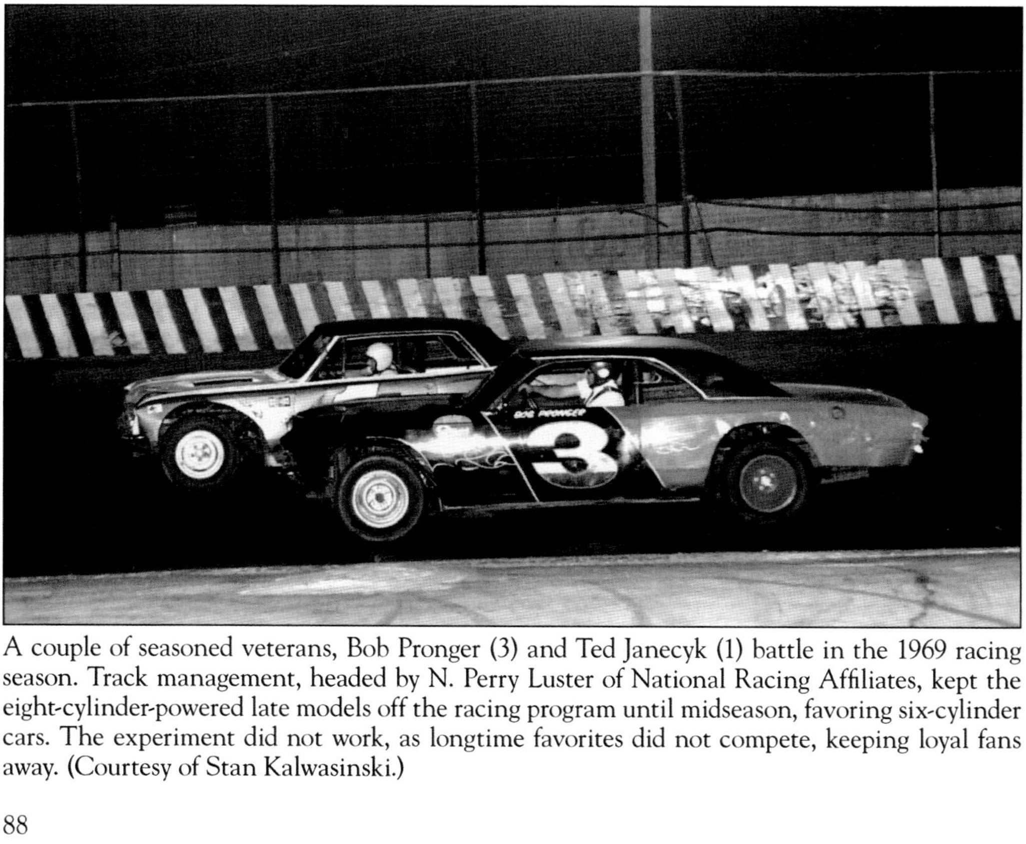

A couple of seasoned veterans, Bob Pronger (3) and Ted Janecyk (1) battle in the 1969 racing season. Track management, headed by N. Perry Luster of National Racing Affiliates, kept the eight-cylinder-powered late models off the racing program until midseason, favoring six-cylinder cars. The experiment did not work, as longtime favorites did not compete, keeping loyal fans away. (Courtesy of Stan Kalwasinski.)

Four

The 1970s

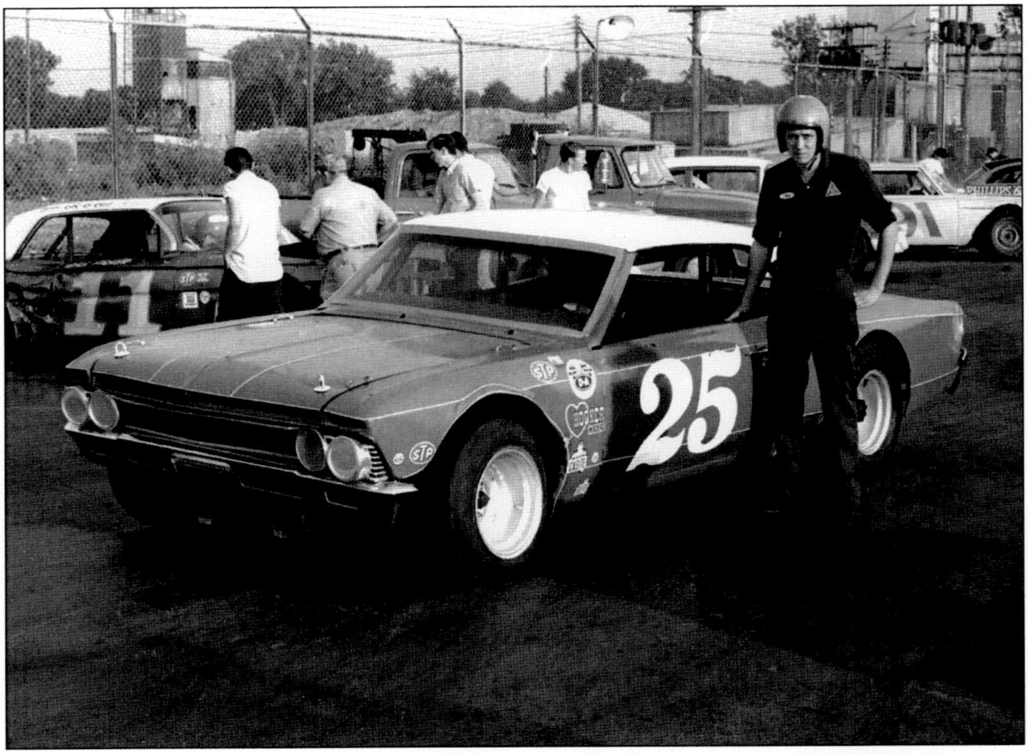

The 1970s ushered in a new era of racing. Pete Jenin took sole ownership and control of the track in 1970. The cars shifted from dealer-bought vehicles, modified in-house, to high-horsepower muscle cars custom built by various fabricating companies. Ray Para of East Hazel Crest poses proudly next to his 1966 Chevelle in the pits in 1970. Para was the terror of the track's amateur division in 1965, winning 21 features and taking home the overall division track championship. Moving into the late models in the late 1960s, Para would win 41 late model features at the speedway during his career. (Courtesy of Stan Kalwasinski.)

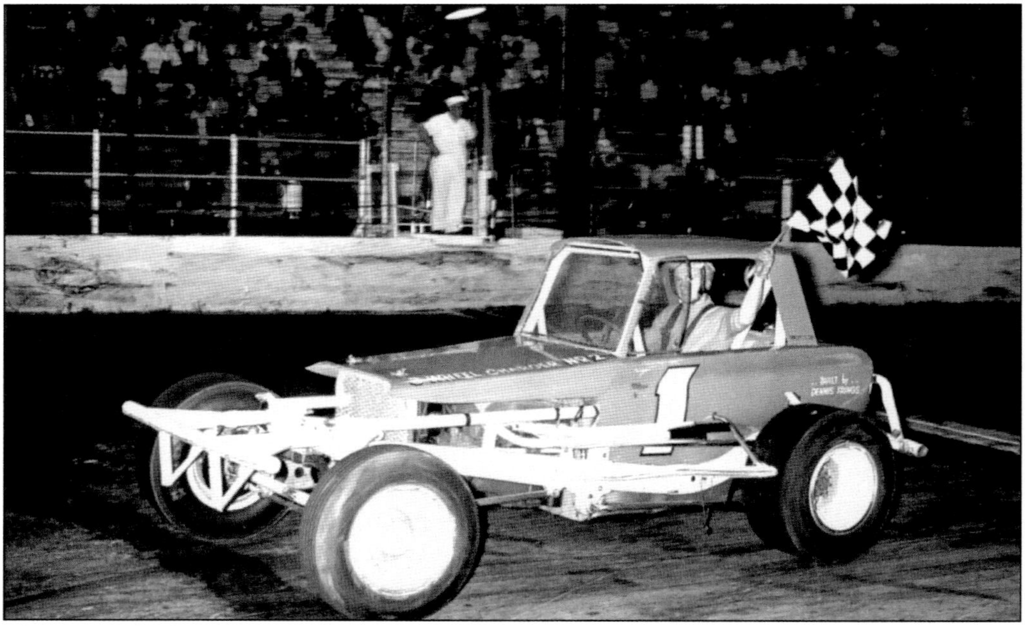

The open-wheel modified stock cars of the Interstate Racing Association (IRA) competed on a regular basis at Raceway in 1970 and 1971. With most of the competitors based in northern Illinois and southern Wisconsin, the association regulars were newcomers to the tight, paved oval. Al Schill (1), who is still racing late models in his home state of Wisconsin, is pictured here after a feature win in 1970. (Courtesy of Stan Kalwasinski.)

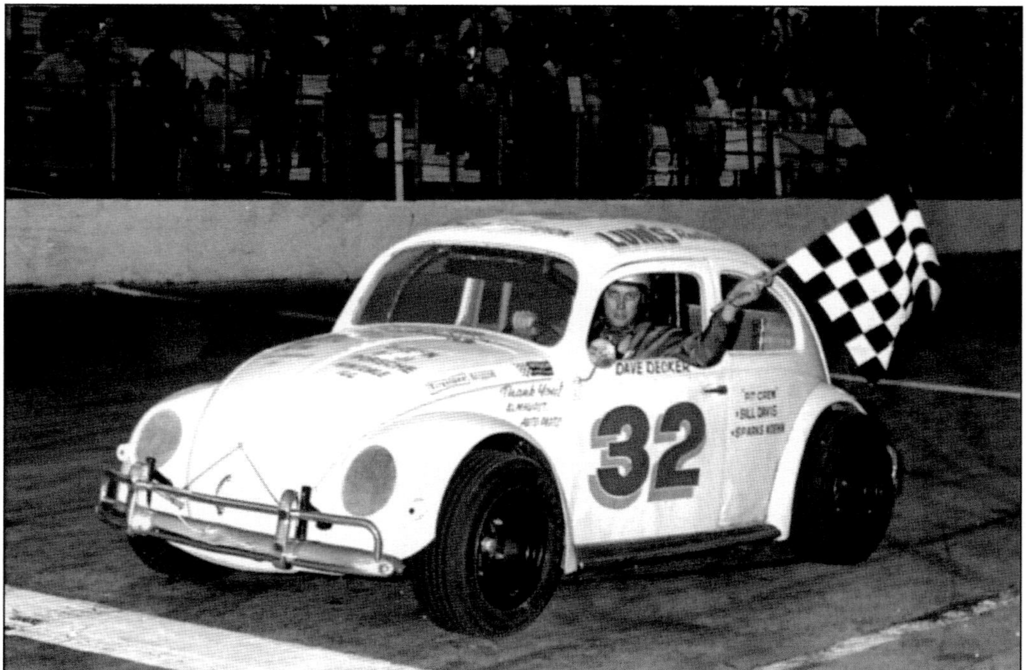

Dave Decker (32) drove his Volkswagen to the 1970 and 1971 ministock championships. Pictured here in 1970, Decker was seriously injured in a USAC event later in his career and never raced again. (Courtesy of Stan Kalwasinski.)

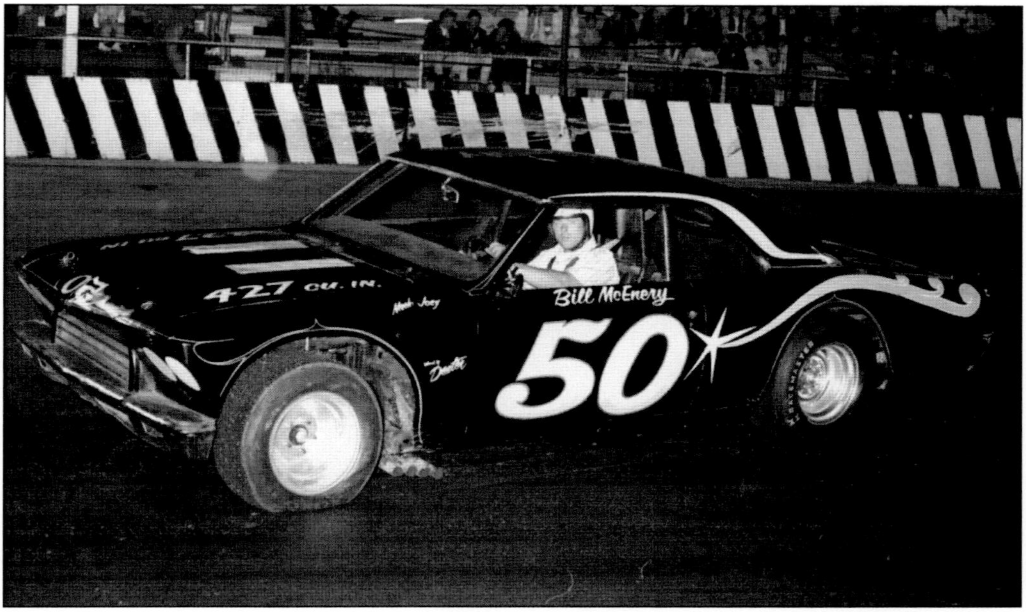

Bill McEnery (50), pictured here in 1970, began racing stock cars at Raceway Park in 1968. McEnery ended up scoring eight feature wins in his best season, 1972, when he finished third in the standings behind champion Bud Koehler and runner-up Ray Young. A successful entrepreneur, McEnery is the founder and owner of Gas City, a chain of gas stations in the Chicago area. (Courtesy of Stan Kalwasinski.)

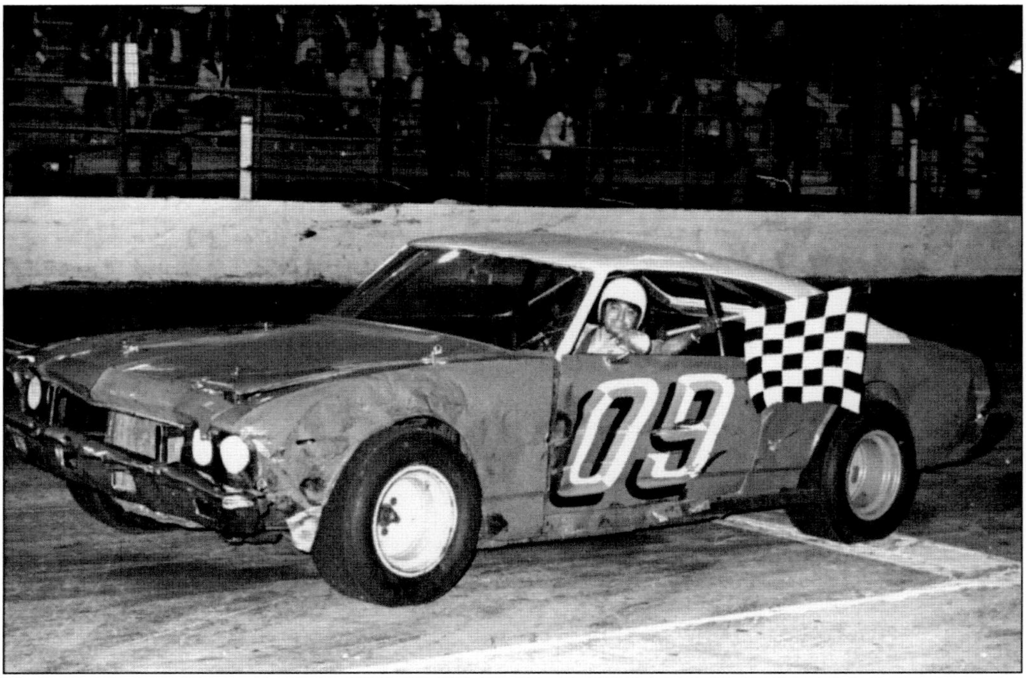

Marks Hernandez (09) drove under the alias of "Speedy Gonzales" and won one late model feature in his long driving career. Speedy used Raceway Park's inverted start to his advantage as he built up a big lead while faster cars behind him were caught up in traffic. Speedy's only feature win was very popular with the fans and is still talked about to this day. (Courtesy of Paul Beck.)

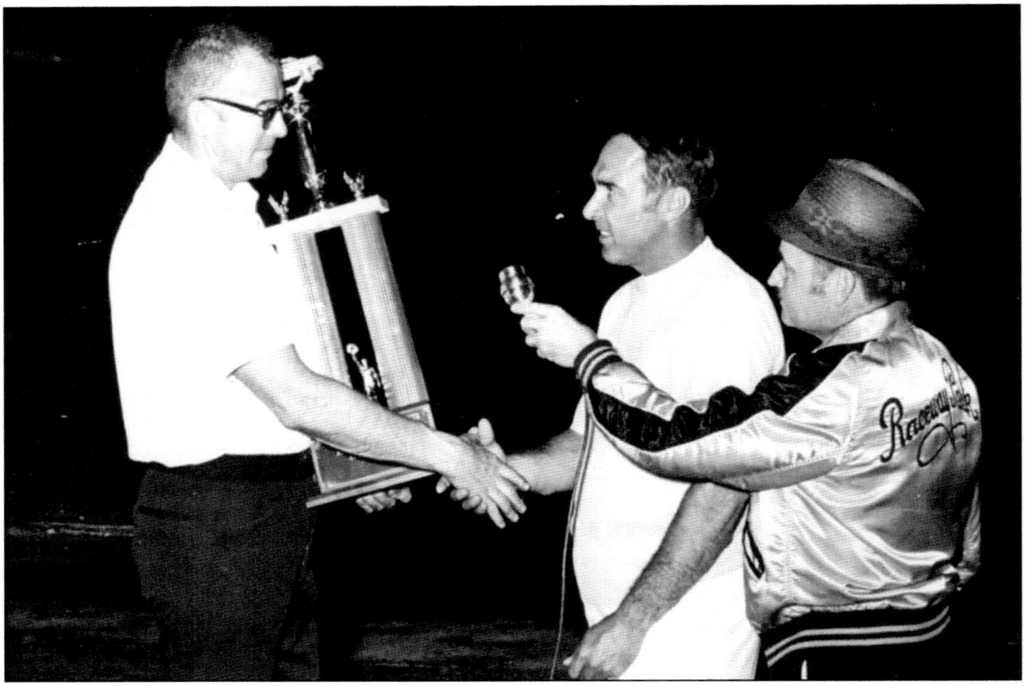

Bob Pronger accepts congratulations from Marv Berry of Watson-Berry Chrysler and Plymouth as announcer Wayne Adams conducts the postrace interview after another Pronger feature victory in the early 1970s. (Courtesy of Paul Beck.)

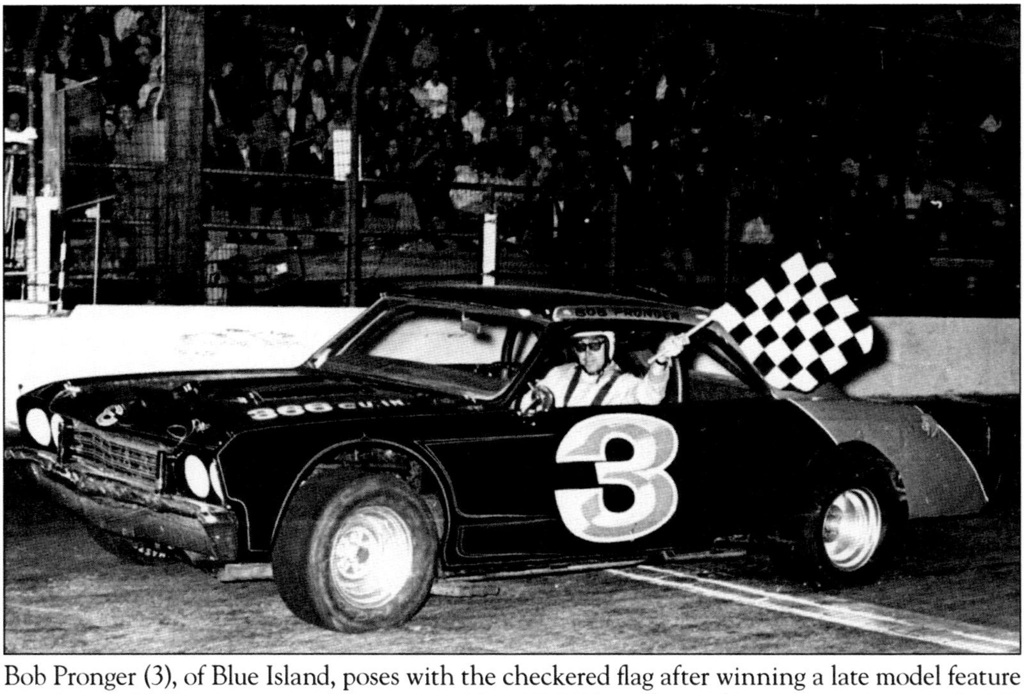

Bob Pronger (3), of Blue Island, poses with the checkered flag after winning a late model feature race in the 1970 racing season. Pronger and his 1967 Chevelle would go on to win a total of 13 features in 1970, but a young George Hill would upset Pronger and Bud Koehler to win the late model driving championship. (Courtesy of Paul Beck.)

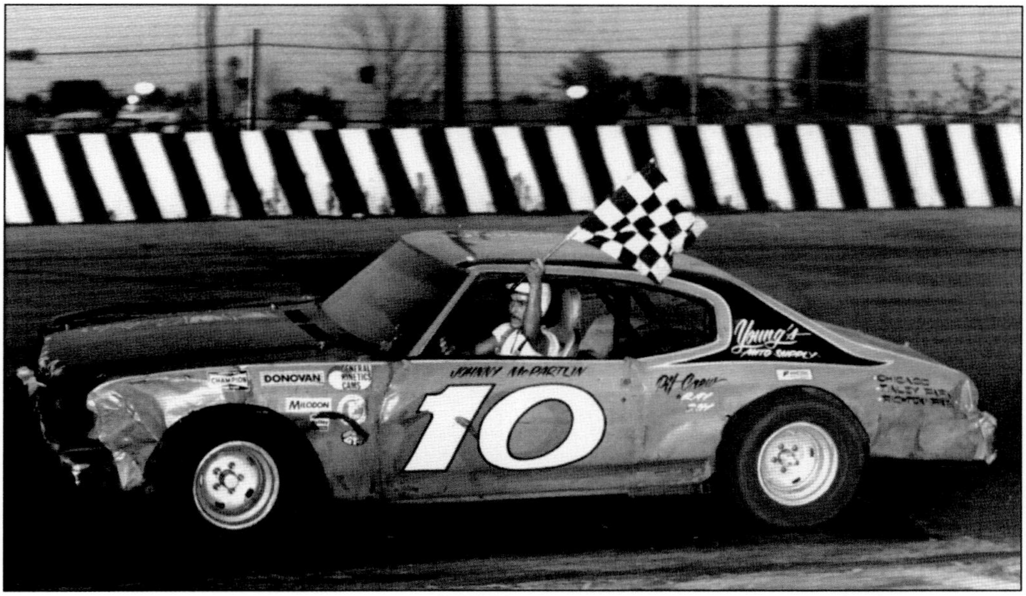

Johnny McPartlin (10) traded in a dragster for a stock car in the early 1970s and had a fair amount of success at Raceway Park. McPartlin grew up in Calumet Park, just a few blocks from Raceway Park, and scored one feature victory. McPartlin would go on to build engines for NASCAR's biggest stars after his driving career ended. McPartlin's son is a National Muscle Car Association (NMCA) drag-racing champion driving a car prepared by his father. (Courtesy of Stan Kalwasinski.)

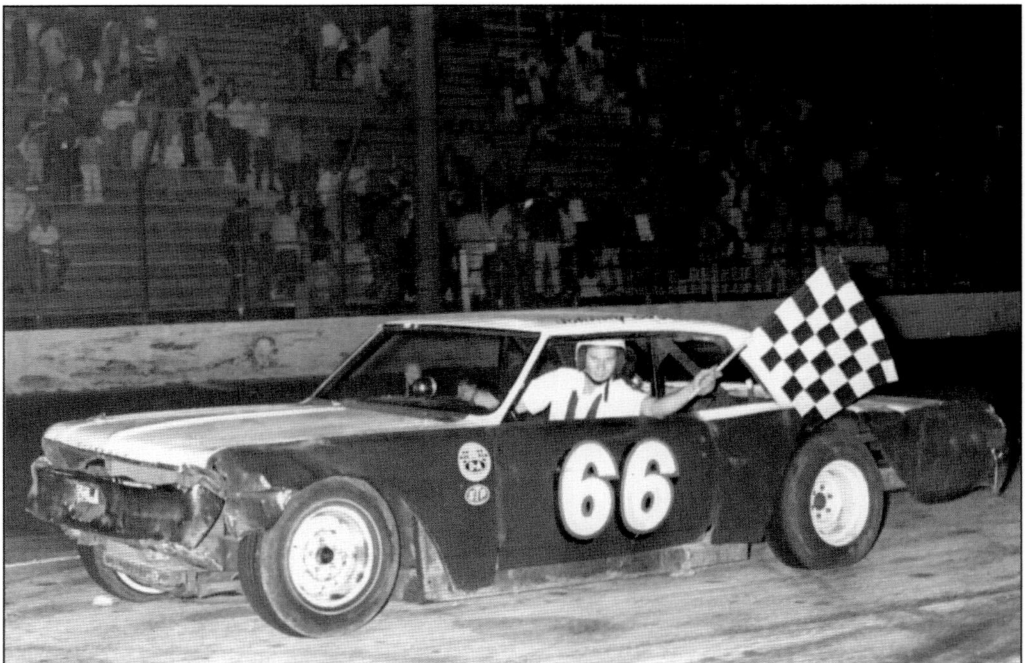

In 1970, Johnny Buben (66) was a tough competitor in the amateur division, driving a Chevelle. Buben won the Golden Knights championship in 1968, and he would later become the track scorer. (Courtesy of Stan Kalwasinski.)

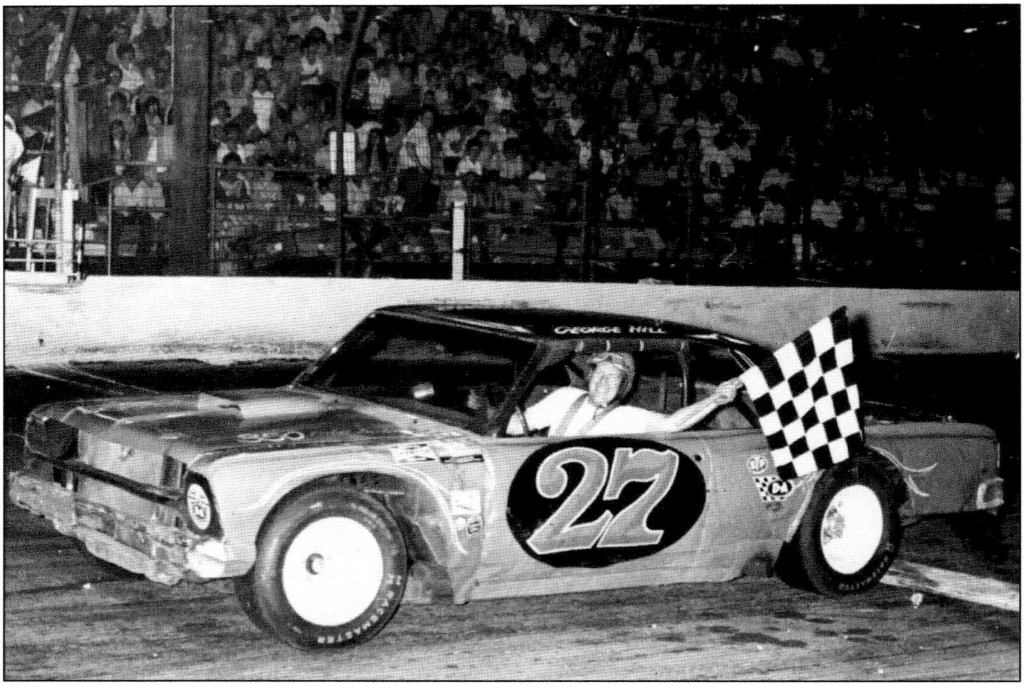

George Hill (27) enjoys another win during his 1970 championship season. The year 1970 also marked the new beginning of Pete Jenin's role as owner/promoter after two years of leasing Raceway Park to N. Perry Luster. (Courtesy of Paul Beck.)

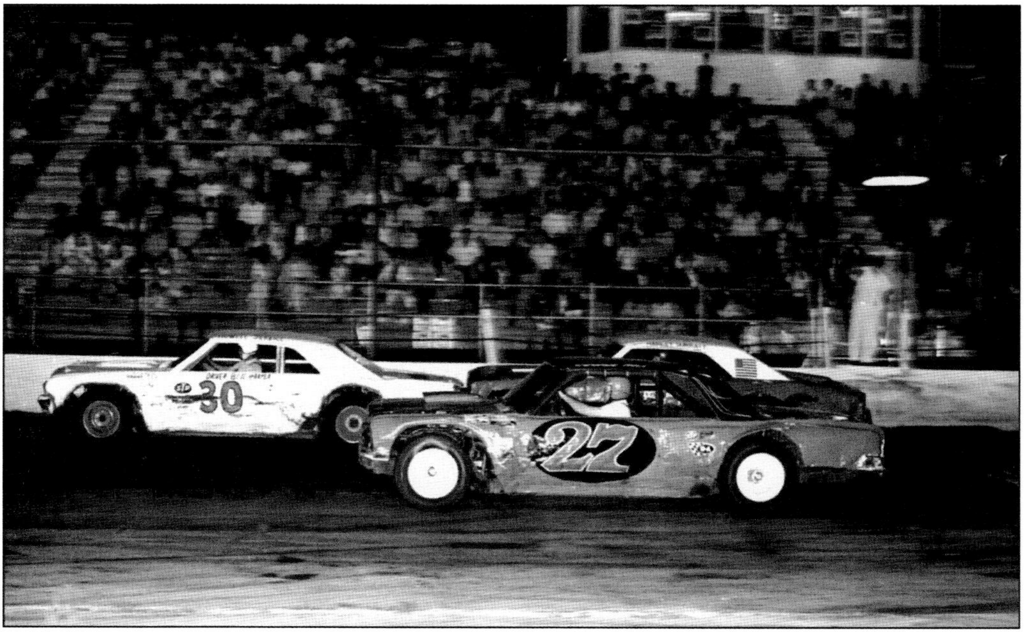

George Hill (27) passes Bill Harper (30) and Harley Surratt (45) on the inside lane in this 1970 racing scene. Hill won his first feature race and track championship in 1970, a feat that had only occurred once before. In 1960, Harry Simonsen, who sold the car that Hill drove to the 1970 championship, won his first feature race and also won the track championship in the same year. (Courtesy of Stan Kalwasinski.)

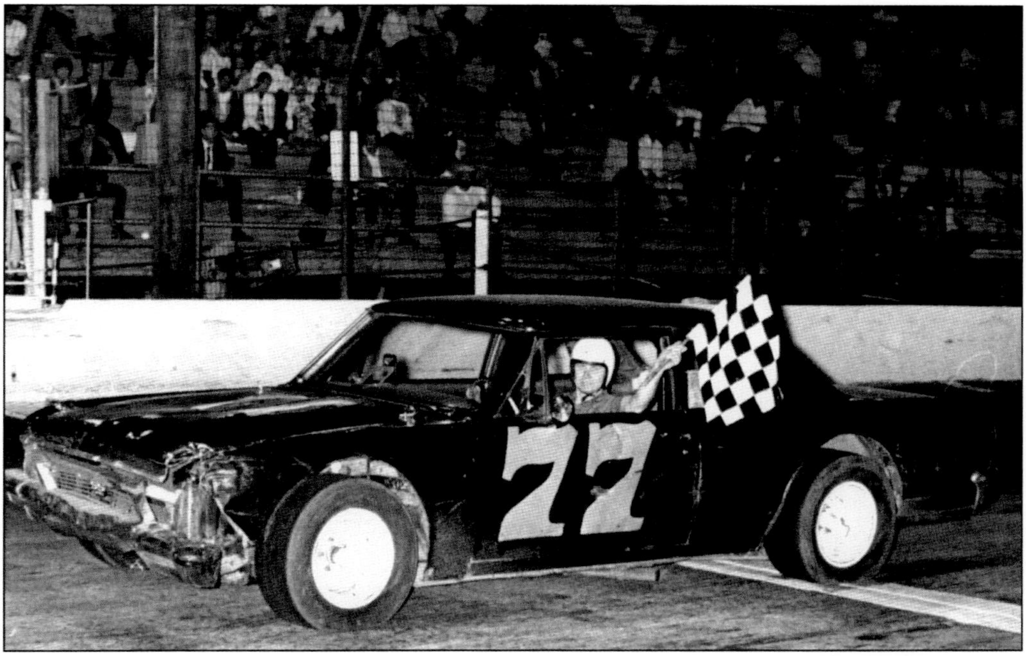

Over his 30-plus years of racing, 11-time track champion Bud Koehler (77), of Blue Island, drove cars that were painted red and white (and sometimes blue). The one exception to this standard was Koehler's 1970 late model ride, a 1965 Chevelle. Painted brown with silver numbers, Koehler struggled early in the season and won few races (above). After adding a spoiler and repainting the car to the customary red and white halfway through the season, the Bill Koenig–owned machine came to life (below). (Courtesy of Paul Beck.)

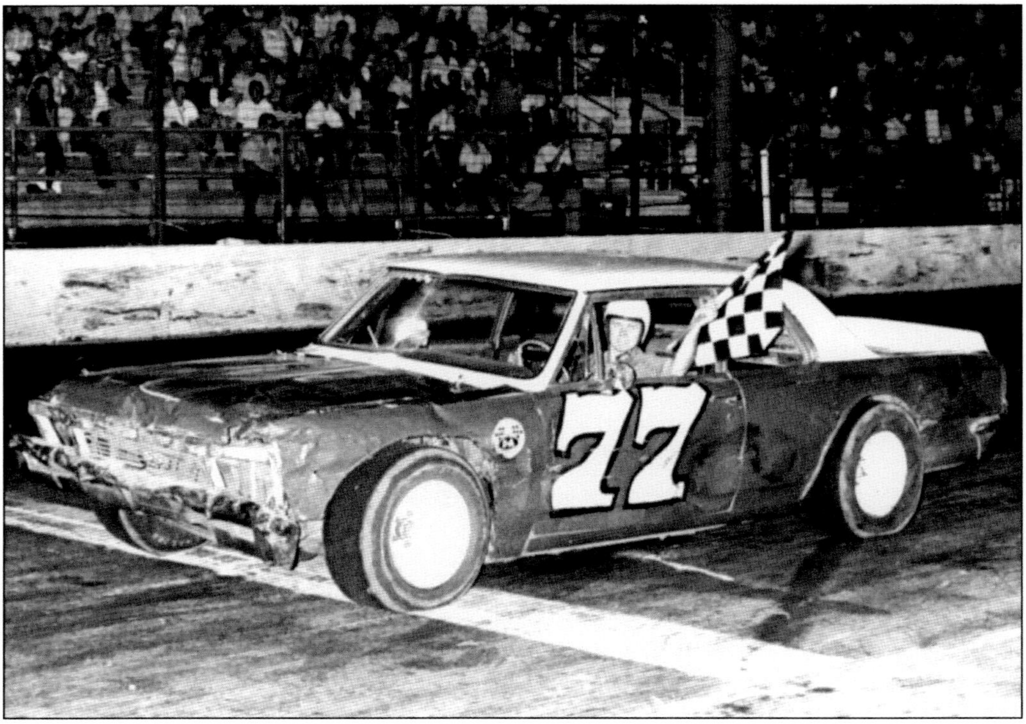

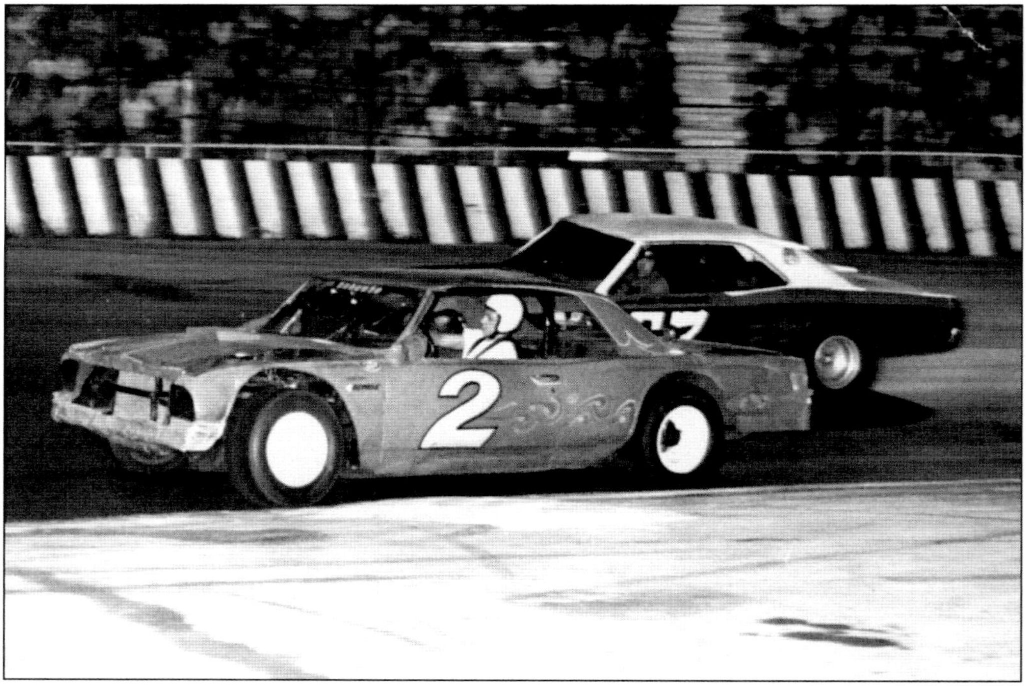

Gary Mitidiero (2), of South Holland, guides his 1965 Chevelle past the 1966 Chevelle of Bob Frederick (57) in this 1970 late model scene. Mitidiero would capture his first late model feature win in that year's 300 Lap Classic. (Courtesy of Paul Beck.)

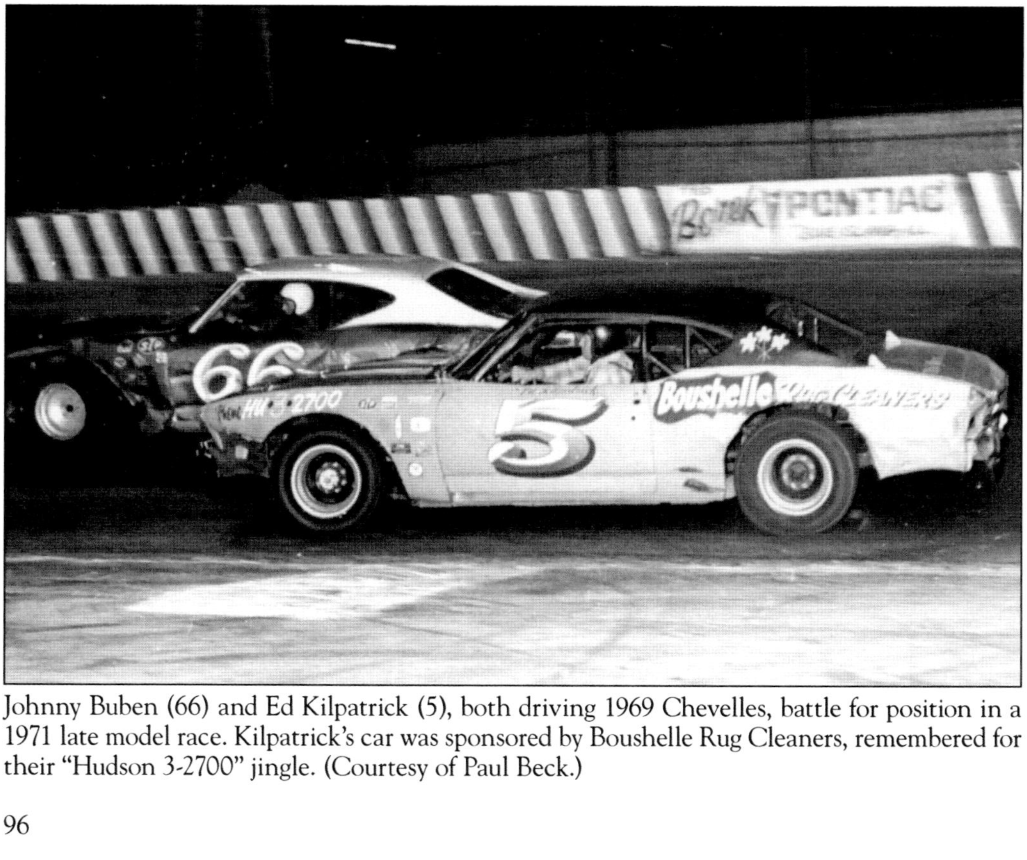

Johnny Buben (66) and Ed Kilpatrick (5), both driving 1969 Chevelles, battle for position in a 1971 late model race. Kilpatrick's car was sponsored by Boushelle Rug Cleaners, remembered for their "Hudson 3-2700" jingle. (Courtesy of Paul Beck.)

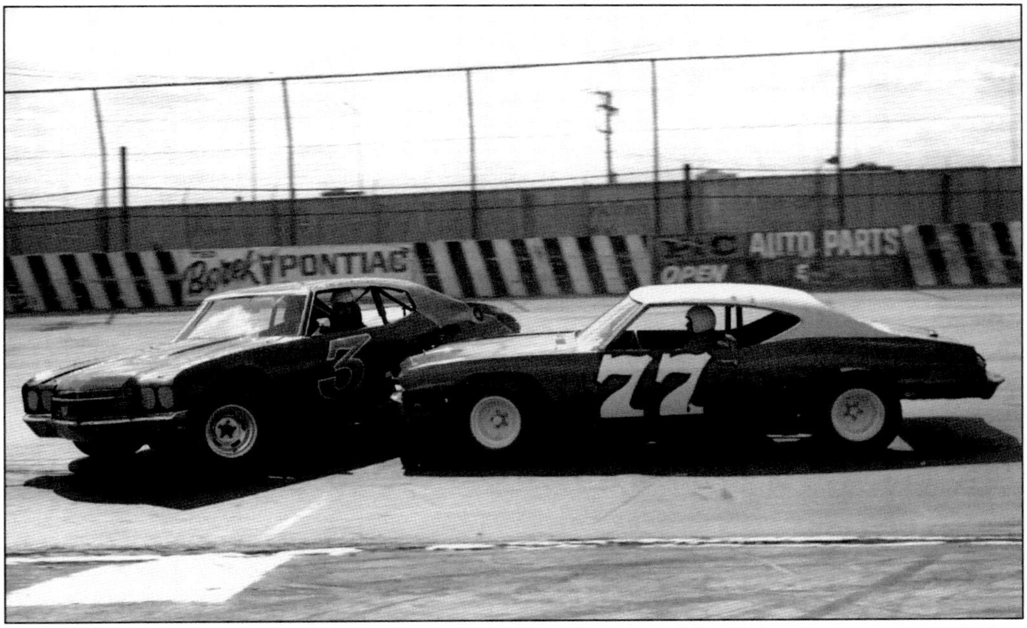

Opening day 1971 finds archrivals Bob Pronger (3) and Bud Koehler (77) going at it as usual. Ray Freeman would win the late model track championship that year, which saw Pronger disappear in June after winning eight feature races in Dave Roulo's fast Chevelle. It was common knowledge that Pronger was involved in car stealing and chopping activities, and his disappearance was believed to be a mob hit. (Courtesy of Stan Kalwasinski.)

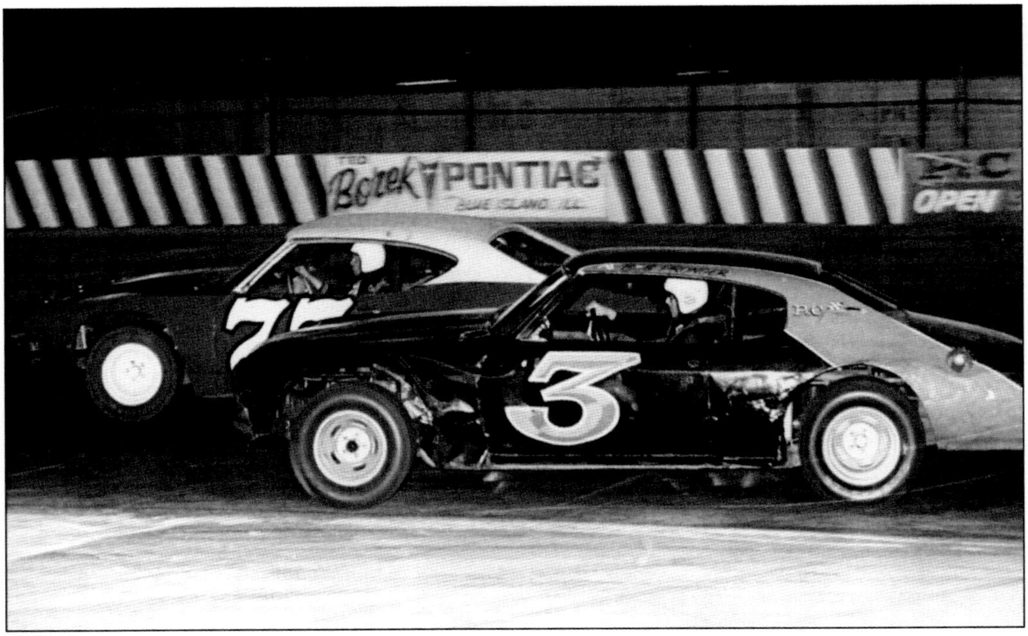

In this 1971 late model scene, Raceway Park's two biggest rivals, in both success and size, face off against each other for the final time. Six-foot-four-inch Bud Koehler (77) leads six-foot-five-inch Bob Pronger as they exit turn two and enter the backstretch. Koehler would finish the year second in points to Ray Freeman, and Pronger would disappear in June. He has never been heard from since. (Courtesy of Paul Beck.)

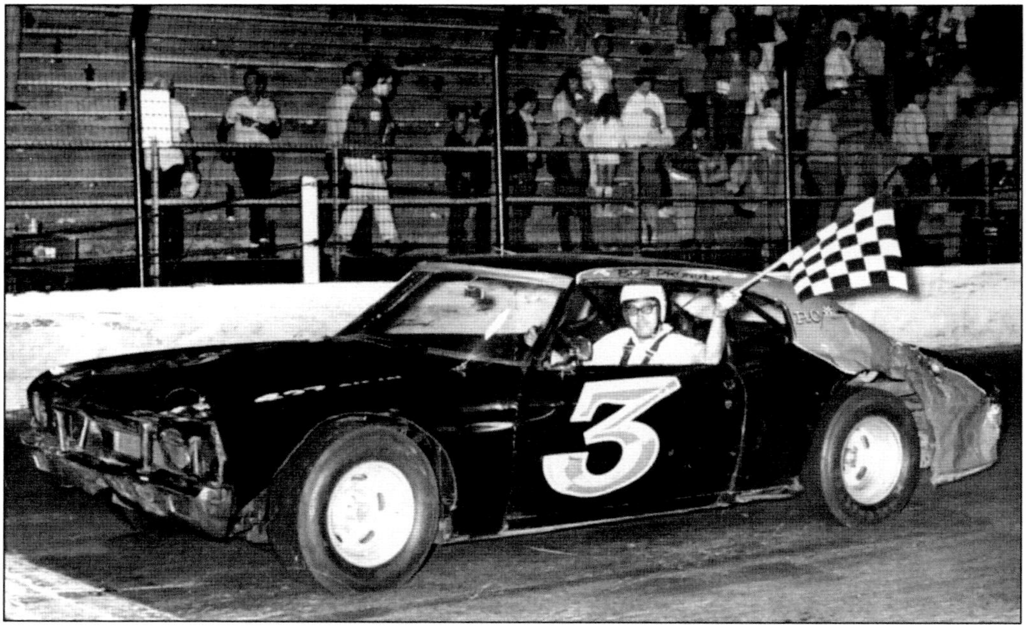

As fans vacate the grandstands after a night of racing in 1971, Bob Pronger carries his final checkered flag after winning the late model feature race. Pronger disappeared the following day, and Stash Kullman briefly took over the driving duties of Pronger's Fran Dandurand and Dave Roulo–owned race car. Dandurand and Roulo were only a couple of weeks away from completing and unveiling a new Camaro for Pronger to drive. (Courtesy of Paul Beck.)

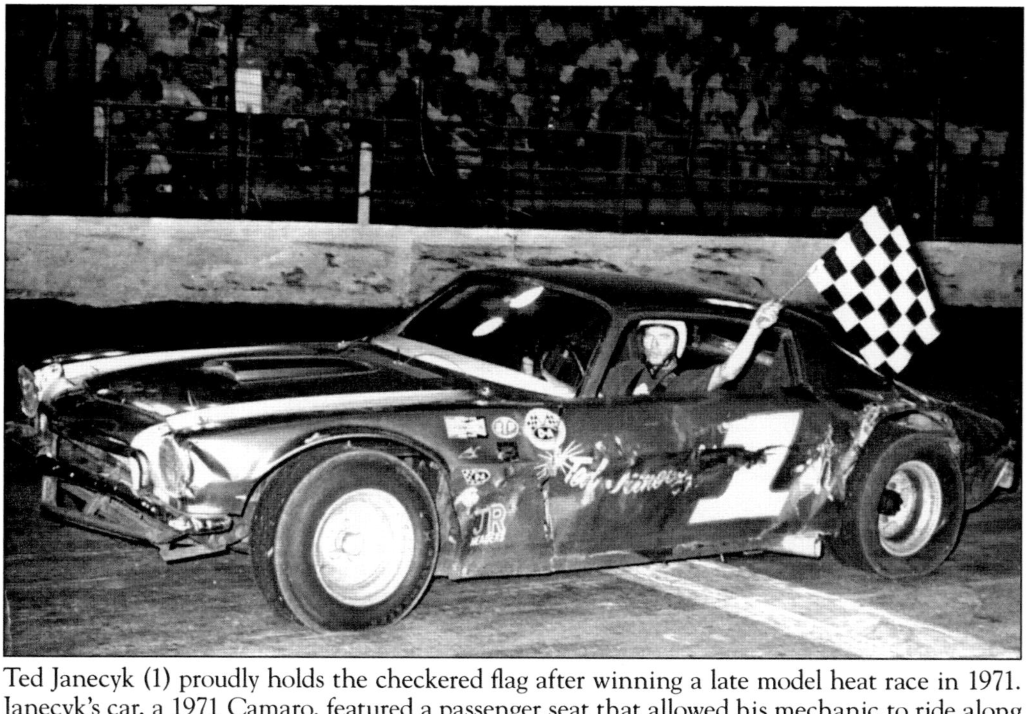

Ted Janecyk (1) proudly holds the checkered flag after winning a late model heat race in 1971. Janecyk's car, a 1971 Camaro, featured a passenger seat that allowed his mechanic to ride along during practice sessions. The Camaro is currently located at Janecyk's home in Calumet Park, which is right across the street from the site of the former track. (Courtesy of Paul Beck.)

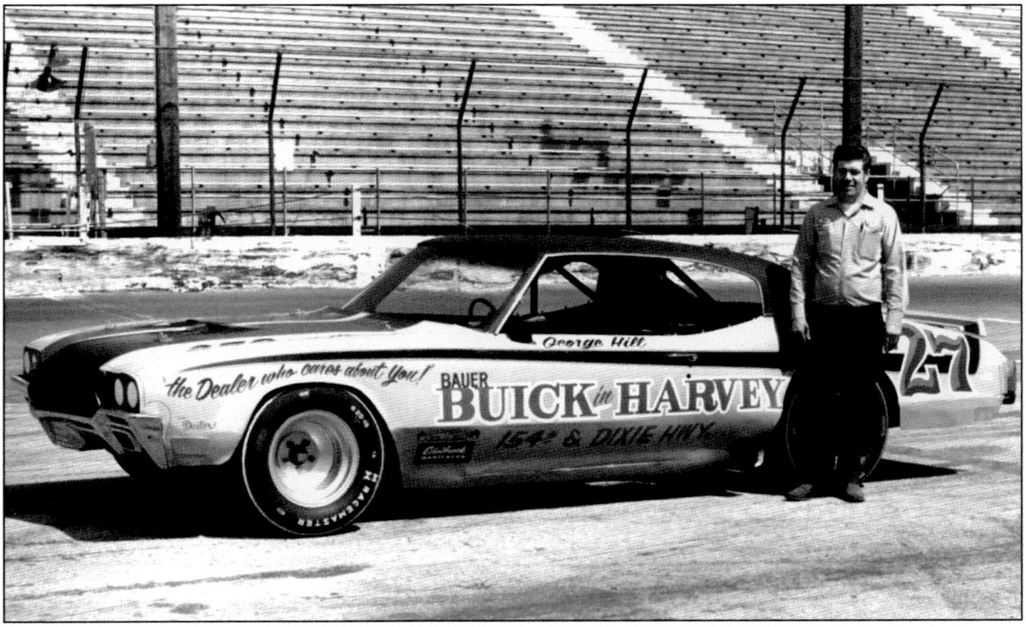

George Hill, a mechanic for Bauer Buick in Harvey, won the 1970 late model championship at Raceway Park. Pictured here with his 1971 Buick Skylark (27), Hill was unable to win another championship the following year. Ray Freeman would go on to win the 1971 championship, becoming the first driver in Raceway Park's history to win a claiming division championship (1963) and a late model championship (1971). (Courtesy of Stan Kalwasinski.)

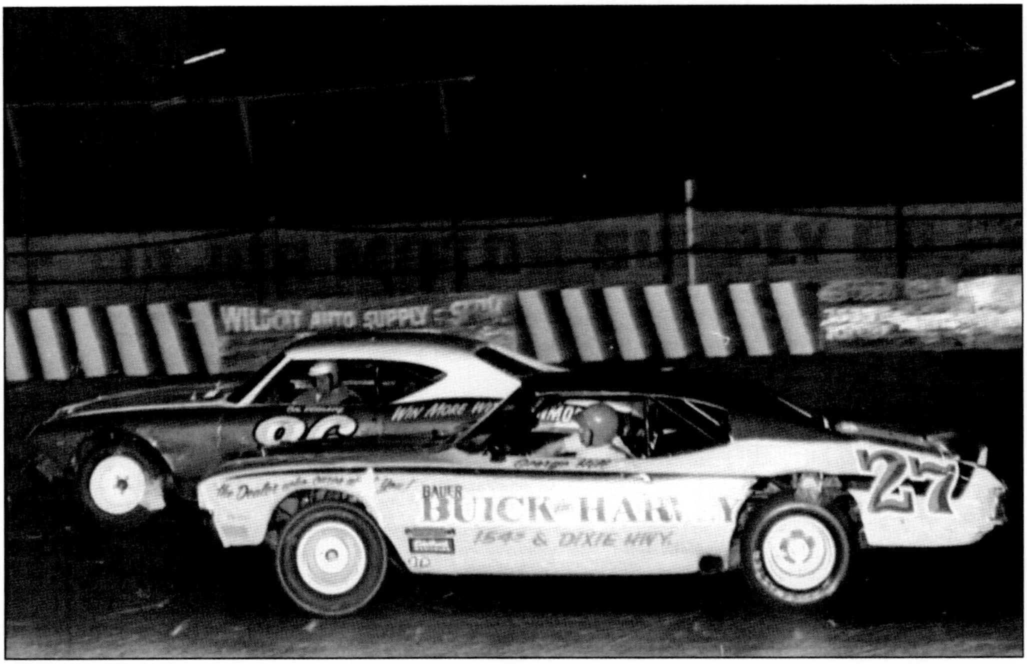

Defending late model champion George Hill (27), of Blue Island, attempts to pass Don Oldenberg (86) of Hammond, Indiana, early in the 1971 season. At the time of this photograph, Hill's career was at its peak while the career of longtime competitor Oldenberg was winding down. (Courtesy of Paul Beck.)

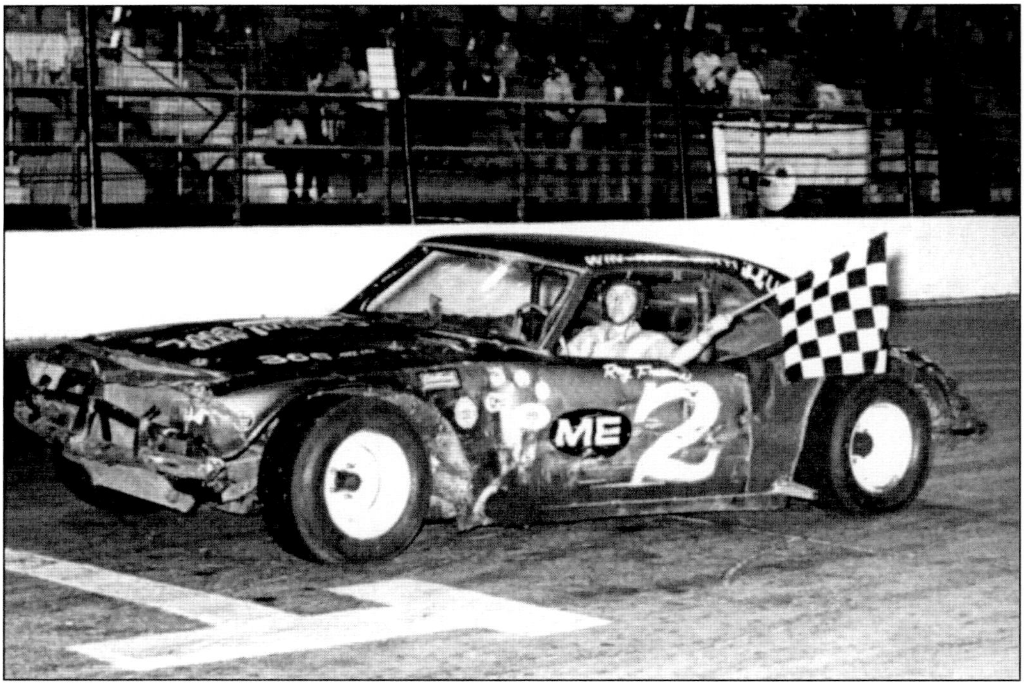

Ray Freeman (ME2) poses with the checkered flag after winning another feature race in 1971. Freeman, driving a 1969 Camaro, would go on to win the 1971 late model championship after battling Bud Koehler for the title all season long. (Courtesy of Paul Beck.)

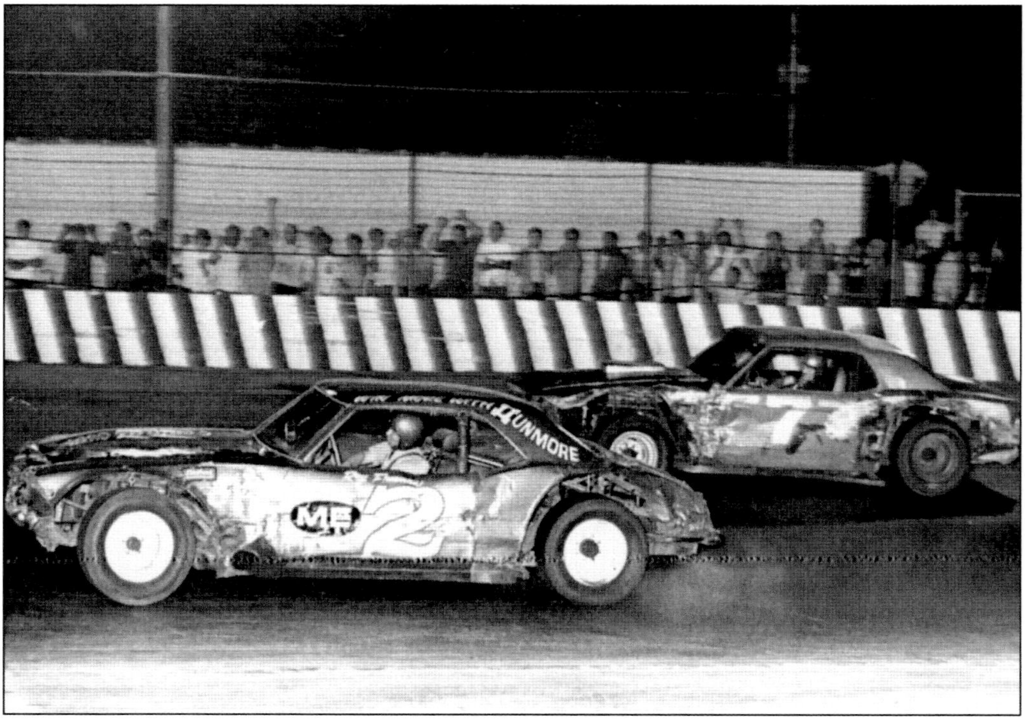

In this 1971 scene, Ray Freeman (ME2) and his 1969 Chevrolet Camaro pass the Ford Mustang of Ralph Reeves (7) in turn four. (Courtesy of Paul Beck.)

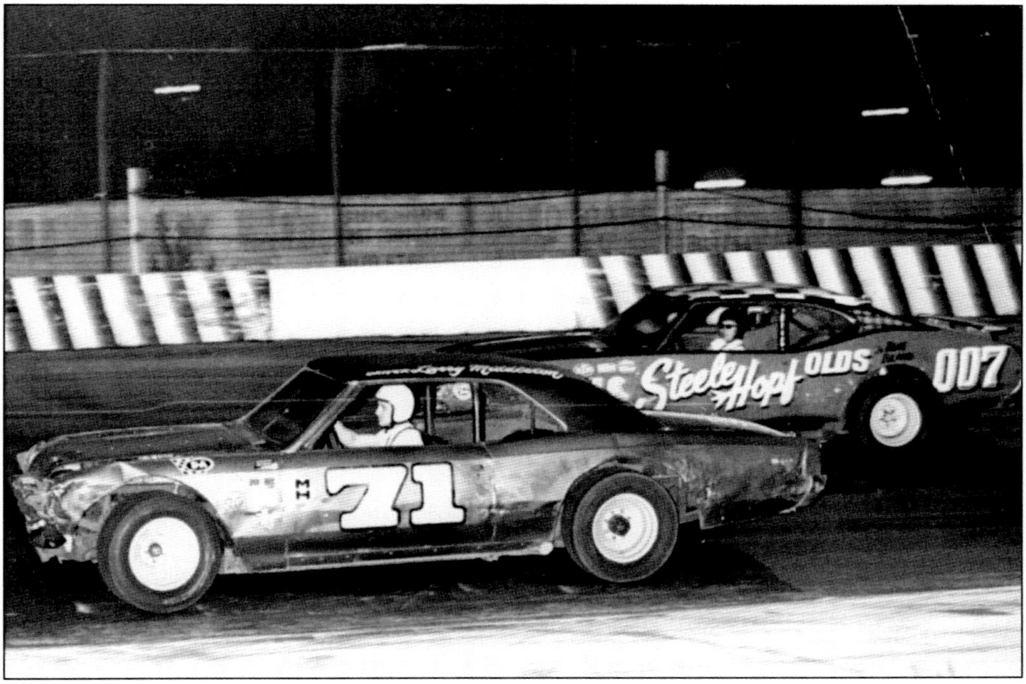

Larry Middleton (71) passes Dan Colyer as "James Bond" (007) in 1970. Seven years later, Middleton would win the first of two consecutive Raceway Park late model driving championships. Colyer, a fan favorite, would win several feature races in his long career. (Courtesy of Paul Beck.)

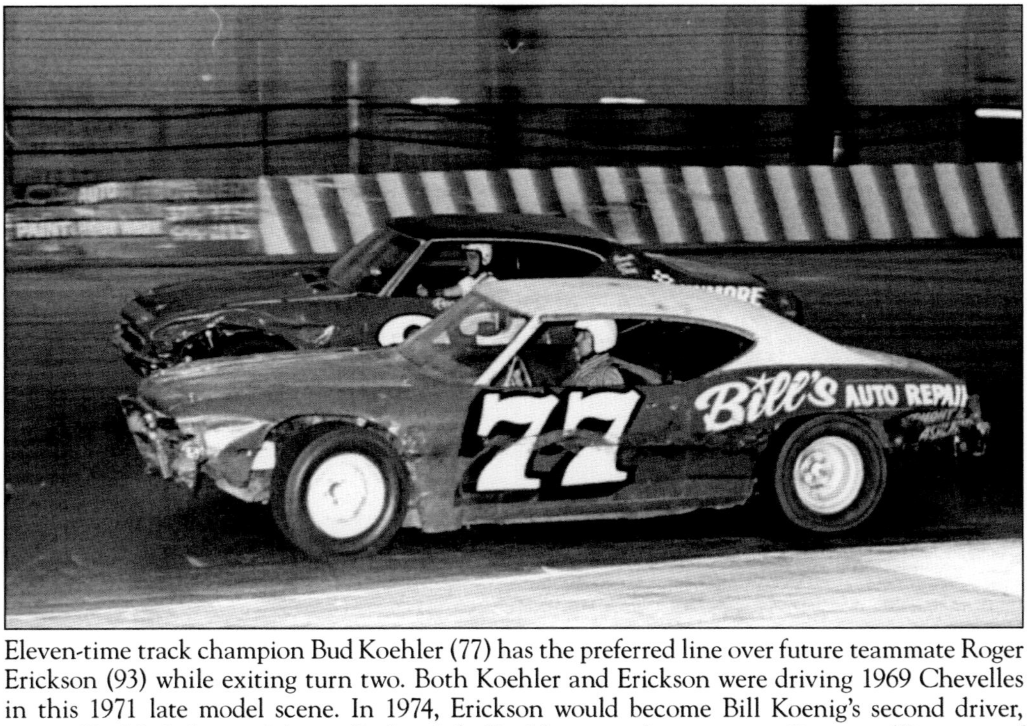

Eleven-time track champion Bud Koehler (77) has the preferred line over future teammate Roger Erickson (93) while exiting turn two. Both Koehler and Erickson were driving 1969 Chevelles in this 1971 late model scene. In 1974, Erickson would become Bill Koenig's second driver, racing Koehler's former Monte Carlo while Koehler moved into a new Camaro. (Courtesy of Paul Beck.)

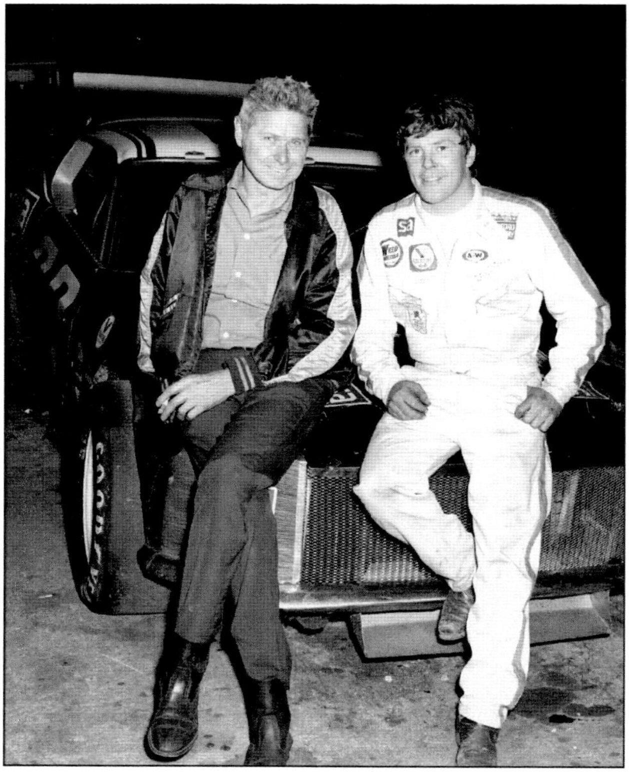

Two Midwestern stock car–racing legends, Bud Koehler and Wisconsin's Dick Trickle, pose for a picture in the pits on May 19, 1974. Trickle, on his way home from a Sunday afternoon race, made an unexpected stop at Raceway Park and competed in the evening program. Koehler won the 30-lap feature that night in his Bill Koenig–owned Camaro, with Trickle finishing third behind Marks Hernandez as "Speedy Gonzales." When posing for pictures, Koehler would tend to hide his right hand, which was deformed after suffering from a railroad-related accident as a child. (Courtesy of Stan Kalwasinski.)

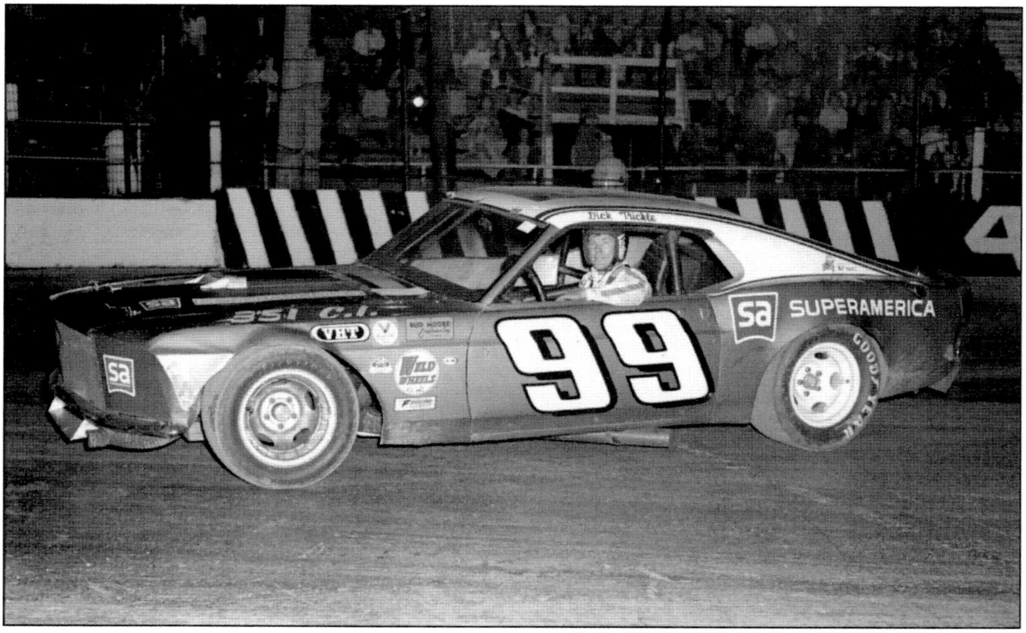

Midwestern racing legend Dick Trickle made an unexpected visit to Raceway Park on May 19, 1974. Winner of over 1,000 feature races during his short track career, Trickle finished third behind Bud Koehler and Marks Hernandez, better known as "Speedy Gonzales." In 1989, the 48-year-old Trickle was crowned Rookie of the Year in NASCAR Winston Cup competition. (Courtesy of Stan Kalwasinski.)

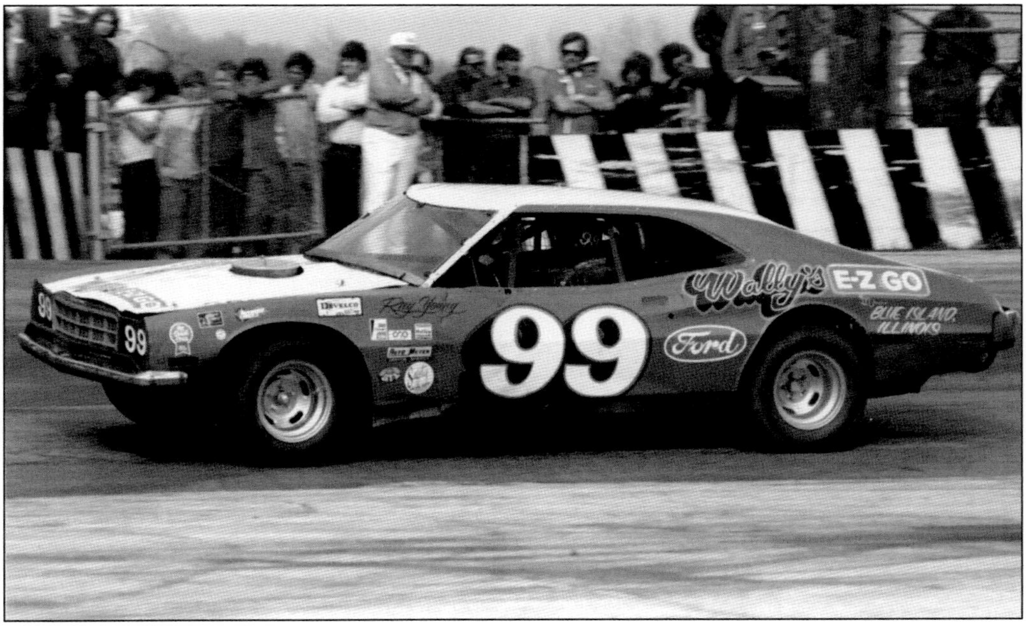

Making fewer and fewer events in the 1970s and 1980s, Ray Young (99) is shown here on opening day in 1975, wheeling his Wally's EZ-Go Ford Torino in feature race action. Young was the track's late model champion in 1962 and again in 1973. Born in Tennessee, Young began his racing career at Raceway Park in 1952 and won 107 features during his exceptional career. (Courtesy of Stan Kalwasinski.)

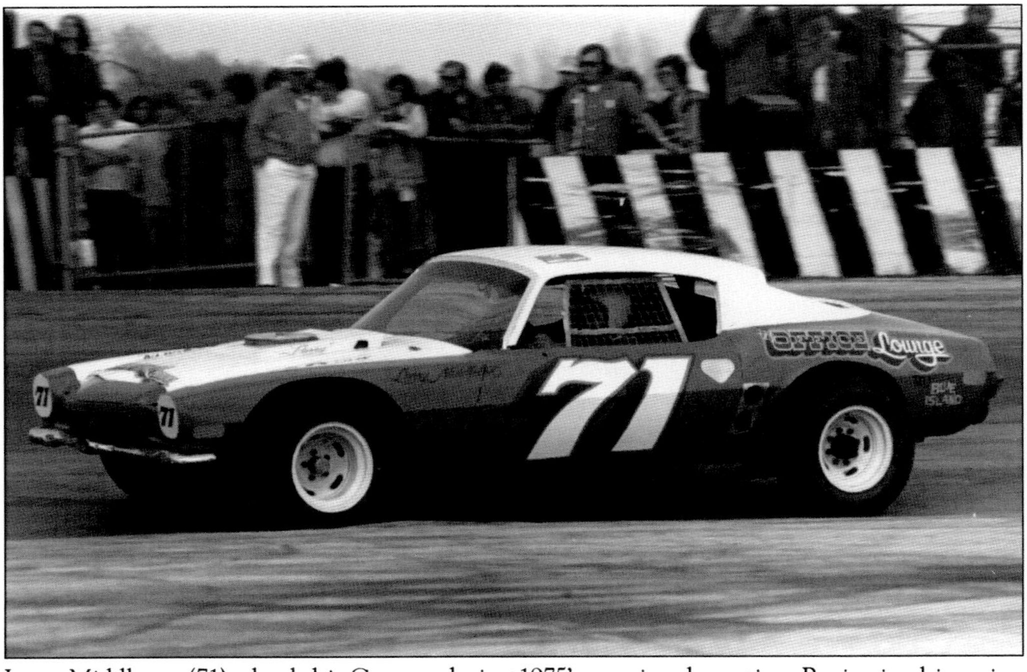

Larry Middleton (71) wheels his Camaro during 1975's opening day action. Beginning his racing career at the track in 1963, Middleton would go on to win back-to-back late model crowns in 1977 and 1978. Middleton posted 65 career wins before he turned his last lap at Raceway Park. (Courtesy of Stan Kalwasinski.)

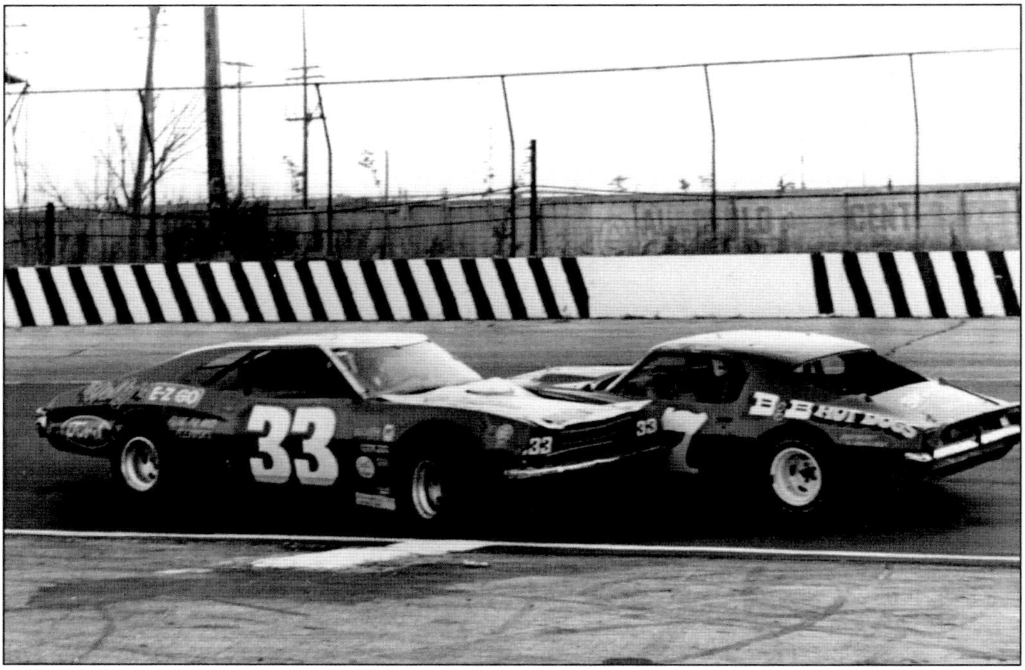

Paul Bauer (33) gets turned around in turn two after tangling with Bud Koehler (77) in 1975. (Courtesy of Paul Beck.)

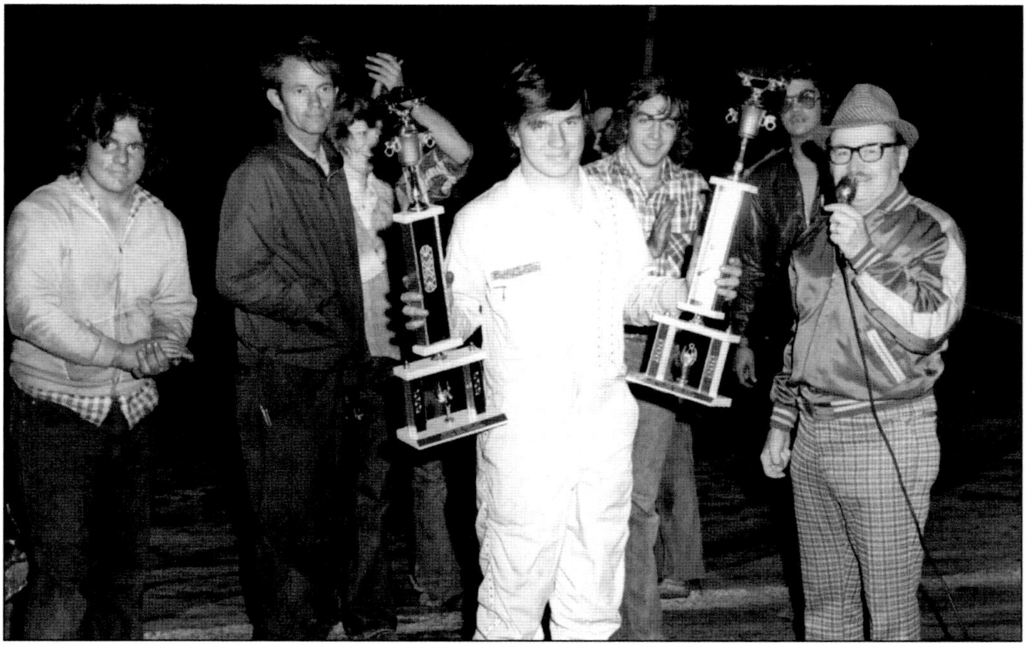

Bobby Dotter was the late model rookie sensation at the track in 1977, winning 17 features during the year. To top that, the 17-year-old Dotter did not begin competing until after Memorial Day. The youngster finished fifth in the point standings as Wayne Adams handles the microphone duties after presenting Dotter with a couple of trophies for two feature wins during a Monza event late in the year. Dotter would go on to compete on several Midwestern circuits and would have some success in several NASCAR divisions. (Courtesy of Stan Kalwasinski.)

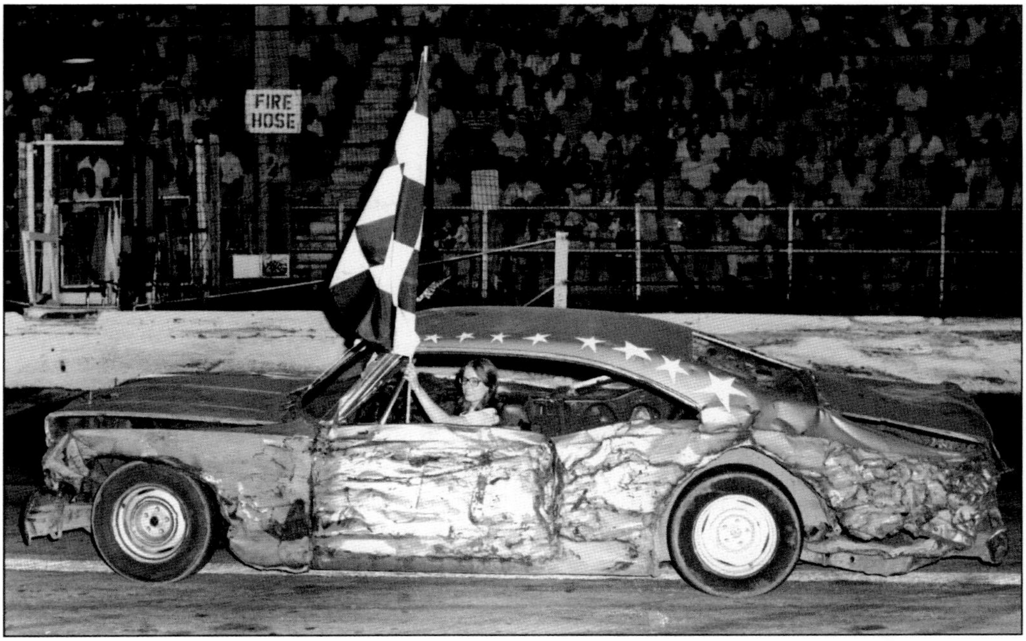

Barbara Bosak (1, above) and Nancy Prince (54, below) were stock car racing rivals for a number of years at the speedway. Women racers seemed to be always in competition, dating back to the 1950s, when Reggie Taylor and Billie Ann Broach were in action. Bosak was the track's 1978 hobby stock division champion, winning eight feature races with Prince winning 13 that season. Bosak even tried her luck in late model competition for a couple of years. (Courtesy of Stan Kalwasinski.)

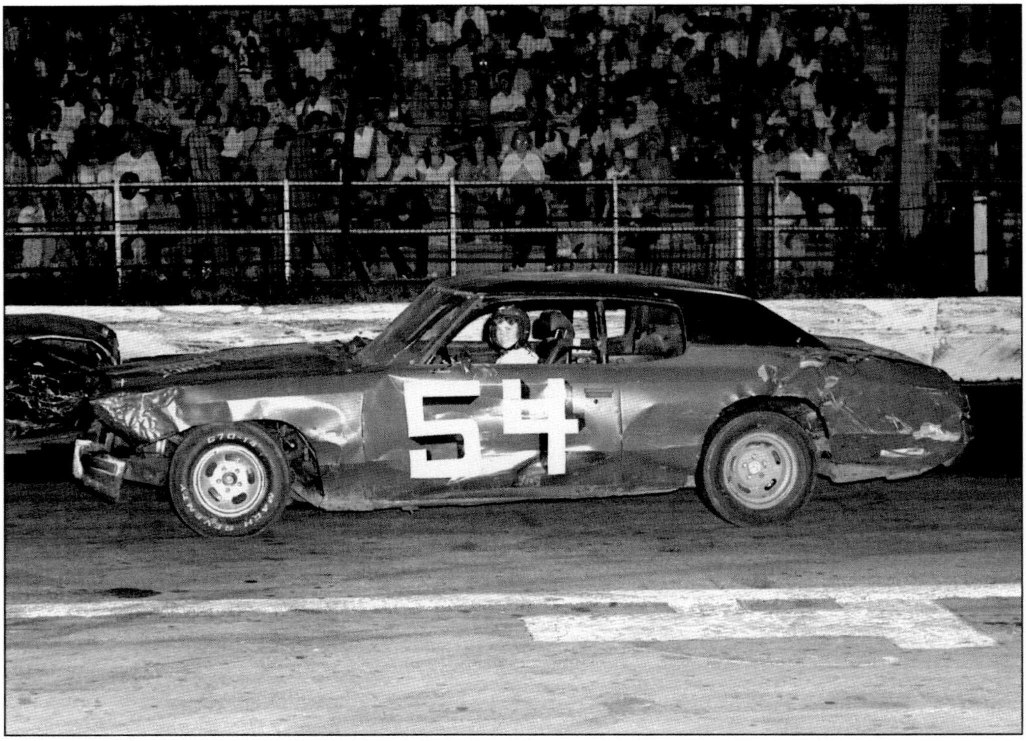

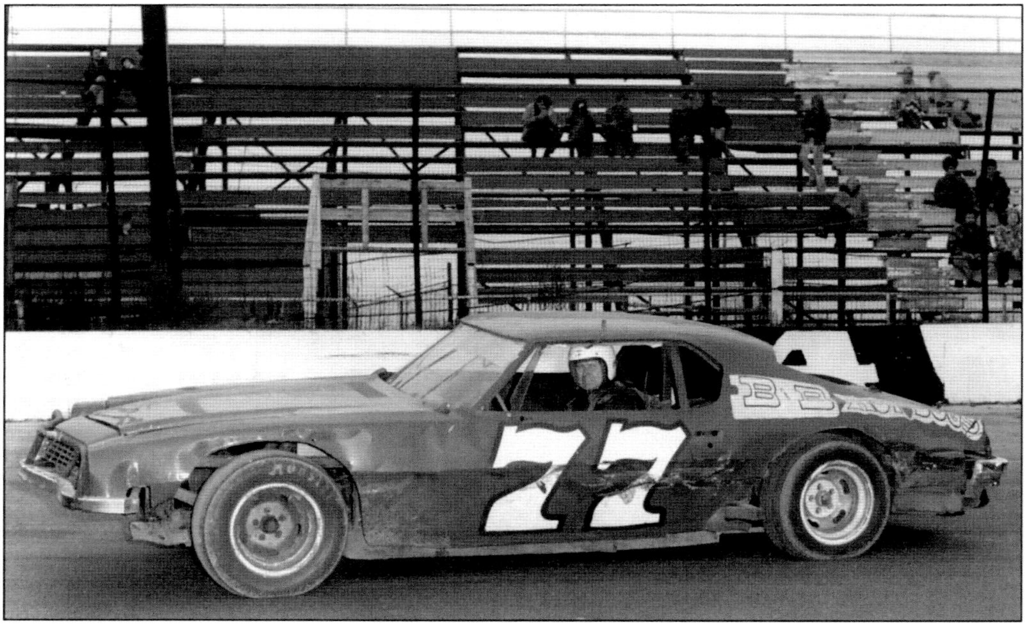

Winding down a racing career that included 490 stock car feature wins and 11 stock car championships at Raceway Park, Robert "Bud" Koehler (77) sits behind the wheel of Bill Koenig's B&B Hot Dogs–sponsored Camaro during the final racing program of 1977. A painter and home decorator by trade, Koehler called it quits after the 1978 racing season. (Courtesy of Stan Kalwasinski.)

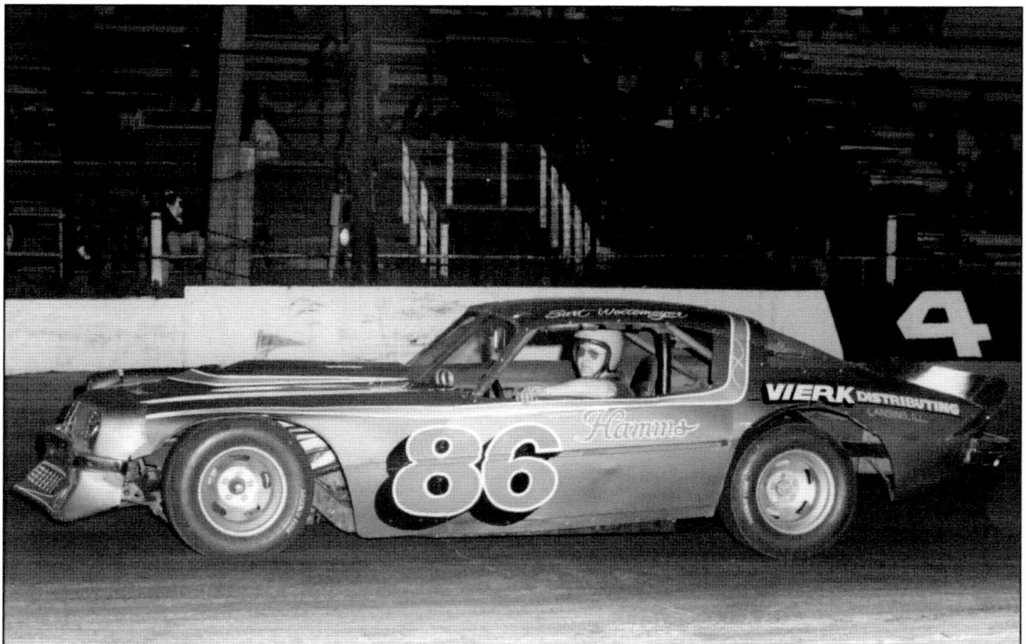

Lansing's Burt Weitemeyer, shown here in 1979, moved from the track's hobby stock ranks into the high-powered late models in the 1970s and 1980s. Before his racing days were over, Weitemeyer (86) would win three late model features at the speedway, in addition to nine non–late model victories. (Courtesy of Stan Kalwasinski.)

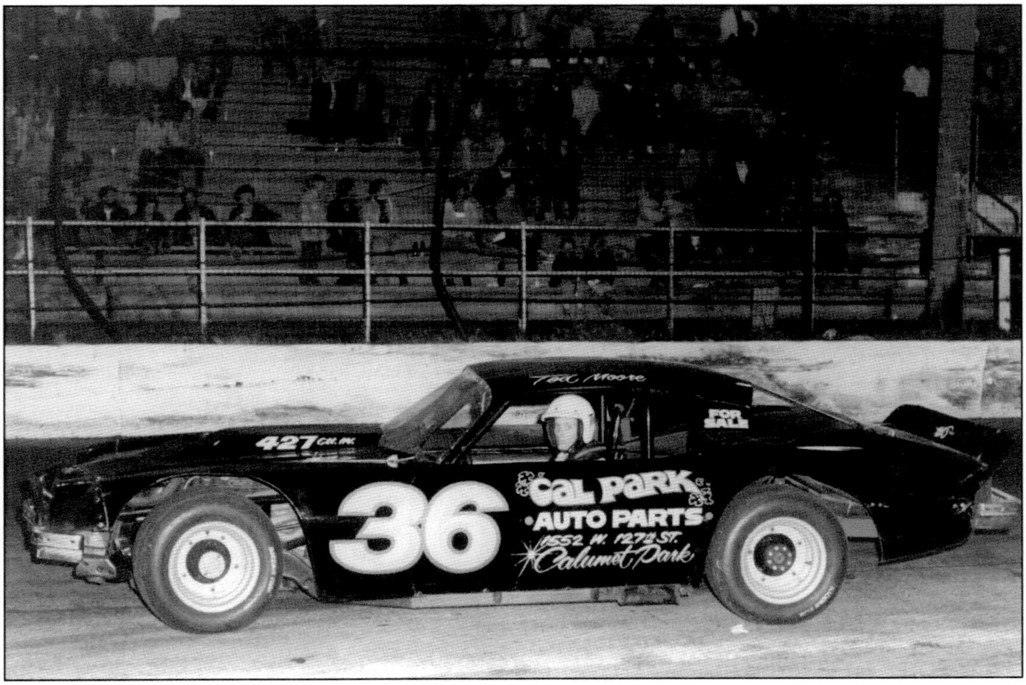

Little Ted Moore (36) was a late model terror during his brief career in the late 1970s and early 1980s. Moore posted a total of 27 feature victories and is shown here driving Ray Wroblewski's Camaro in 1979. (Courtesy of Stan Kalwasinski.)

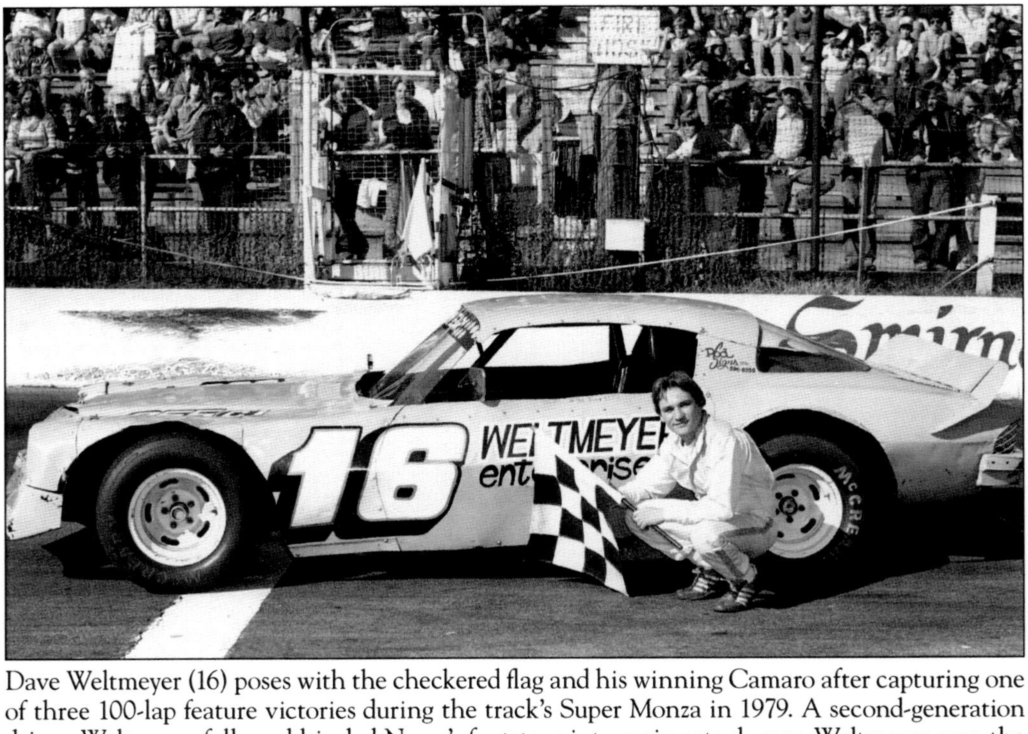

Dave Weltmeyer (16) poses with the checkered flag and his winning Camaro after capturing one of three 100-lap feature victories during the track's Super Monza in 1979. A second-generation driver, Weltmeyer followed his dad Norm's footsteps into racing stock cars. Weltmeyer won the late model championship in 1979, 1980, and 1983. (Courtesy of Stan Kalwasinski.)

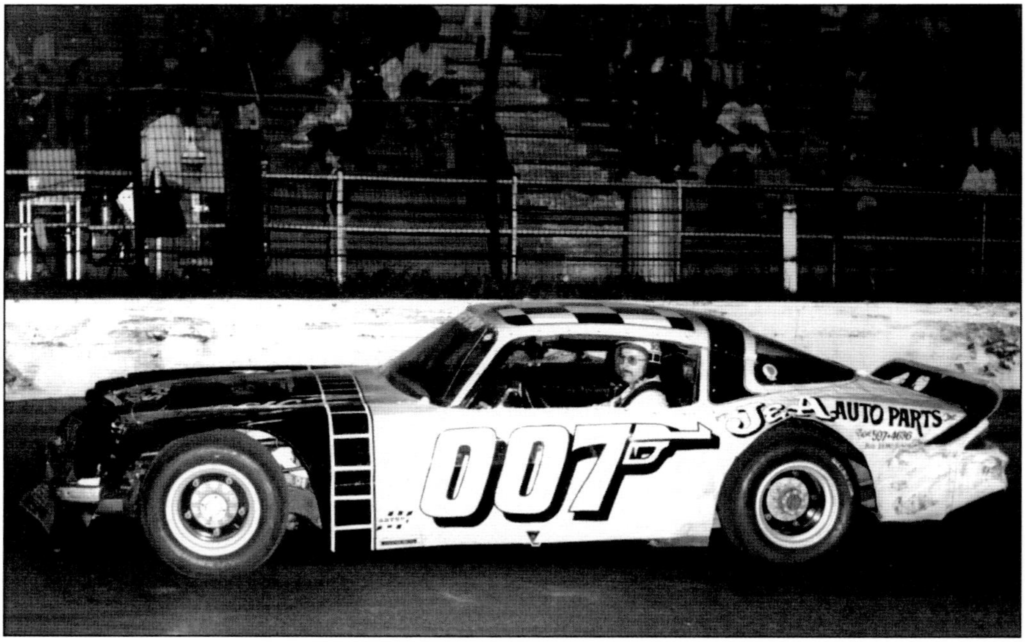

Dan Colyer (007) always drove sharp-looking race cars, and his Camaro for the 1979 racing season was no exception. Driving under the alias of James Bond in the 1960s and 1970s, Colyer did a fair amount of the painting and lettering of the cars during this time period. Colyer is still operating his sign-painting business in Blue Island, and he is also the operator of a vintage limousine service. His cars have been featured in movies such as *Flags of Our Fathers*. (Courtesy of Stan Kalwasinski.)

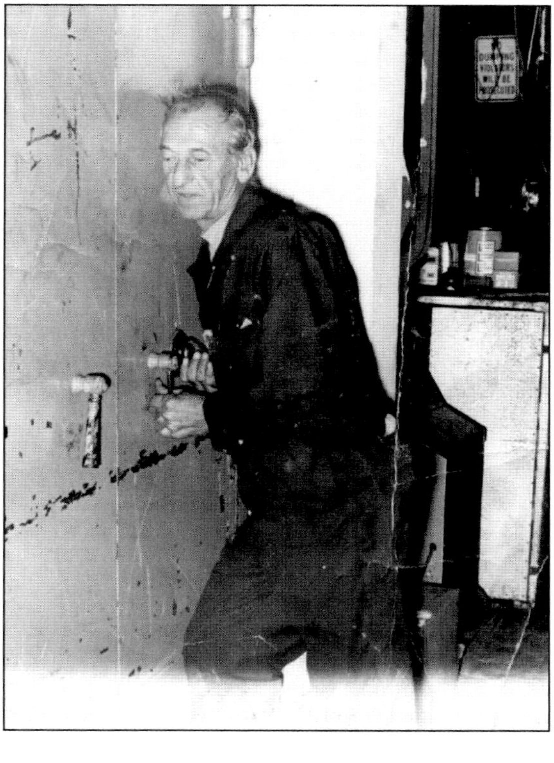

Raceway Park owner and promoter Pete Jenin attempts to open a safe inside the track's workshop. After each race night, Jenin, along with at least one Andy Frain usher, would take that night's profits to one of Blue Island's banks for deposit. (Courtesy of Paul Beck.)

Five

THE 1980s

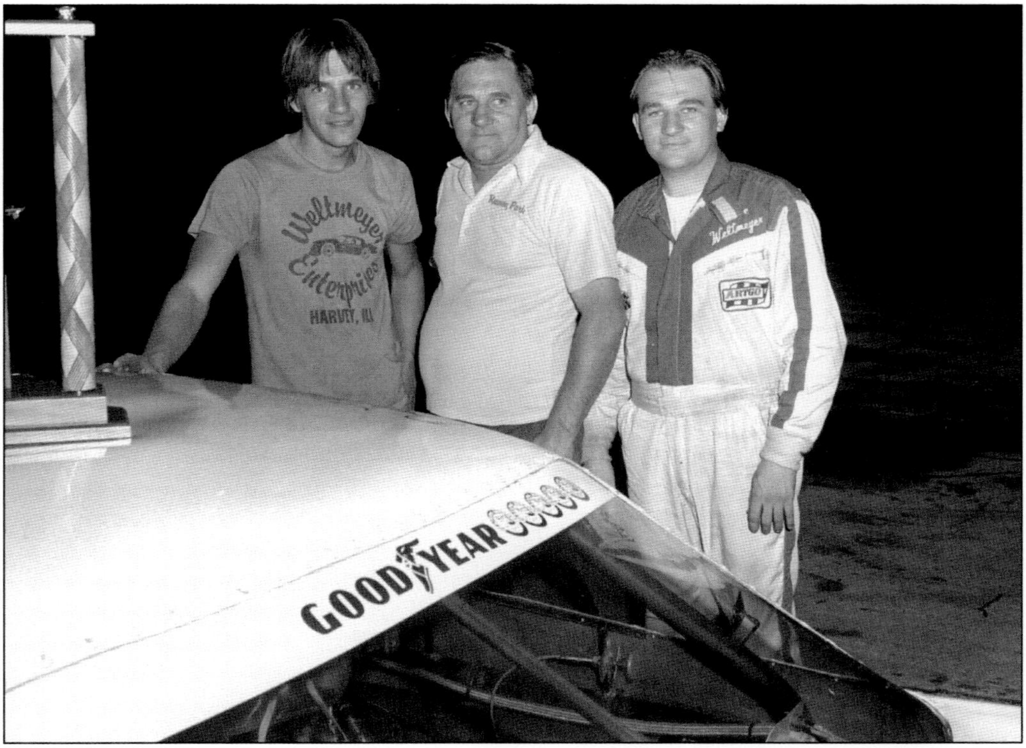

The 1980s looked like a promising decade, as young stars such as the Weltmeyer brothers, Frank Gawlinski, and others became the top late model drivers. However, the 1980s spelled the demise of the racetrack, as all of the legends had retired, and attendance was continually decreasing. Norm Weltmeyer (center) was proud of all his children, but he probably relished the fact that two of his sons were late model champions at Raceway Park. Following in their father's footsteps, Bobby (left) was the late model champion in 1981 and 1982 and older brother Dave captured the championship in 1979, 1980, and 1983, the year that this photograph was taken. (Courtesy of Stan Kalwasinski.)

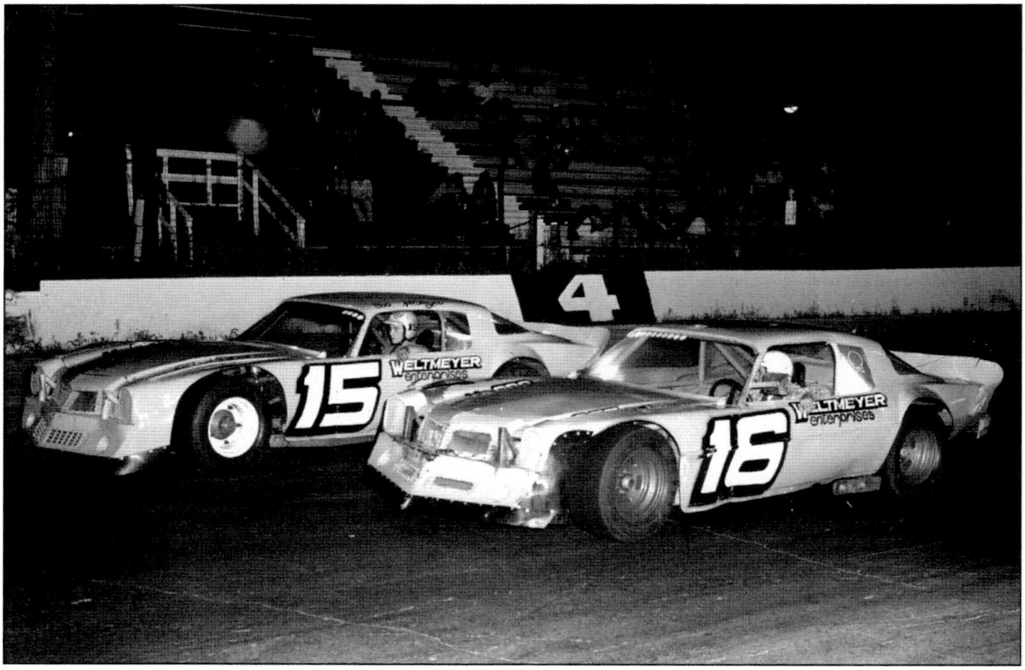

Ready to battle each other and the rest of the late model field, brothers Bobby Weltmeyer (15) and Dave Weltmeyer (16) line up for a 1980 feature race. Between the two of them, the Weltmeyers won five consecutive late model championships. (Courtesy of Stan Kalwasinski.)

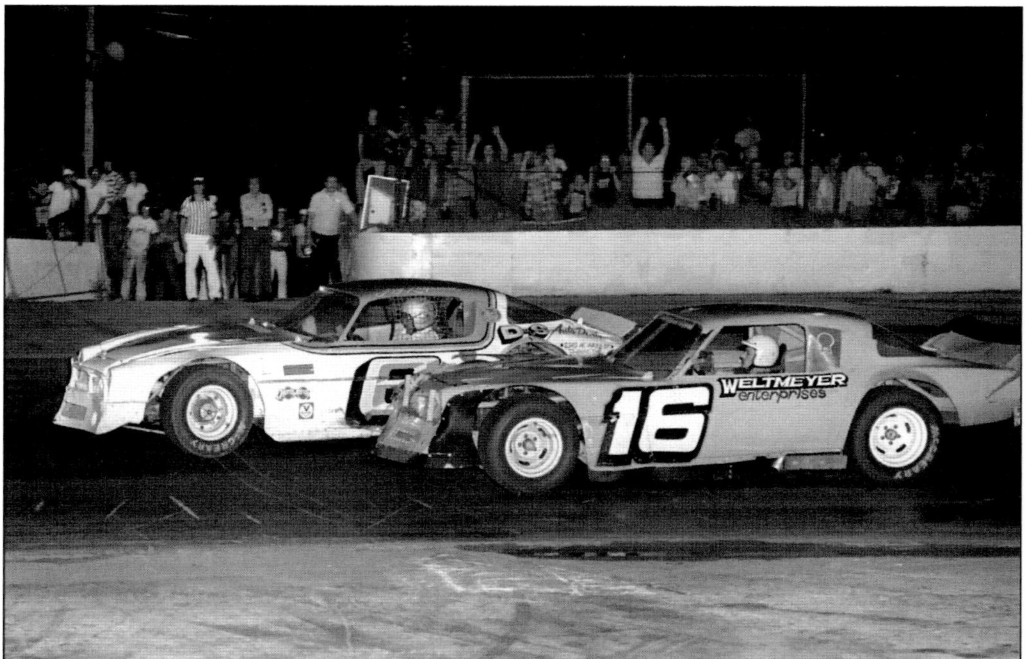

Jerry Kemperman (6) and Dave Weltmeyer (16) battle side-by-side through turn four during a 1980 feature race. Dave Weltmeyer was on his way to winning his second-consecutive late model championship and won 20 features that season. (Courtesy of Stan Kalwasinski.)

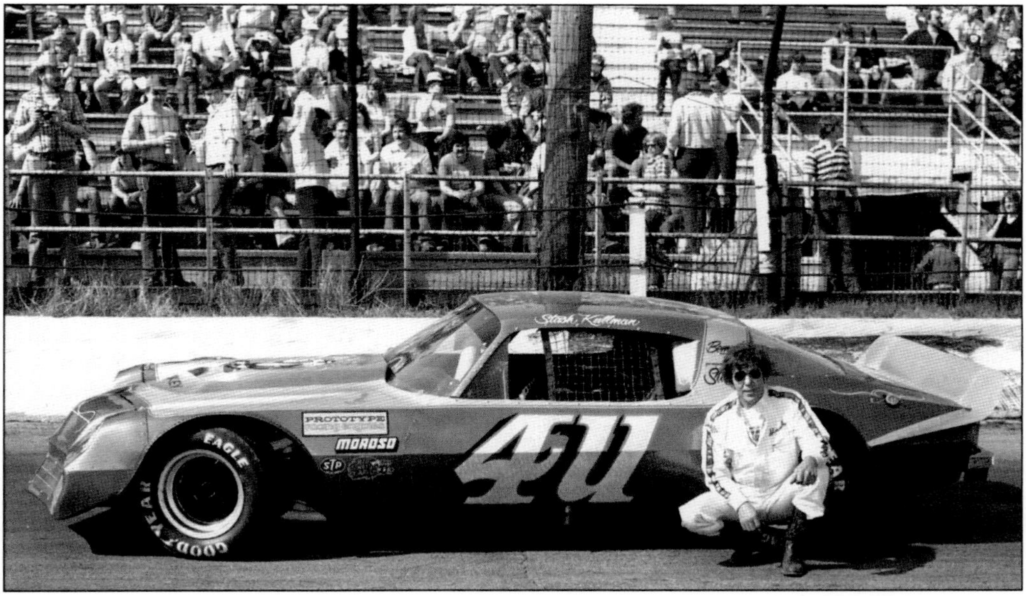

Winding down his racing career that started back in 1952, Stanley "Stash" Kullman poses next to his fresh Camaro (4U) before the 100-lap season-opening event in 1981. Kullman and his pink race cars were a familiar site at the track year after year, with Kullman winning a total of 30 feature races at Raceway Park. Always a character, Stash's Camaros featured Looney Tunes characters painted on the hood, and his Chevelles of the 1970s had the Playboy Granny exhibited on the trunk lid, see-through negligee and all. (Courtesy of Stan Kalwasinski.)

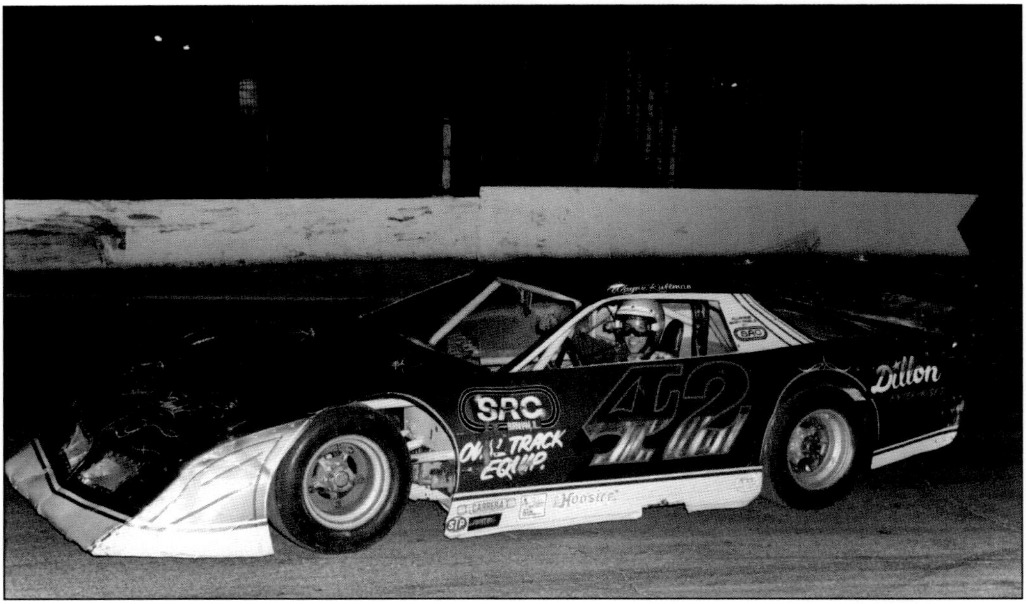

Wayne Kullman (42), son of late model competitor and race car builder Stash, smiles as he awaits the start of a 1983 late model race. While the spoilers and noses on the cars were increasing in size, the crowds attending the races were continually decreasing in number. Wayne only competed for a couple of years, preferring to help his father fabricate race cars. He also was a founding member of the Beatles cover group American English, as he was the band's first "George Harrison." (Courtesy of Stan Kalwasinski.)

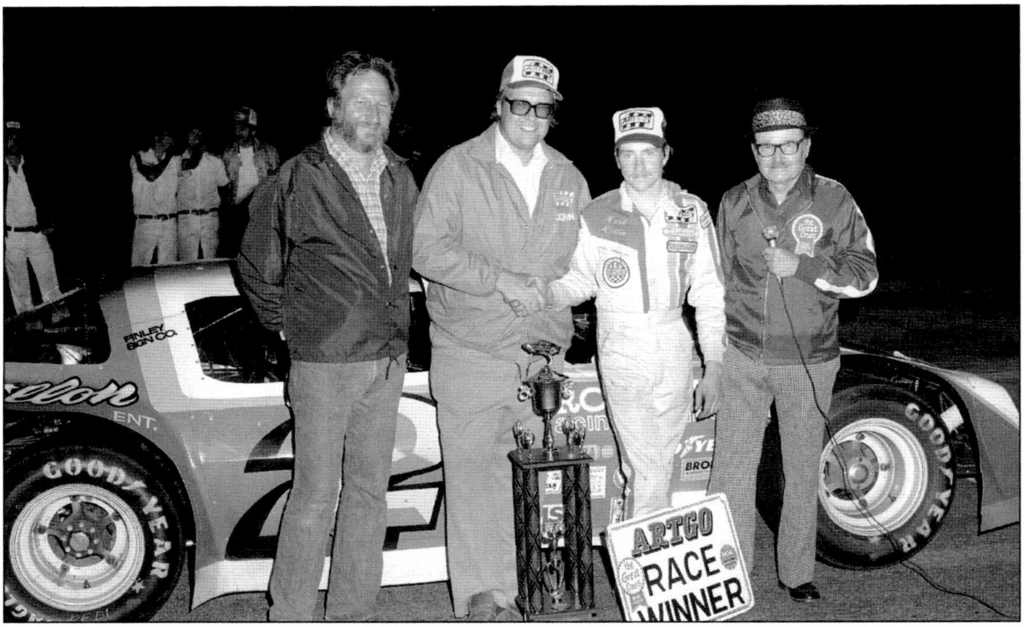

Before his success in NASCAR, Mark Martin competed in the Midwest, racing with a number of organizations. John McKarns's ARTGO late model tour visited the track on June 16, 1981, for the series's first and only appearance at Raceway Park. Martin, along with Wisconsin ace Jim Sauter, shared victory honors in the two 75-lap features that night. After his victory in the second 75 lapper, Martin poses with, from left to right, Ron Malec, McKarns, and Wayne Adams. Malec was representing the Calumet Raceway Associates, the promotional group at the track for a little over a year. (Courtesy of Stan Kalwasinski.)

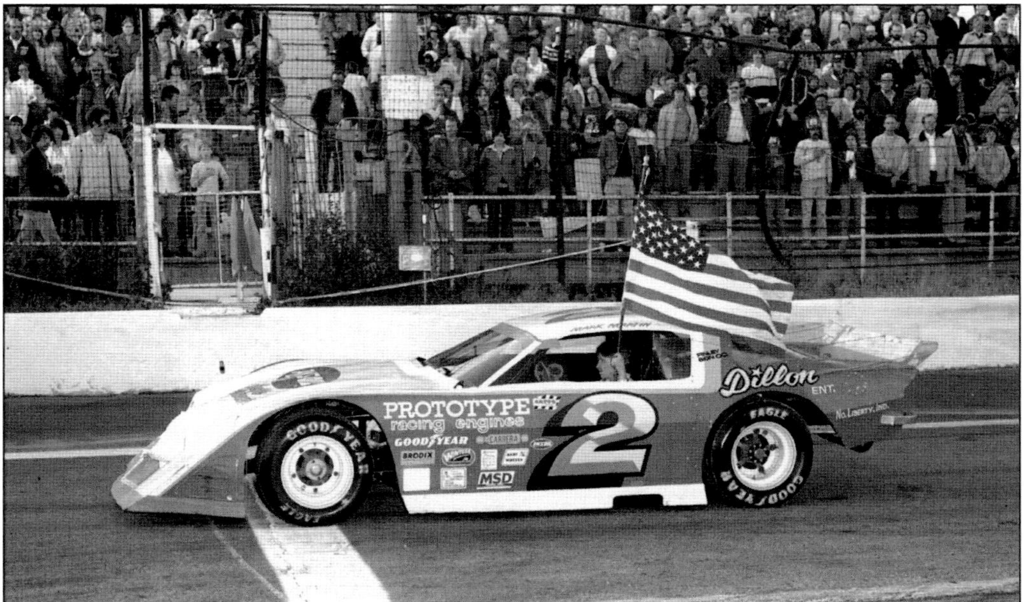

After being the fastest qualifier, Mark Martin carries the American flag during opening ceremonies before the 1981 ARTGO event held at Raceway Park. Martin would split the twin 75-lap features with Jim Sauter. (Courtesy of Stan Kalwasinski.)

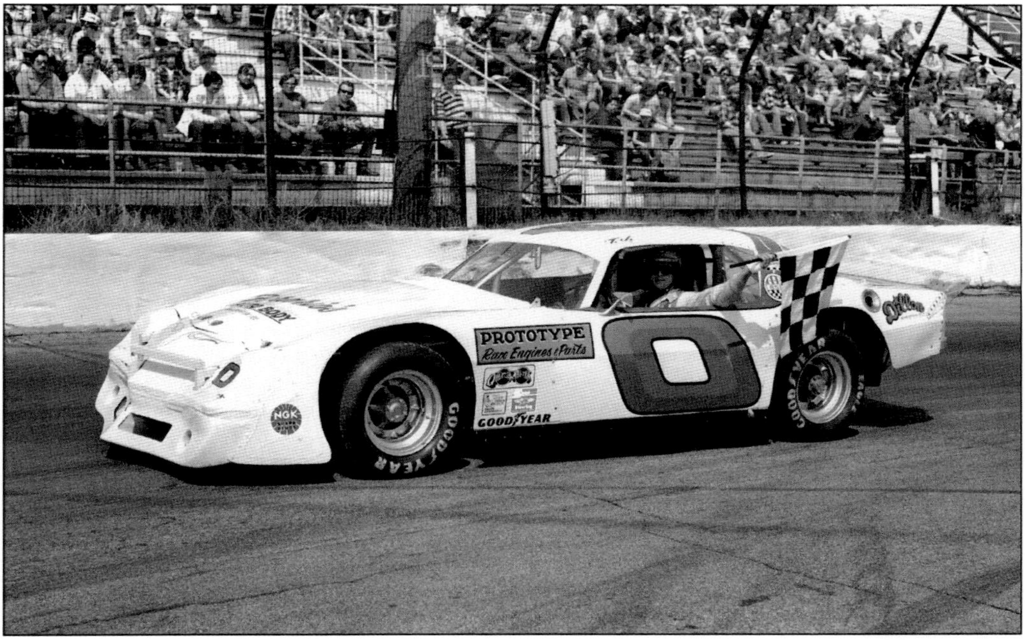

Tom Jones (0) was a track champion at several Chicagoland speedways and was a top runner in the American Speed Association (ASA). Never a regular at Raceway, Jones made numerous appearances at the track and is shown here after winning a heat race on 1981's opening day. (Courtesy of Stan Kalwasinski.)

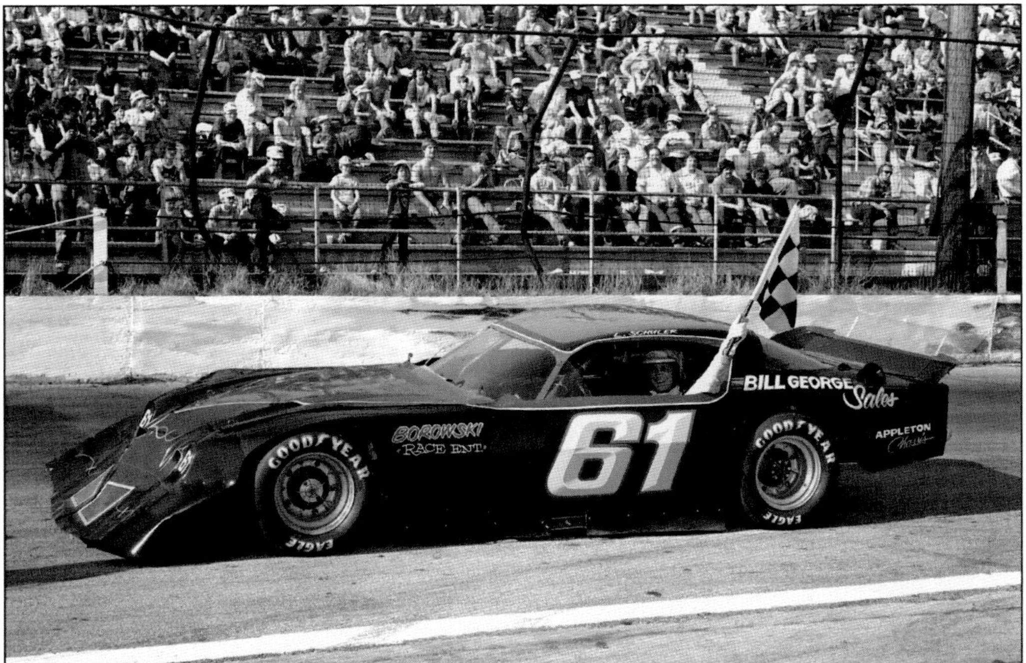

A familiar winning figure at other area speedways, Larry Schuler (61), son of frequent Raceway Park competitor Lee Schuler, drove his Camaro to victory in the opening day 100-lap feature on April 26, 1981. (Courtesy of Stan Kalwasinski.)

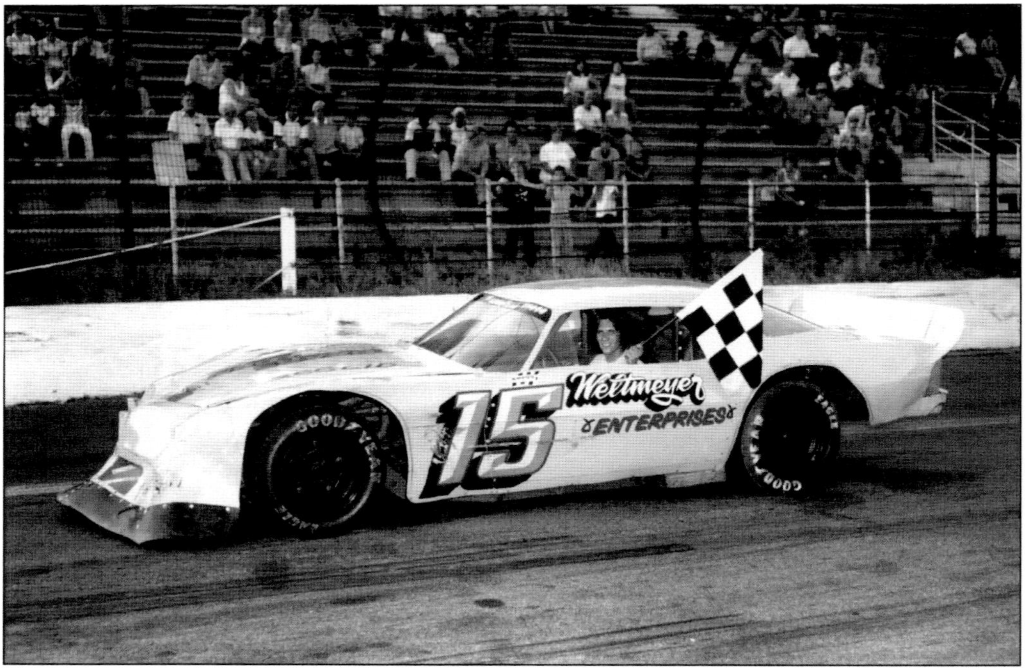

Bobby Weltmeyer (15) enjoyed a lot of success at the speedway, winning the late model track championships in 1981 and 1982. Shown here with his Camaro in 1981, Bobby watched his older brother Dave win back-to-back titles the two previous years. (Courtesy of Stan Kalwasinski.)

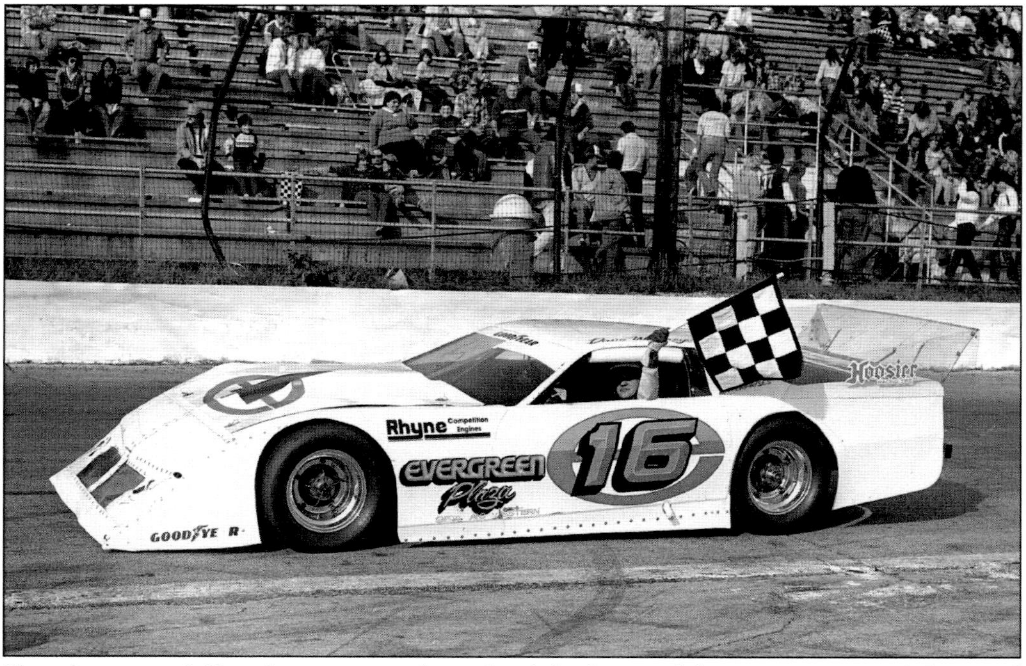

Sloped noses and Plexiglas wings on the tails of the late model cars were some of the speed secrets in 1983. Dave Weltmeyer, a native of nearby Harvey, carries the checkered flag after a late-season afternoon victory. Weltmeyer (16) was in the process of wrapping up his third late model championship that season. (Courtesy of Stan Kalwasinski.)

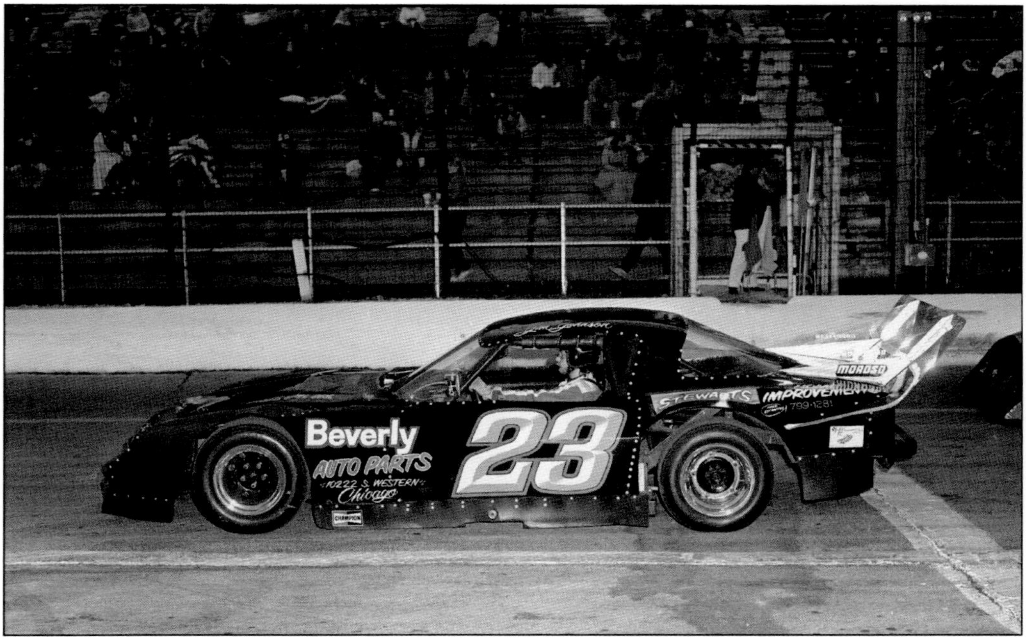

Jim Johnson (23) sits behind the wheel of his Camaro prior to the start of a 1983 race. Johnson would win the 1987 late model championship and won 17 features during his championship year. (Courtesy of Stan Kalwasinski.)

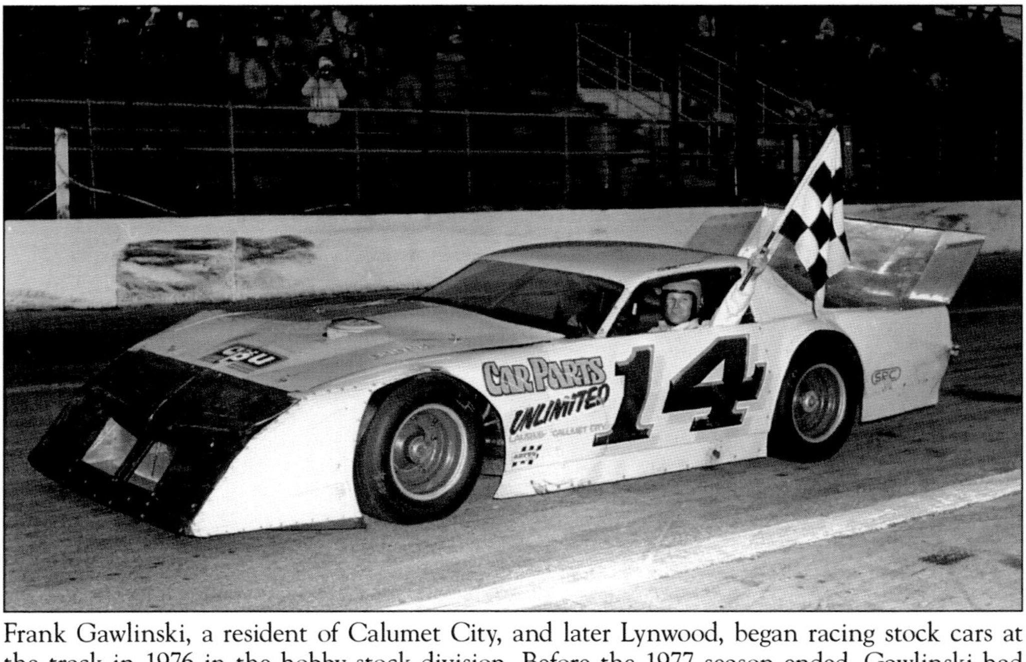

Frank Gawlinski, a resident of Calumet City, and later Lynwood, began racing stock cars at the track in 1976 in the hobby stock division. Before the 1977 season ended, Gawlinski had purchased a late model Chevelle and began learning the ropes of late model racing. Gawlinski won a total of 52 late model features at Raceway Park with his best points finish being 1978, when he finished second behind champion Larry Middleton. Gawlinski, who would go on to win nine track championships at Illiana Motor Speedway in Schererville, Indiana, is shown here after a win at Raceway in 1983. (Courtesy of Stan Kalwasinski.)

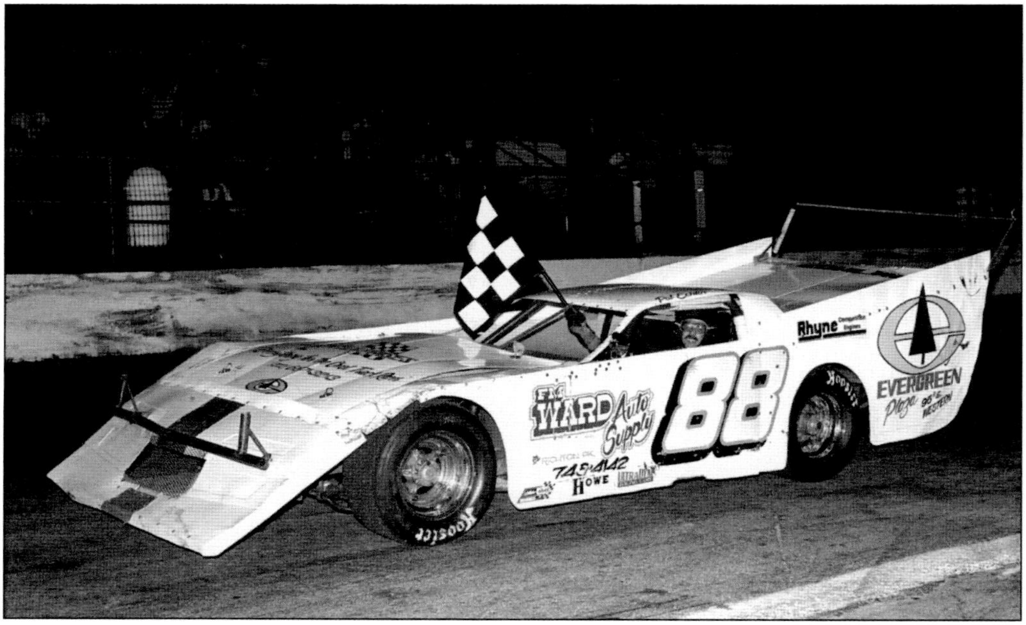

Pat Echlin paired up with car owner Joe D'Ambrose for a track championship in 1984. Echlin drove D'Ambrose's wedge late model to a record-tying total of 33 feature wins during the season. Bobby Weltmeyer had also won 33 features in one season, setting the record first in 1982. Before the track held its last race in 2000, Echlin would win three more late model crowns (1991, 1992, and 1993). (Courtesy of Stan Kalwasinski.)

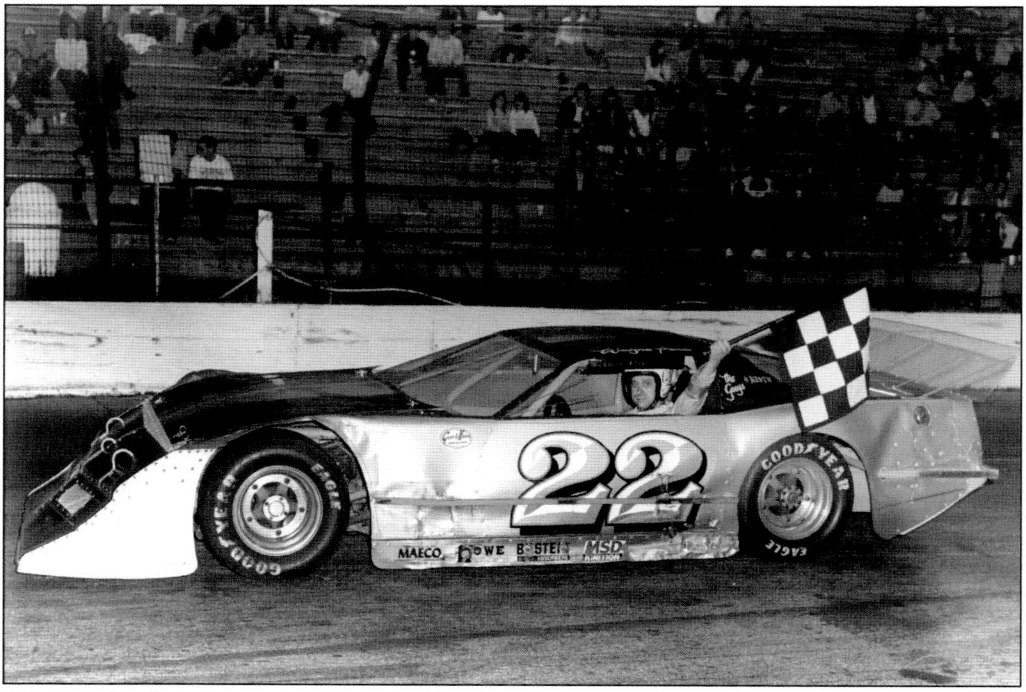

The Para brothers (Ray, Wayne, and Jim) always seemed to be racing at the track in the 1960s, 1970s, and 1980s. Wayne (22) was the late model track champion in 1985 and won a total of 41 late model feature races during his career at Raceway Park. (Courtesy of Stan Kalwasinski.)

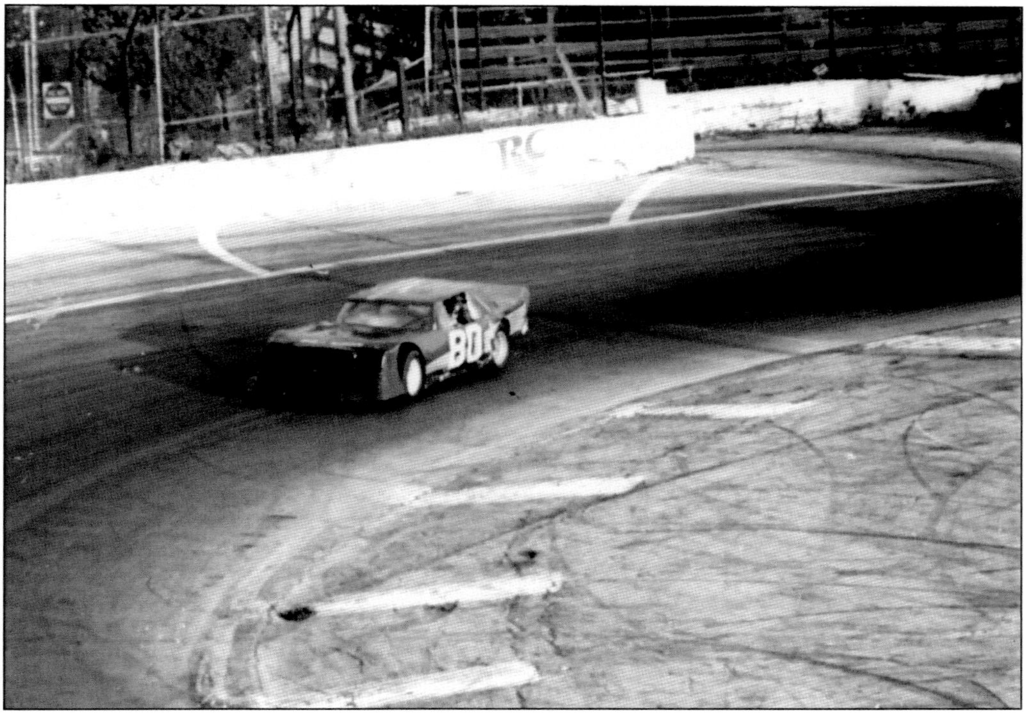

Steve Seligman (80) guides his late model into turn four during a 1981 qualifying run. Notice the empty backstretch grandstands—during the 1950s and 1960s, both sets of stands would be filled as qualifying would end. The 1980s saw a smaller car count and a smaller attendance as drivers and fans began going elsewhere for short-track racing. (Courtesy of Paul Beck.)

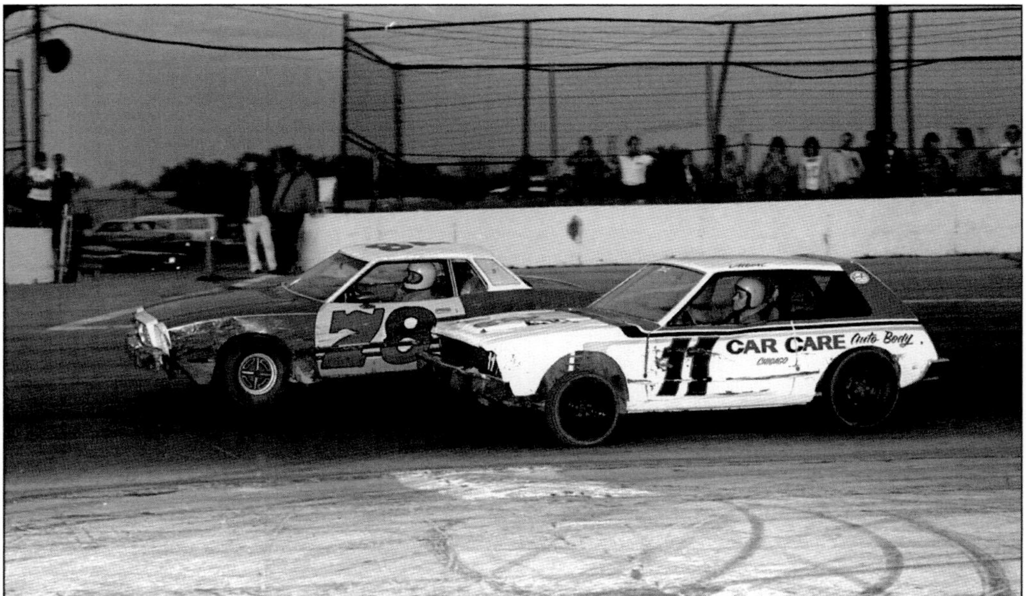

Alberto Cabrera (11) always seemed fast when he competed at the track in the ministock division, and he was that division's champion from 1984 through 1986. Cabrera is shown here passing a competitor during 1985 racing action. (Courtesy of Stan Kalwasinski.)

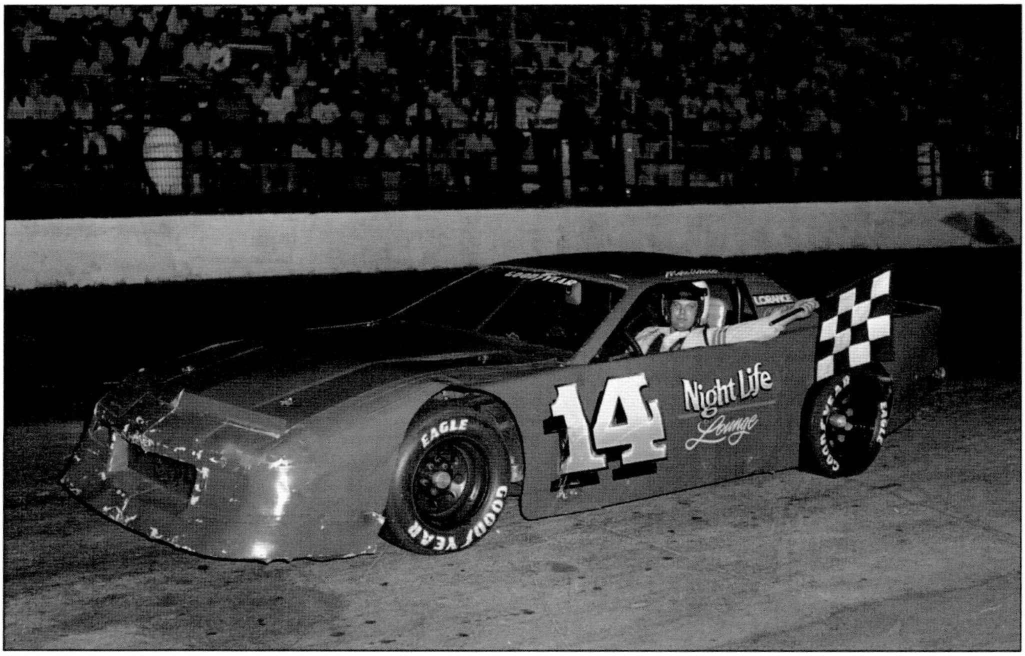

Mike White (14) put together a fast-running late model Camaro to compete at Raceway Park in 1988. That year's track champion, White won 22 feature races during his title season. (Courtesy of Stan Kalwasinski.)

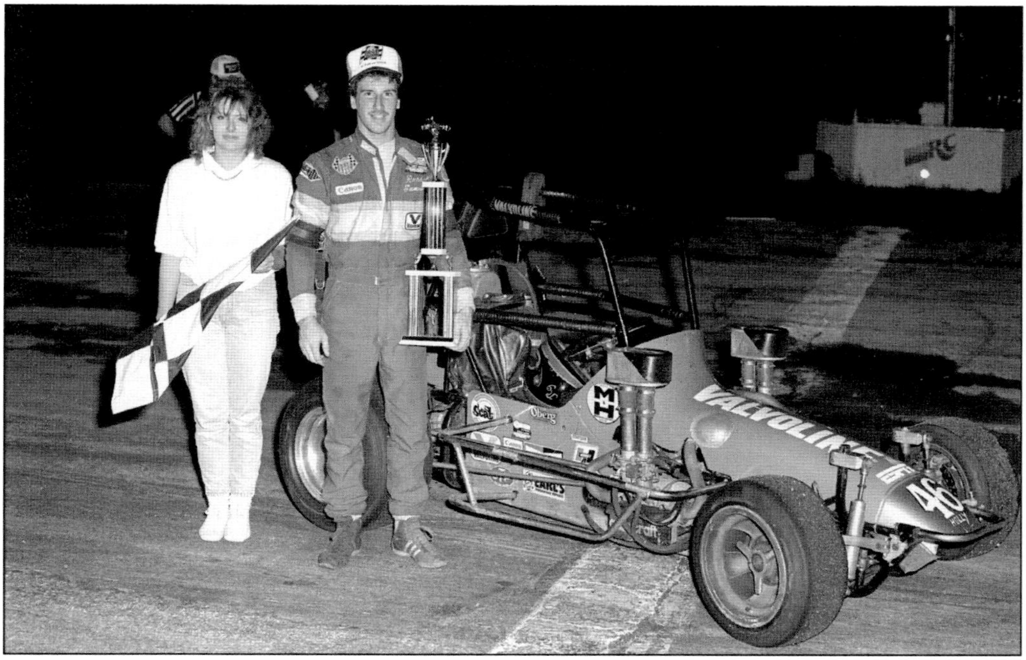

Starting out as a track for midget auto racing, Raceway Park would be the scene of scattered midget racing dates during most of its stock car–racing days. One of the last midget feature races held was in 1987 when Russ Gamester (46) won a feature during the United Midget Auto Racing–sanctioned action. A Peru, Indiana, native, Gamester was the 1989 USAC national midget champion. (Courtesy of Stan Kalwasinski.)

Six

THE 1990S AND INTO THE 21ST CENTURY

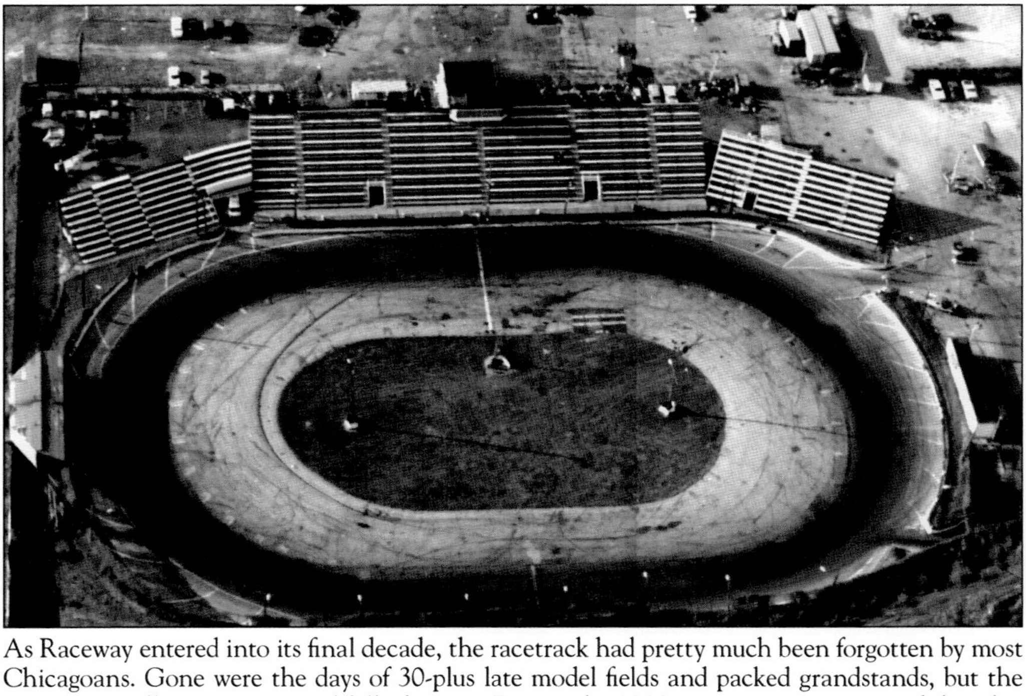

As Raceway entered into its final decade, the racetrack had pretty much been forgotten by most Chicagoans. Gone were the days of 30-plus late model fields and packed grandstands, but the racing was still competitive and full of action. During the 2000 season, it was suspected that this was Raceway Park's final season. Early in 2001, the property was sold, the track was torn down, and the land was redeveloped into a retail shopping complex. This early-1990s aerial photograph of the racetrack allows readers to get a general idea of where everything was on the property. Today this site is the home of a shopping complex conveniently named Raceway Park Center. (Courtesy of Bob Pilsudski.)

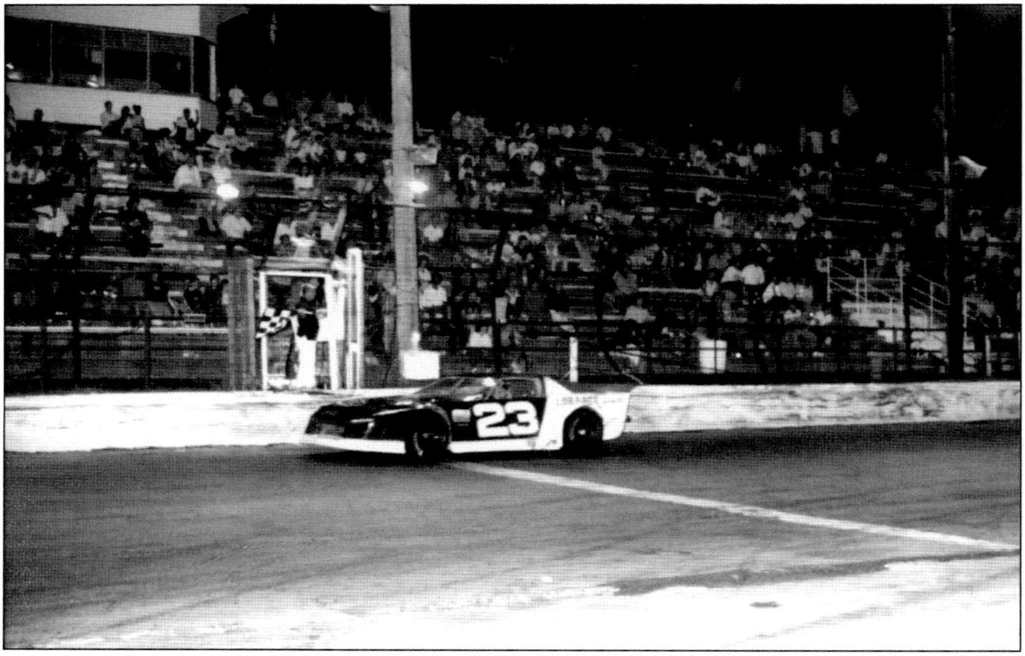

Joe Witkowski (23) takes the checkered flag during a 1990 late model feature race. Witkowski, a native of Hammond, Indiana, was the track's late model champion in 1989 and 1990. Although Witkowski competed at other area racetracks, he did not have the same success as he did at Raceway Park. (Courtesy of Bob Pilsudski.)

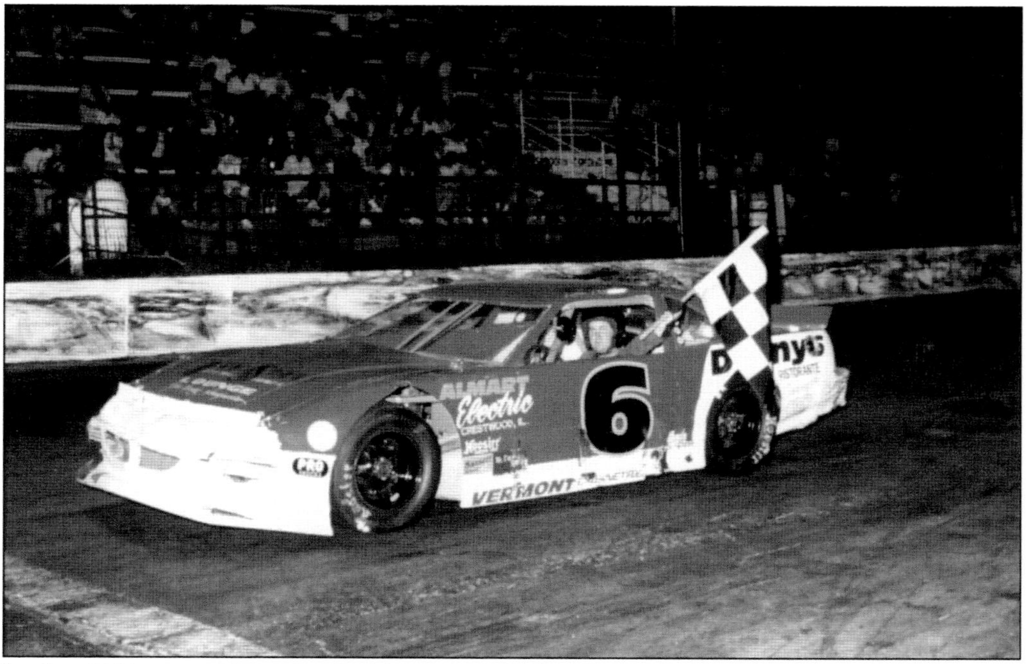

In this 1991 scene, Kevin Reidy (6) poses with the checkered flag. Reidy was the track's late model champion in 1995, 1999, and 2000. His last two championships were for car owner Ray Wroblewski, who won championships previously with Jimmy Johnson and Pat Echlin at the helm of his cars. (Courtesy of Bob Pilsudski.)

Pat Echlin (0) hoists his 1992 late model track championship trophy after winning back-to-back championships, while announcer George Rowlette prepares to interview the late model star. Echlin would go on to win the championship for a third straight time in 1993, a feat that was last achieved by Bud Koehler in 1974, 1975, and 1976. (Courtesy of Bob Pilsudski.)

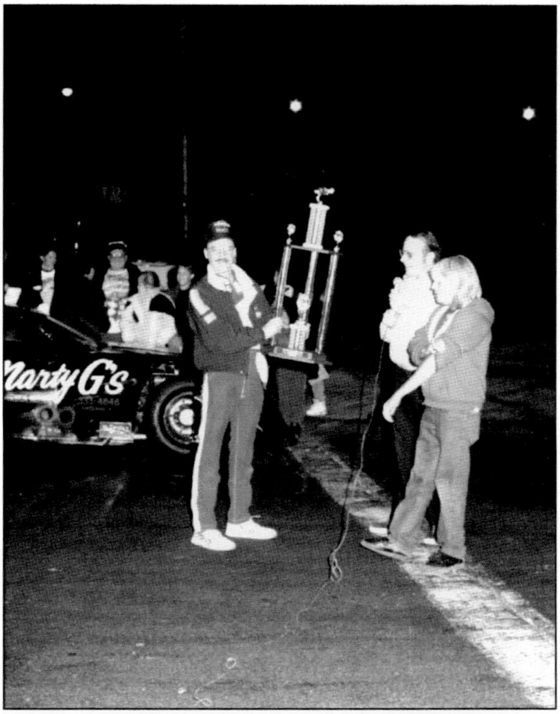

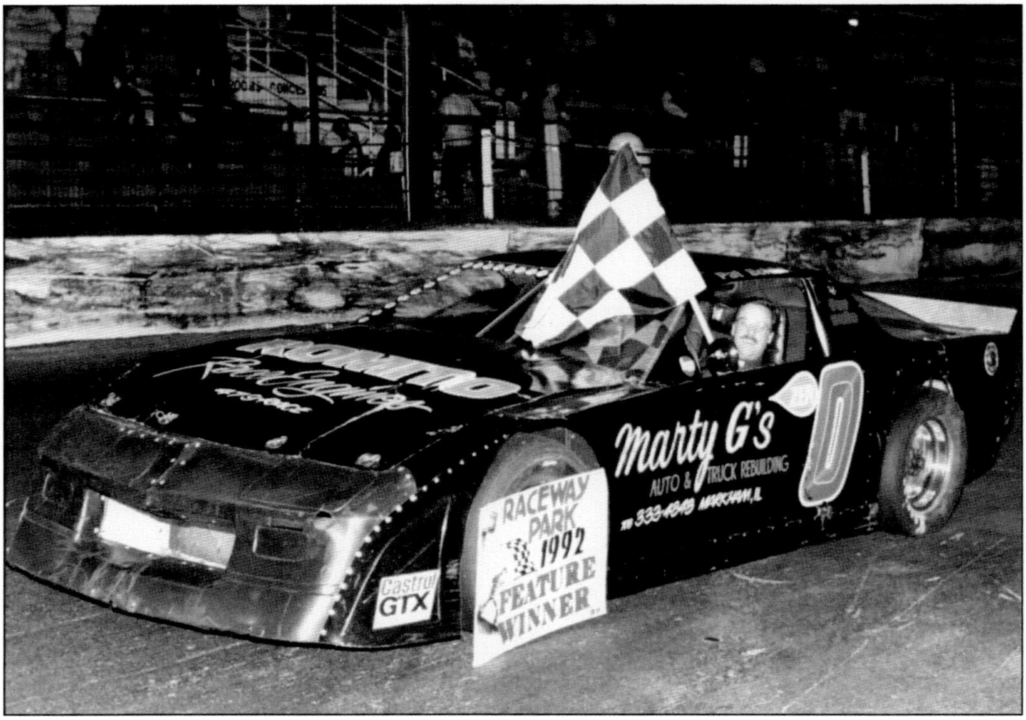

Late model track champion for 1992, Pat Echlin (0) poses with the checkered flag after winning one of his 26 features that year. Echlin won a total of four late model track championships at Raceway Park and set the qualifying record by posting a lap of 11.191 seconds in 1984. (Courtesy of Bob Pilsudski.)

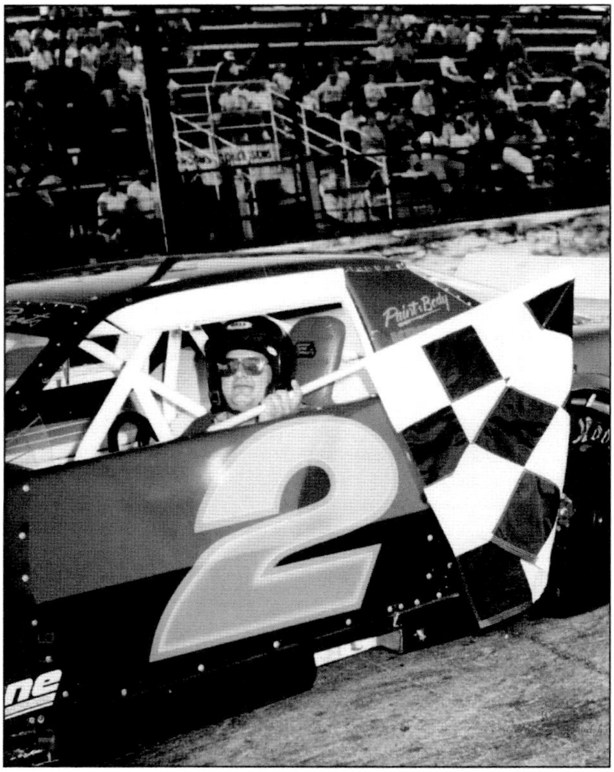

Two-time late model champion John Brolick (2), of Calumet City, holds the checkered flag after winning another victory in the early 1990s. The 1994 and 1997 late model champion won a total of 82 features at Raceway Park in his career. (Courtesy of Bob Pilsudski.)

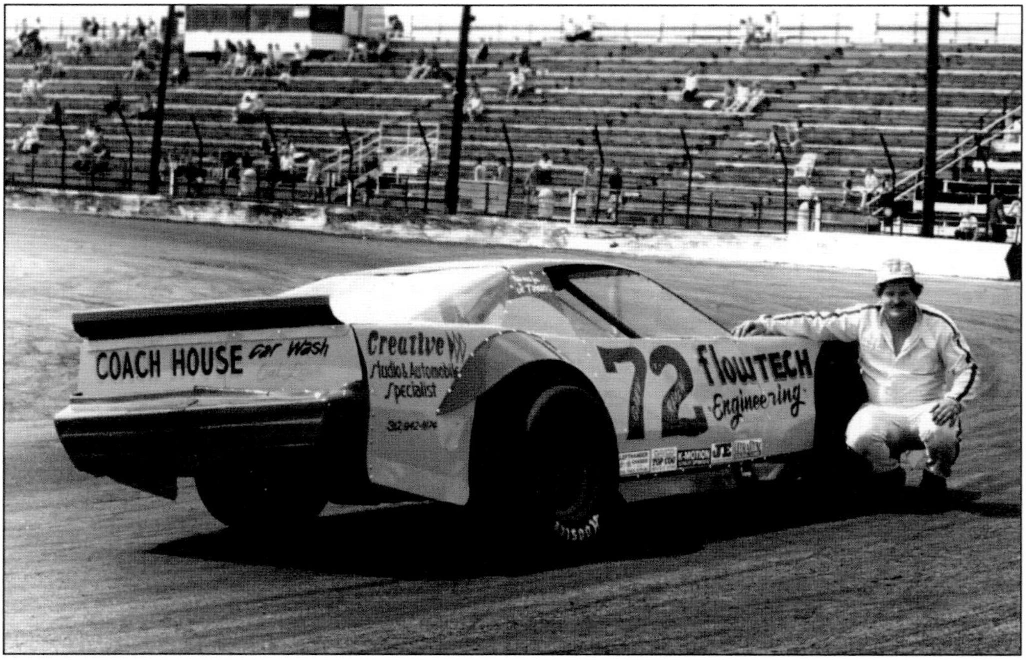

Second-generation late model driver Gary Raven (72), of Hometown, poses with his late model ride on 1992's opening day. Gary Raven's father, Dick, competed at Raceway Park in the 1960s and 1970s, but Gary would achieve much greater success. The younger Raven won two late model championships as well as more than 50 feature victories. (Courtesy of Bob Pilsudski.)

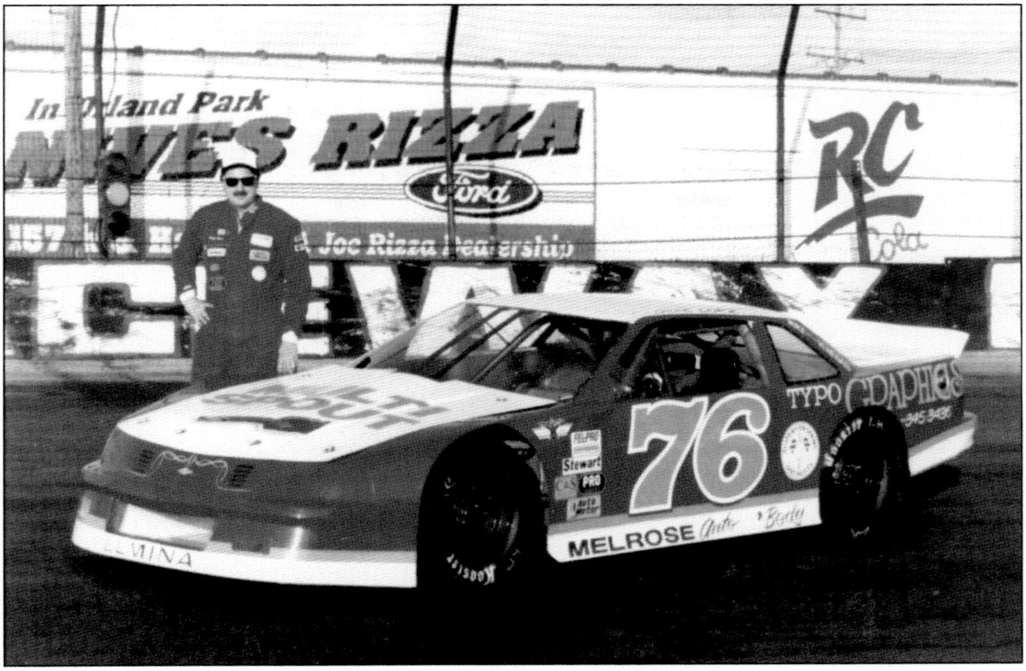

Although never a late model champion, Mike Lorz (76) was one of the top competitors at Raceway Park. In this 1993 scene, Lorz poses with his Chevy Lumina on opening day. Lorz would go on to become a car owner in the ASA series. (Courtesy of Bob Pilsudski.)

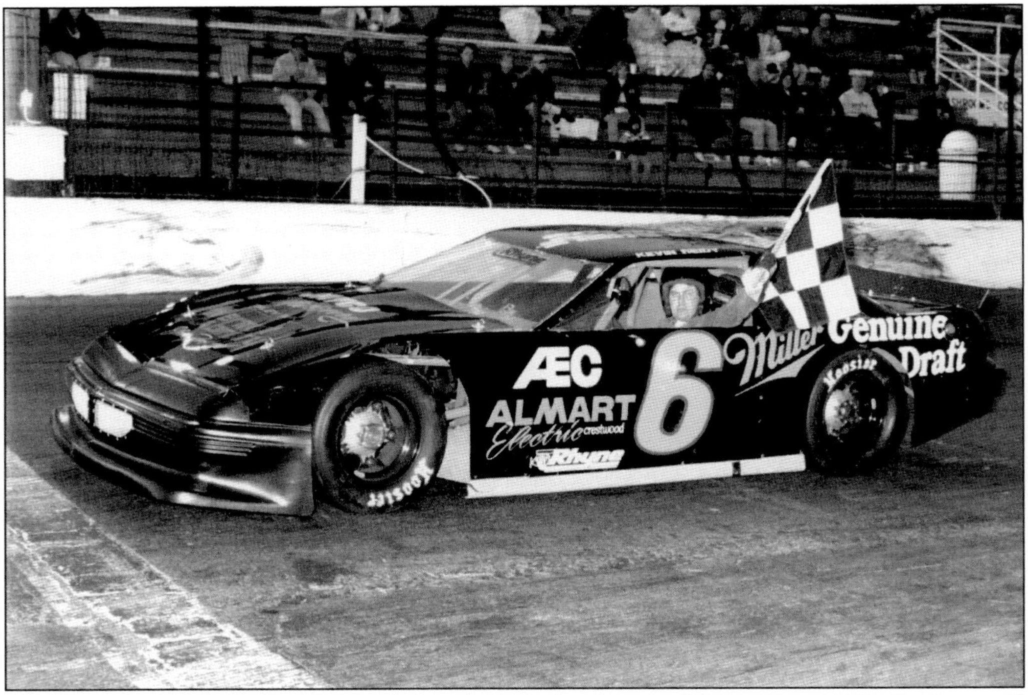

Kevin Reidy (6) holds the checkered flag after another late model victory in 1992. Reidy would drive a similarly painted ride to the late model championship in 1995, and he would also take home the late model crown in 1999 and 2000. (Courtesy of Bob Pilsudski.)

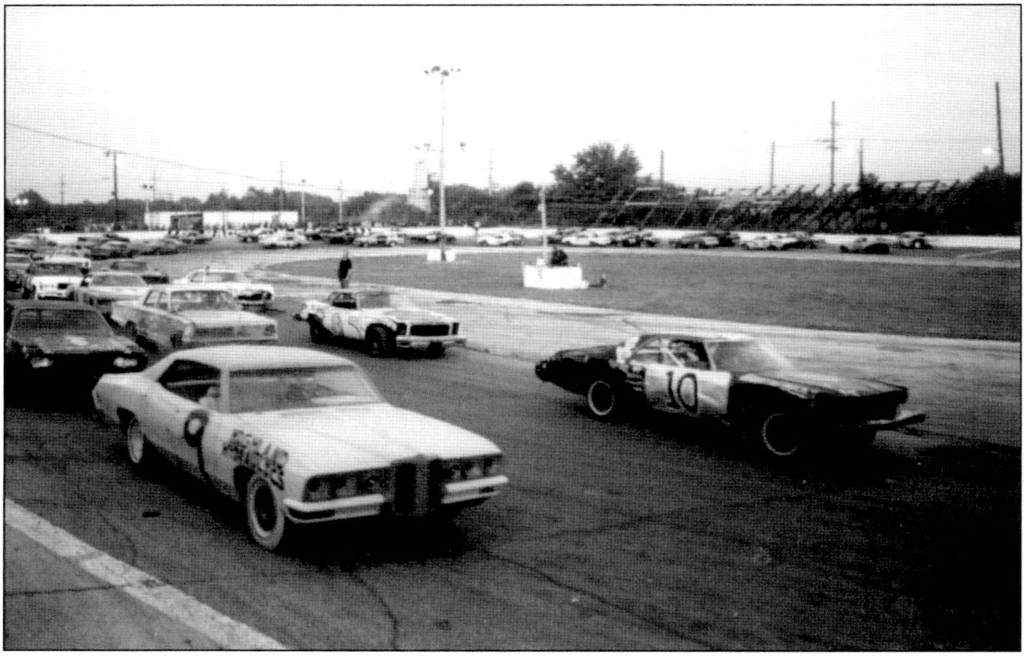

The track is nearly full of stock cars as an Enduro is about to begin in 1996. The Enduro, a grueling 300-lap endurance race, was a fan favorite and would usually pack the grandstands whenever one was held. Most competitors were upstart drivers who took old street-legal vehicles, added a roll cage and fuel cell, and raced the cars. (Courtesy of Bob Pilsudski.)

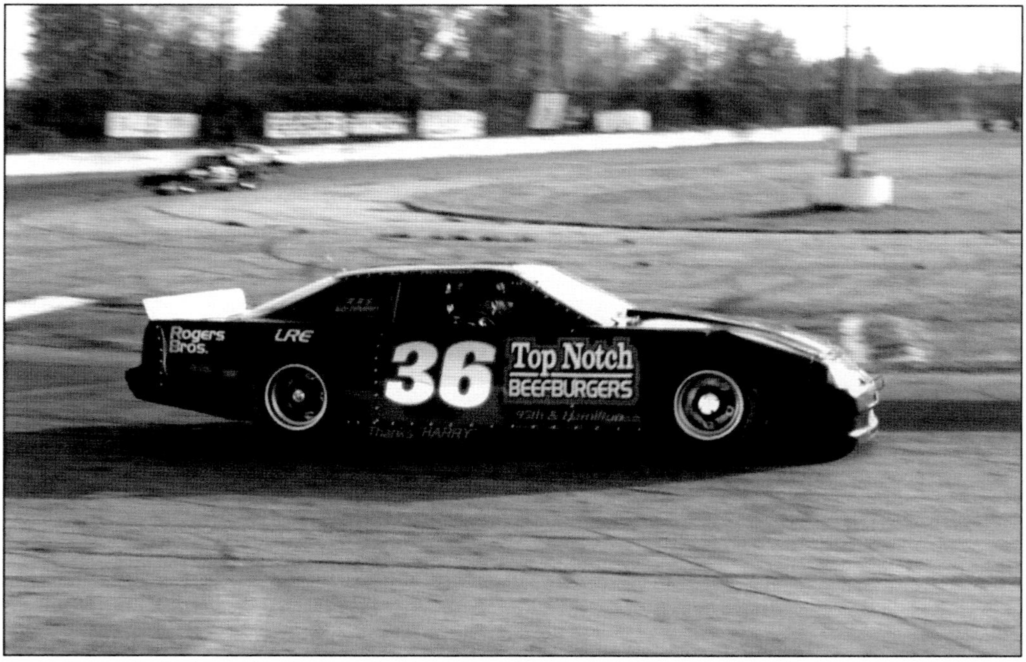

Dan Deutsch (36) guides his Michael and Richard Rogers–owned Ford Thunderbird around turn four during prerace hot laps in 1998. Although he never won a late model championship, Deutsch did win 59 features during his driving career and was one of the top late model drivers in Raceway's last decade of operation. (Courtesy of Paul Beck.)

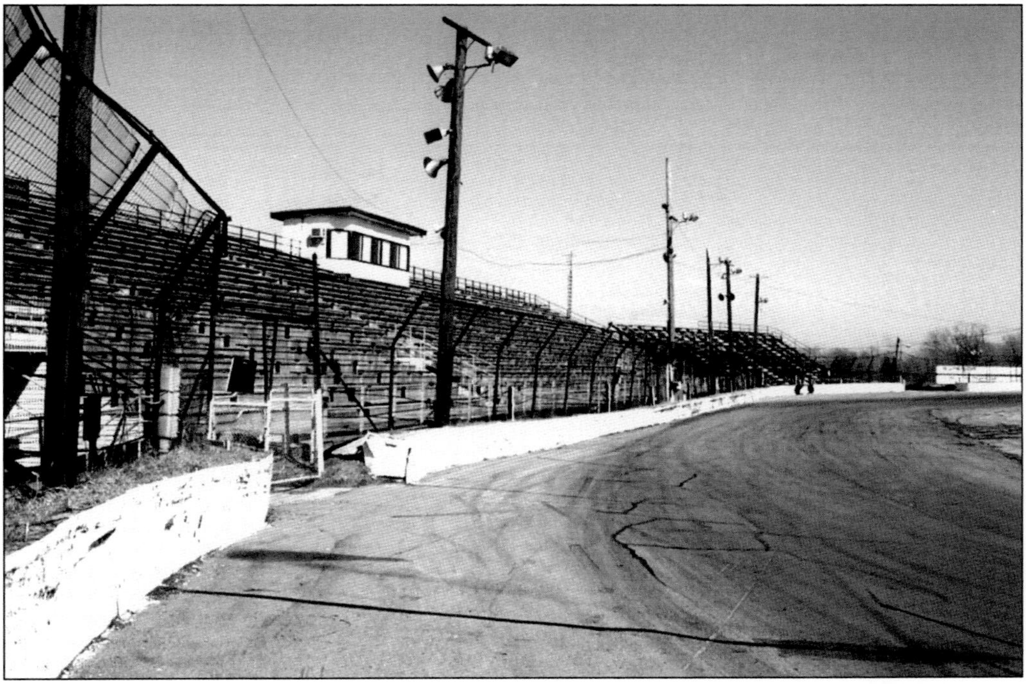

After the announcement that the track was sold and would be torn down for commercial development, Raceway Park sits idle in March 2001 with no cars racing or fans in the stands. A few months later, Blue Island's Raceway Park was gone and only a great memory to countless fans. (Courtesy of Stan Kalwasinski.)

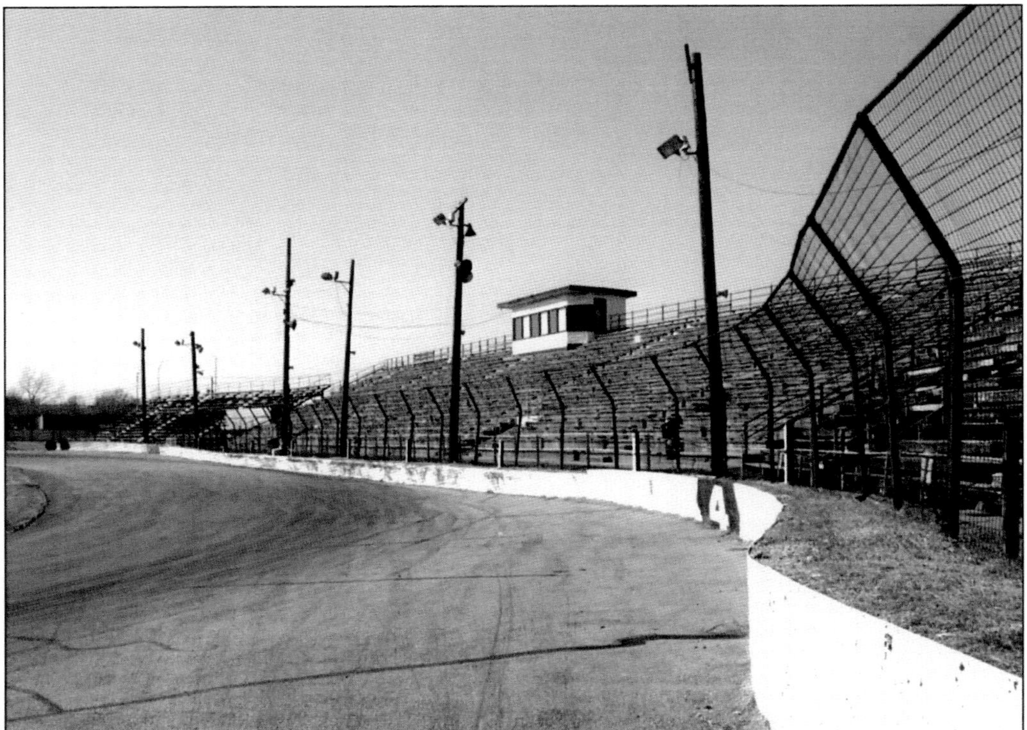

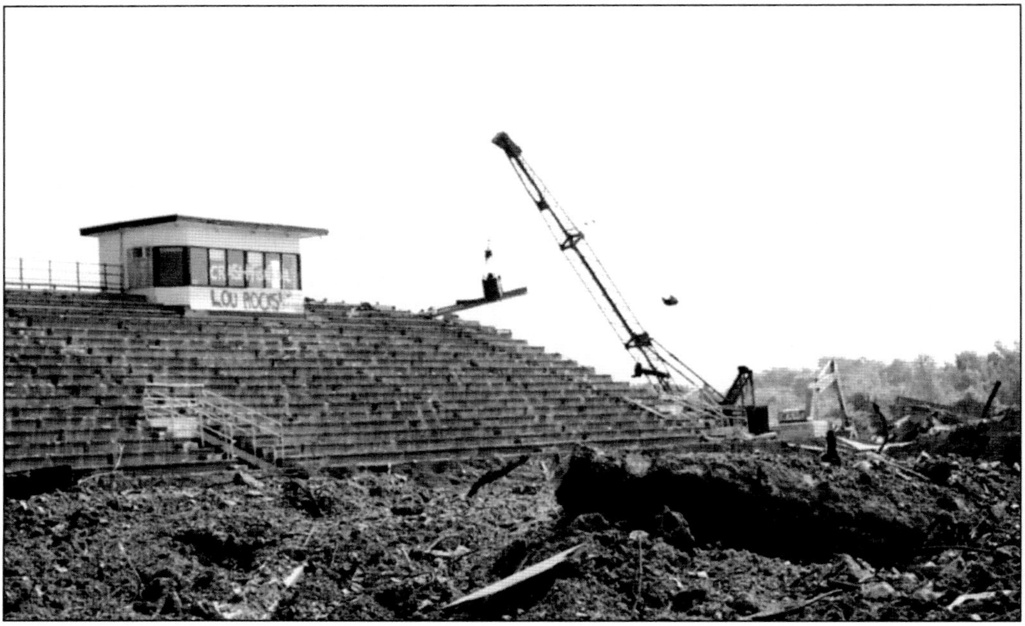

Demolition crews have a good start at tearing down the "World Famous Motordrome" in the spring of 2001. Racing photographer Bob Sheldon visited the racetrack every few days to document the end of the historic speedway and longtime Chicagoland entertainment venue. From 1938 through 2000, except for 1943 and 1944 when the track remained silent during World War II, the speed plant entertained countless fans, young and old, and provided a wide variety of automobile racing competition. (Courtesy of Bob Sheldon.)

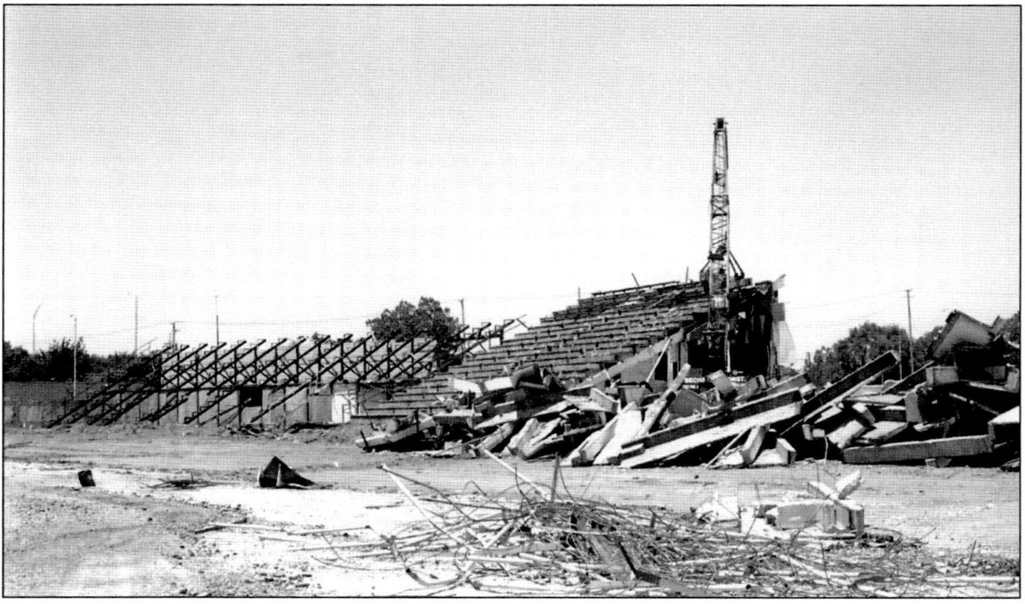

Stock Car Champions
(Referred to as Late Model champions as early as 1951)

2000	Kevin Reidy	1982	Bob Weltmeyer	1964	Bud Koehler
1999	Kevin Reidy	1981	Bob Weltmeyer	1963	Bill Cornwall
1998	Gary Raven	1980	Dave Weltmeyer	1962	Ray Young
1997	John Brolick	1979	Dave Weltmeyer	1961	Bob Pronger
1996	Gary Raven	1978	Larry Middleton	1960	Harry Simonsen
1995	Kevin Reidy	1977	Larry Middleton	1959	Bob Williams
1994	John Brolick	1976	Bud Koehler	1958	Bill Van Allen
1993	Pat Echlin	1975	Bud Koehler	1957	Bud Koehler
1992	Pat Echlin	1974	Bud Koehler	1956	Bob Button
1991	Pat Echlin	1973	Ray Young	1955	Tom Cox
1990	Joe Witkowski	1972	Bud Koehler	1954	Bud Koehler
1989	Joe Witkowski	1971	Ray Freeman	1953	Bryant Tucker
1988	Mike White	1970	George Hill	1952	Bud Koehler
1987	Jim Johnson	1969	Bob Pronger	1951	Bill Van Allen
1986	Mike Pockrus	1968	Jerry Kemperman	1950	Hal Ruyle
1985	Wayne Para	1967	Bud Koehler	1949	Bud Koehler
1984	Pat Echlin	1966	Bud Koehler		
1983	Dave Weltmeyer	1965	Ted Janecyk		

Other Stock Car Racing Champions

2000	Bill Neering (SPR) Scott Gardner (SS)	1976	Jerry Clark (HS) Bruce Odell (6C)
1999	John Senerchia (SPR) Ryan Dix (SS)	1975	Burt Weitemeyer (HS) Al Stuchel (6C)
1998	Louie Pasderetz (SPR) D.J. Helwig (SS)	1974	Dave Urewicz (HS) Tom Nielsen (6C)
1997	Bob Cagle (SPR) Russ Vankuiken (SS)	1973	Jack Thomas (HS) Guy Carnagey (6C)
1996	Mark Olejniczak (SPR) Guy Baumann (SS)	1972	George Abbott (6C)
1995	Joe O'Connor (SPR) Mike Szekely (SS)	1971	Mel McKeever (6C) Jeff Koehler (SPR)
1994	Joe Jones (SPR) Ron Haney (SS)		Dave Decker (MS)
1993	Mike Carpenter (SPR) Rob Delinsky (SS)	1970	Chuck Manis (AM) Dave Decker (MS)
1992	Don Kritenbrink (SS)	1969	Vern Mullennix (6C)
1991	Mike Tobuch (HS) Scott Cicuto (SP)	1968	Johnny Buben (GK)
1990	Mike Tobuch (HS) John Brolick (SP)	1967	Jerry Welch (NO)
1989	Tony Meier (HS) Chuck Janko (SP)	1966	Wayne Adams Jr. (NO)
1988	Hank Pugh (HS) Randy Gifford (SP)	1965	Ray Para (AM)
1987	John Hargus (HS) Bob Wall (SP) Ben Slachta (MS)	1964	Ray Para (AM) Ron Wilkerson (CL)
1986	Bob Copley (HS) Bob Wall (SP) Alberto Cabrera (MS)	1963	Ray Freeman (CL)
1985	Dennis Ponton (HS) John Rastovsky (SP) Alberto Cabrera (MS)	1962	Don Saynay (RK)
1984	Dan Deutsch (HS) Ron Deutsch (SP) Alberto Cabrera (MS)	1961	Wayne Bowdish (RK)
1984	Dave Duckworth (AHS)	1960	Rich Miller (NO)
1983	Dan Weltmeyer (HS) Ron Deutsch (SP) Paul Yancick (AHS)	1959	Ed Kilpatrick (NO)
1982	Craig Johnson (HS) Jim Gilbert (SP)	1958	Bill Heyser (NO)
1981	Scott Sterkowitz (HS) Jake Oudshoorn (SM)	1957	Augie Wolf (NO)
1980	Mike Varner (HS) Terry Laxton (SM)	1955	Bob Button (CN)
1979	Don Helwig (CHS) Leo Mens (SM)		
1978	Barbara Bosak (HS) Jack Annen (CHS)		
1977	Al Ponton (HS)		

(SS)-Street Stock, (HS)-Hobby Stock, (SP)-Spectator Division, (MS)-Mini Stock, (AHS)-Class A Hobby Stock, (SM)-Sportsman, (CHS)-Cadet Hobby Stock, (6C)-Six Cylinder, (AM)-Amateur, (SPR)-Semi Pro, (GK)-Golden Knights, (NO)-Novice, (CL)-Claiming, (RK)-Rookie, (CN)-Convertible

Midget Racing Champions

1987	John Warren	1952	Bud Koehler	1942	Tony Bettenhausen
1982	Mac McClellan	1951	Bud Koehler	1941	Tony Bettenhausen
1977	Bob Richards	1950	Eddie Russo	1940	Ted Duncan
1971	Tom Steiner	1949	Bud Koehler	1939	Ted Duncan
1961	Mel Kenyon	1948	Ray Richards		
1960	Russ Sweedler	1947	Tony Bettenhausen		
1959	Bob Tattersall	1946	Mike O'Halloran		

Listed above are all those drivers, of both midgets and stock cars, who claimed the title of champion from 1939 through 2000 at Blue Island's Raceway Park. (Authors' collection.)

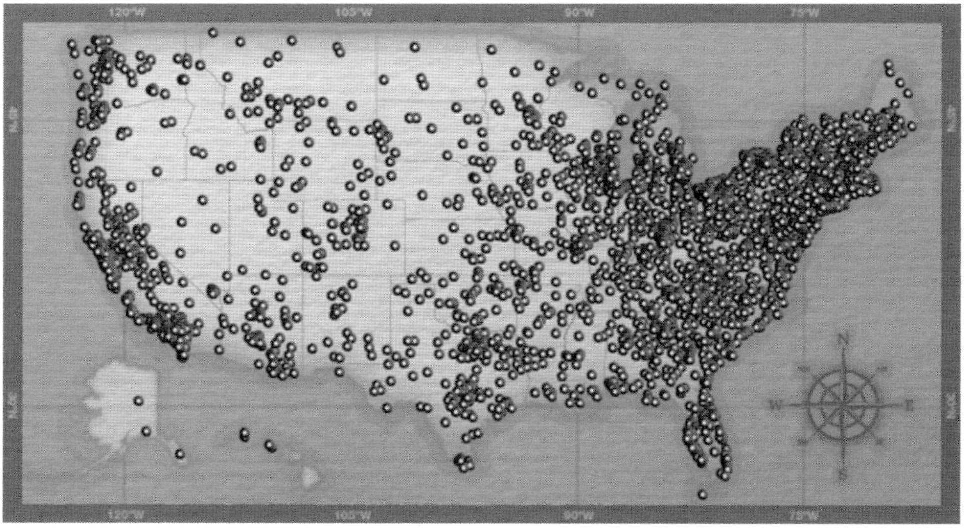